UEDA AKINARI

UEDA AKINARI

Blake Morgan Young

UNIVERSITY OF BRITISH COLUMBIA PRESS
VANCOUVER

UEDA AKINARI

This book has been published with the help of a grant from the Canadian Federation for the Humanities, using funds provided by the Social Sciences and Humanities Research Council of Canada.

Canadian Cataloguing in Publication Data

Young, Blake Morgan, 1943-
   Ueda Akinari

   Bibliography: p.
   Includes index.
   ISBN 0-7748-0153-0

   1. Ueda, Akinari, 1734-1809. 2. Authors,
Japanese — 18th century — Biography. I. Title.
PL794.8.Z5Y66   895.6'33   C82-091169-0

ISBN 0-7748-0153-0

Printed in Canada

To Leon Zolbrod

Contents

Preface

Ueda Akinari emerges in historical perspective as perhaps Japan's outstanding popular author of the years between the early eighteenth and early nineteenth centuries, but he cannot be seen as a mere link in the chain from Ihara Saikaku (1642-93) to Takizawa Bakin (1767-1848). A dedicated student of the Japanese classics, he does not really fit into the pedigree of scholars extending from Keichū (1640-1701) to Hirata Atsutane (1776-1843). Although he strove for excellence in composing poetry, his work does not belong to that of any particular school. He drew inspiration from many sources, refusing to adhere to any one teacher or faction, and while he has influenced generations of younger writers, there are none who can be called his disciples. Whatever the pursuit, he maintained his independence, standing alone and unique in all of his intellectual and literary endeavours. In his personal life, he was much the same. He was born during the administration of the eighth Tokugawa Shogun, Yoshimune (1684-1751, in office 1716-45), who had instituted a series of stringent social and political reforms, and he lived through the administration of Tanuma Okitsugu (1719-88, president of the Council of Elders 1779-86), with its laxness and extravagance, and the renewed retrenchments of the Kansei Era (1789-1801), yet his writings show little evidence that he felt affected by the political and economic events of his time, or that he was even aware of them. Through it all, he refused to follow blindly the trends in society and tried to live as he himself saw fit.

Akinari never attained the recognition that he sought as a scholar and a poet, but he achieved fame inadvertently through a collection of nine short stories. He was an outspoken rationalist and intolerant of those who were not, yet he was also notably superstitious, and quite equally intolerant of those who scoffed. While suffering from an inferiority complex, he did not hesitate to challenge the leading intellects of his day. Although inclined by temperament toward literary pursuits, the more utilitarian values of the merchant class in which he was raised led to an inner conflict that he resolved, if at all, only during the last few years of his life. While scorning wealth and material possessions for himself, he experienced acute feelings of guilt when he failed to provide them for his family. He was known as a misanthropic recluse, and his temper was lengendary; yet he loved his wife, was fond of children, and sometimes stayed up all night talking with friends. The riddle of his parentage has only been partially solved, and he left no descendants; he was born in an Osaka brothel and died penniless, thinking himself a failure. Nevertheless, his reputation was considerable even during his lifetime, and has continued to grow in the years since his death.

If, as Westerners have long maintained, Japan is a nation of paradoxes, then Akinari was a true product of his homeland, for he has been widely misunderstood even by his fellow countrymen. But the contradictions in his life must be recognized and accepted, for they are all true aspects of the total man.

I began the task of preparing this biography with the intention of concentrating on Ueda Akinari's life story, with only passing reference to his writings. However, as the work progressed, I realized that it is neither desirable nor, in the long run, possible to consider a writer apart from his works. At the same time I realized that commenting in detail upon all of his works would not only be an endless task, but would also ultimately overshadow the biographical emphasis of this study. I had to compromise and be selective, and to a degree my choices were arbitrary. The works discussed are those which I liked best, and which I considered most interesting and relevant. I have virtually ignored some of Akinari's major scholarly writings, feeling that they were not particularly meaningful apart from study of the Japanese classics that they explicate, while his literary works can be enjoyed on their own merits.

Another thing that I came to realize is that much of the misunderstanding about Akinari has arisen from a lack of sound evidence. I had resolved to find the facts, meticulously separating verifiable truth from speculation, but often I found that I could do no more than identify conjectures as such. Where firm conclusions could not be drawn, I felt it best to heed Akinari's own advice on such problems and not force an interpretation of evidence that is insufficient, ambiguous, or nonexistent. There are, consequently, many blank spaces in the narrative that follows and many outstanding questions for others to seek the answers to. I hope they will take up the challenge, and I wish them well in their search.

My good wishes are also extended, along with heartfelt thanks, to all those persons and institutions who, in so many different ways, helped to make this study possible. The initial research was supported by fellowships from the University of British Columbia and the Canada Council. Later, a research grant from the University of Auckland, where I was then employed, enabled me to examine relevant materials that I had missed during my stay in Japan, or that had been published afterwards. The generous support received from all three institutions is gratefully acknowledged.

Professors Moriyama Shigeo and Takada Mamoru of Tokyo Metropolitan University, who gave amply of their time discussing my research with me, answering numerous questions, offering many valuable suggestions, and pulling whatever strings they were able in my behalf, deserve a special word of thanks. The same is true of Professor Nagashima Hiroaki of Jissen Women's University, who so graciously shared with me his then unpublished findings on Akinari's natural mother. My work also benefitted from discussions with Professors Nakamura Hiroyasu of Shizuoka University, Morita Kirō of Akita Prefectural Agricultural Junior College, and Katanuma Seiji of Hokkaido University of Education. Satō Saburō, assistant curator at the Homma Art Museum in Sakata; Fuji Fujio, priest at the Kaguwashi Shrine in Osaka; and people at the Saifukuji Temple in Kyoto must all be thanked for showing me their collections of Akinari relics, and for sharing their own knowledge of Akinari with me. Nor could I have completed this study without the assistance of numerous secondhand book dealers and library personnel, most of them anonymous, through whom I gained access to necessary materials.

Toshio Akima, Tetsuo Takagaki, and Setsuko Itō, my colleagues at the University of Auckland, offered considerable assistance and advice while I was writing up the results of my research, while many useful comments were received from Professor Ken'ichi Takashima and Mrs. Kathryn Herbert, who critically read through the completed first draft. Those whose assistance came in the form of encouragement and moral support are too numerous to mention, but special thanks must go to Ronald and Toshiko Lee, to my parents, and to my wife.

Most of all, I am indebted to Professor Leon Zolbrod, who directed my own interests toward Akinari, who put in long hours instructing me over the years, both in and out of class, who meticulously reviewed my research at all stages, and who on many occasions restarted my engines when they were stalled. I dedicate this study to him in lieu of the medal that he so richly deserves.

B.M. Young
University of Victoria

1

Akinari's Early Life

It is relatively certain that Ueda Akinari was born in Osaka in 1734, very likely in the Sonezaki pleasure quarter, to an unwed mother by the name of Matsuo Osaki. Akinari seems to have been reluctant to discuss his origins, for he referred to the circumstances of his birth only twice in his known writings, both times in his old age. Shortly before his death he stated, "Born in Naniwa [Osaka] I have been a guest in the Capital for sixteen years. I had no father; I do not know the reason why. When I was four years old my mother also cast me away. Fortunately I was taken in by Mr. Ueda." A few years earlier he had written that he knew nothing of his true father's life or death and had met his real mother only once.[1]

The records of the Saifukuji, the temple in Kyoto where Akinari's remains are interred, show that he died in the sixth year of the Bunka Era, sixth month, twenty-seventh day (8 August 1809) at the age of seventy-six; thus he must have been born in 1734.[2] Supporting evidence is offered by Akinari's friend, the writer Ōta Nampo (1749–1823), who made mention of a party held in Osaka in the third year of the Kyōwa Era (1803), sixth month, twenty-fifth day in honour of Akinari's seventieth birthday.[3] But while this confirms 1734 as the year of his birth, it really says nothing more. By 1803 Akinari's residence was in Kyoto, and his presence in Osaka on this occasion was due only to a brief visit. As the party was held during an important religious festival, it was more likely a convenient time for him and his friends to get together, rather than the actual anniversary of his birth. Some twenty-two years after Akinari's death, one of his former associates wrote that his original surname had been Tanaka and that he had been born in Sonezaki.[4] From these statements arose the view, widely accepted until recent years, that Akinari's mother was a courtesan by the name of Tanaka, and that his father was an anonymous customer.

But although Akinari denied having more than a superficial acquaintance with his natural mother, he definitely knew more than he revealed. It is clear that he was informed of his mother's death, in 1768; that he knew her posthumous Buddhist name, Myōzen; and that he assumed filial responsibility for holding the proper memorial rites on her behalf.[5] Moreover, it is now apparent that he was acquainted with members of her family. In his account of an excursion to the province of Yamato in the spring of 1788, he mentioned visiting four different relatives, one of whom, a cousin, he identified as headman of the village of Nagara (now a part of Gose-shi, Nara-ken).[6] Akinari did not say through which of his parents he was related to the man (in addition to his natural parents he had an adoptive father and two foster mothers), but other information indicates that he was a nephew of Akinari's natural mother. Official records reveal that this village headman would have been Sueyoshi Shōzō (1735–1812), whose family held the heriditary post until the late nineteenth century.[7] Meanwhile, Sueyoshi family records show that Shōzō's mother, known posthumously as Eishun (1708–78), was the daughter of Matsuo Kyūbei (d. 1725), of the neighbouring village of Hino (also now a part of Gose-shi). The same records further reveal that Eishun had a younger sister, known as Osaki, whose posthumous name was Myōzen.[8] Since a child of Myōzen would have been a cousin to Sueyoshi Shōzō, this woman must have been the mother of Ueda Akinari.

While information about the Matsuo family is limited, extant gravestones indicate that it was an old family in the area, dating from no later than the mid-seventeenth century. In the nineteenth century, members of the family served as headmen of their village, which suggests that they were relatively well-to-do farmers. Osaki's father, Kyūbei, is known to have left Hino and gone to live in Osaka, where he operated a shop called the Kamakuraya. Presumably Osaki herself spent at least the early years of her life in Osaka, although she may have gone to live with her married sister in Nagara, or with relatives in Hino, after her father's death.

The identity of Akinari's father remains uncertain, but the following item has made possible some informed speculation.

In the Capital there was a man called Ueda Yosai, who lived by studying the national learning. He had formerly been the master of a brothel in

Shinchi, in the northern part of Osaka, but, coming to a decision, he fled that existence and lived in the Capital thereafter. Having recently heard these facts, I make note of them. Yosai was the descendant of a noted *hatamoto* family of Edo. His grandfather was an official whose son had been called to serve as a page boy and bedchamber attendant. By nature this youth delighted in debauchery and pleasure, and would often go directly to the gay quarters upon leaving his post. One night, while disporting himself in full ceremonial dress, he held a courtesan at his side and left the brothel, concealing her under his clothing. His father quite lost patience with such dissipated conduct and considered what action he should take. He decided to place his son under house arrest in an area under his administration, on the pretext that the boy had become deranged. He summoned an official from the village to Edo and sent his son back with him. While staying in that village, in the province of Yamato, the son had relations with the village headman's daughter; the child that was born was Yosai. For some reason the girl went to a brothel in Osaka when she gave birth. The child read books and learned how to compose *waka* poetry. He was called Tōsaku. When someone told him the truth about his birthplace and lineage he verified the report and then regretted all the more having fallen into that brothel, so he ran away and became a recluse. At first he lived in the north of Osaka, but later he made his home in the Capital. He took the name of Akinari, but was also known as Muchō. It has been less than ten years since his death. He was more than seventy when he died.[9]

The above lines were written about 1814 or 1815 by the distinguished Confucian scholar, Rai Shunsui (1746–1816), in *Shōroku*, the collection of notes that he jotted down from time to time between 1802 and 1815 while in service at his lord's mansion at Kasumigaseki in Edo (now Tokyo).[10] Before taking up that position, Shunsui had studied and taught in Osaka from 1764 until 1781, and while it is not known whether he ever met Akinari in person, his associates included at least two of Akinari's close acquaintances, Kimura Kenkadō (1736–1802) and Hosoai Hansei (1727–1803), who may have proven to be sources of reliable information.

Although there is no evidence to suggest that Akinari ever earned his living by running a brothel, certain other statements of Shunsui are quite correct. Yosai, Tōsaku, and Muchō are all names by which Akinari was known at one time or another. He did have periods of residence in or near all the places that Shunsui names. While his literary career was wider-ranging than indicated, he did engage in all of the pursuits mentioned. His death in 1809 was "less than ten years" before Shunsui made his record, and he was indeed "more than seventy when he died." Moreover, Akinari did have family ties in Yamato. Therefore, although Shunsui's note on Akinari must be interpreted with caution, it does merit careful attention.

At the time of Akinari's birth, Nagara and its neighbouring villages were under the administration of the Kobori family of Edo, whose members, just as Rai Shunsui indicated, were indeed *hatamoto,* or "bannermen," high-ranking direct retainers of the shogun. If a son whose conduct had become an embarrassment to the family was sent to Yamato for confinement, it would probably have been to the administrative centre of the Kobori lands, the village of Mashi, which was adjacent to Nagara. The home of Nakamura Tadasuke, chief magistrate in Mashi at the time, was scarcely ten minutes' walking distance from the Sueyoshi home in Nagara. The two families were parishioners of the same Buddhist temple, and Tadasuke's first wife (d. 1704) had come from the Sueyoshi family. Thus a love affair involving a youth in Nakamura's home and the sister of Sueyoshi Shōzō's mother is by no means inconceivable.

But was there a member of the Kobori family who meets Rai Shunsui's description of Akinari's father? At this crucial juncture, the proof eludes our grasp. Investigation of the Kobori family tree does reveal that Kobori Masamine (d. 1760) had a son, Samon, who died in 1733 at the age of seventeen. By that age the son of a man of Masamine's position would normally have been called upon to perform ceremonial duties for the government, but no record of such service exists for Samon. Conceivably the boy fell into disgrace and his record was blotted out. Thus it is certainly possible that this Kobori Samon, having exhausted his father's patience with his incorrigible behaviour, was discreetly exiled to the countryside where, as one of the final acts of his short life, he seduced a young woman in the district and then died before the child he had sired was born.[11] Regrettably, there is no direct evidence that either Kobori Samon or Matsuo Osaki was in the area in 1733, but in the light of what is verifiable, the circumstantial evidence in favour of Shunsui's account seems impressive. If it is indeed what did happen, then Akinari, though an illegitimate child, was a descendant of the renowned tea master and garden designer, Kobori Enshū (1579–1647).

In Osaka's Dōjima Era-chō, near the present-day site of the *Mainichi Shimbun* newspaper office, there was an oil and paper shop called the Shimaya, owned and operated by a former samurai named Ueda Mosuke. His ancestors had for generations lived in the village of Ueda in the Hikami district of Tamba Province, where they served as retainers to the local lord, or daimyo. Mosuke's father, however, had resigned his post after quarrelling with his superior, and had brought his wife and two sons to Osaka where he hoped to find employment. But he found his training as a warrior to be of little value in the commercial world. His savings were quickly exhausted, and his wife took sick and died. Mosuke, the elder son, managed to find day-to-day employment in a government office, and so helped the family to eke out a bare living until the father died also. Then his fortunes took a turn for the better. His younger brother, Jizō, was adopted by a *sake* brewer in the village of Kuroi, in his old home district of Hikami, while about the same time Mosuke himself was similarly taken in by the proprietor of the Shimaya. Very likely he also married his benefactor's daughter.[12] In any case, by the time Akinari was born, Mosuke had a wife and a daughter and was doing very well as a vendor of oil and paper.

Mosuke may have had business contacts with the Sueyoshi family, for its members earned part of their livelihood preparing oil from rapeseed (a product for which the Nagara area was noted) and sending it to Osaka for distribution.[13] Perhaps he had known Matsuo Kyūbei as a fellow merchant in Osaka. Possibly he even arranged for Osaki to go to Sonezaki to give birth to her child, away from the prying eyes and wagging tongues of the Nagara villagers, for he lived just across the river from the pleasure quarter. Or perhaps he merely learned of the child's existence while supplying his merchandise to houses in Sonezaki and met the mother's family later.[14] What is known is that when Akinari was four years old he became the adopted son of Ueda Mosuke and was thereafter brought up at the Shimaya.

The next year very nearly saw his life cut short. He contracted smallpox; the disease grew severe, and the attending physician gave up hope of recovery. In desperation, Mosuke journeyed to the Kashima Inari Shrine on the northern outskirts of the city to pray. It was late at night when he arrived, and he must have fallen into a doze while offering his petition, for the shrine deity appeared to him in a dream and promised that his son would not die, but would be granted a life of sixty-eight years. Indeed, to the parents' great joy, the boy's condition began to improve almost immediately, and in due course he made a complete recovery. Every month, from that time, Akinari's parents took him back to the shrine to pay homage to the deity and offer thanks. Akinari himself believed that he owed his life to divine intervention, and he remained a faithful patron of the Kashima Inari Shrine for the rest of his days. In 1801, when he reached the promised age of sixty-eight, he composed sixty-eight *waka*, the standard thirty-one-syllable verses of Japanese poetry, which he presented to the shrine as a token of gratitude.[15]

Although he had overcome his illness, he remained permanently scarred by it. An infection settled in the joints of his fingers and caused two of them to atrophy, leaving the second finger on his left hand too short to be of much use, and the third finger on his right hand about the same length as the fifth. When he tried to hold a writing brush, he later lamented, the third finger might as well have been missing altogether. Because of this deformity he was never able to master the arts of calligraphy or painting.[16] About the middle of the same year, his foster mother died. It is not certain whether this happened before or after his own illness, but presumably she had exhausted her strength in caring for him and perhaps succumbed to the smallpox herself. Even though Akinari said later that he had no recollection of her, the loss of two mothers in the space of a single year must have left its mark on his young mind.[17]

Mosuke did not remain a widower for long, but took a new wife, a young woman about twenty-six years old,[18] who proved to be devoted to her step-children. Although she was the third person to fill the maternal role for Akinari, whenever he used the word "mother" in his writings without qualifying adjectives, it was she to whom he was referring. He was plagued with a weak constitution, subject to frequent illnesses and occasional infantile convulsions, and he gave credit to this woman and her loving care for bringing him safely through childhood.[19]

Thus he grew up. It was the time when the Osaka region had passed the peak of its economic prosperity and was losing its position as the nation's centre of commerce and the arts. Edo, long the political centre, was now becoming independent in the economic and cultural fields as well and would in time surpass Osaka. Government policies in the early part of the century, designed to assert the central administration's political power over the merchants' economic strength, had had their effect. Among the townsmen the emphasis had shifted from unrestrained economic growth to consolidating their holdings and preserving the status quo. In their lifestyles as well, they had become more subdued and conservative. But all this was relative, of course. The free-wheeling spirit of the Genroku Era (1688–1703) may have been broken, but Osaka remained a bustling commercial city, and Dōjima, where Akinari was raised, was the centre of the nation's rice market. Well over a thousand exchange houses and brokerage agencies were located there, with financial representatives from all over the country in attendance. It was the scene of feverish speculation, with huge sums being made and lost, and the abundance of ready cash supported thriving entertainment districts with their theatres, eating and drinking establishments, brothels, bath houses, and the like.[20] A high demand for oil and paper gave the Shimaya its share of the general prosperity. It was surely a stimulating environment to grow up in, and the young Akinari would probably have been surprised to hear that he was living in a time of economic and cultural decline.

It is impossible to reconstruct a coherent picture of his childhood and adolescence. After his bout with smallpox, the record falls virtually silent until he was nearly twenty. When he was ten years old, he was attacked while at play by a stray dog and was rescued by a nearby fishmonger,[21] but this is the only other childhood event that he specifically described. Frightening though the experience must have been, it would be difficult and pretentious to relate it to any subsequent development in his life.

Akinari himself claimed that his youth was misspent. He was often away from home, he said, making the moors his dwelling place.[22] "Moors" may have been a euphemism for questionable houses of pleasure, but it might just as well mean that he spent considerable time in the countryside, alone. He was never gregarious and he certainly had much to brood over. He was by this time aware of the unsavoury circumstances surrounding his birth, and apparently he was the subject of some community gossip because of them. Later in life he stated defensively that as long as he was not a member of the outcast *Eta* class, he was free to mingle in society and do as he pleased, and he proclaimed his own self-sufficiency.[23] His early childhood had been unsettled. He had lost two mothers in the space of a year, at an age when he would feel the deprivation. Moreover, there were his hands. Acutely self-conscious about his deformity, he never completely adjusted to it. He could not help but be reminded of his handicap every time he picked up a writing brush, and this may well have made the psychological wound deeper as the years passed. Later, he self-mockingly called himself Muchō, "The Crab," because he fancied that his hands resembled a crab's claws, and he chose Senshi Kijin, "The Pruned Eccentric," as a pen name for one of his works. As long as he lived, he hated meeting people for the first time, ashamed of his appearance.[24] He probably did spend considerable time alone, reflecting on his situation and perhaps indulging in the fantasies that were later to appear in his stories.

He also said that he was lax in his studies and prone to be led away from them by frivolous companions who had neither education nor interest in acquiring it. Indeed, he maintained that although his father tried to make him study, he had not known how to read as a youth, and one of his later associates stated that while young he had indulged solely in pleasure, becoming the laughingstock of his neighbourhood by his twentieth year because he could not even read *kana*, the simple syllabic characters of Japanese script.[25] Caution is needed in interpreting these remarks, however. In the first place, Akinari's early life was probably much like that of the average son of a well-to-do merchant family—and most such youths received some formal education. Not only had the ability to read and write become essential for carrying on trade, but in the more subdued commercial atmosphere of the day, many townsmen had much time to devote to intellectual and cultural pursuits. It was partly for this reason that many of the scholars, artists, and literary figures of the middle and late Tokugawa period (1600–1867) came from mercantile backgrounds. Moreover, Ueda Mosuke was a strict man, and it is hard to believe that Akinari was rebellious enough to avoid getting even a rudimentary education for so long. And finally, by the time Akinari was twenty, his poetry was appearing in published collections, and in his early thirties he wrote two long pieces of popular literature which sold well and today are recognized as masterpieces of their genre. This is hardly what would be expected of a man who was illiterate all through his adolescent years.

Akinari's autobiographical writings make it clear that, in his declining years, he felt that he had fallen short of both his own and his parents' expectations. Feelings of self-reproach probably made him portray himself as worse than he actually was. Moreover, as he became more and more immersed in classical scholarship, he came to despise his earlier activities in the realm of popular literature. When he said that as a young man he had not known how to read, he may well have meant simply that his literary tastes had not yet fully developed and that he had foolishly spent his time reading material of little value. Certainly he received more education as a youth than he claimed credit for, but it remains difficult to identify its sources or judge its extent. He received some instruction from his father, but schools for the merchant class were then becoming popular, and probably Akinari attended one. The Kaito-kudō, one of the more famous of such institutions, was convenient to his home. There is no actual record of his attending that school, but he was acquainted (and on bad terms) with Nakai Chikuzan (1730–1804) and his brother Riken (1732–1817), two Confucian scholars whose father, Nakai Shūan (1693–1758), had founded the school in 1726. He also spoke respect-fully of Goi Ranshū (1698–1762), a Confucian scholar and commentator on the Japanese classics, who taught at the Kaitokudō, even referring to him as *Sensei*,[26] a respectful title that he applied to only a select few. The Kaitokudō was one of those schools that provided for commoners the same kind of full-scale education in the Chinese classics that the officially sponsored schools provided for the samurai class, and Akinari definitely began his study of such works in his youth.[27] Thus, assuming that he did attend the Kaito-kudō, his basic texts would probably have been *kambun* editions of the Four Books and the Five Classics, in which the Chinese text was read with Japanese pronunciation and word order, with rote memorization stressed over rational inquiry. In addition, he must have received practical training in business matters at home in the shop, and he seems to have read a fair amount of popular literature in his spare time.

Thus, despite his repeated self-criticism, the young Akinari was probably more serious than he depicted himself. There is little justification for the common view that sees him as a prodigal son, neglecting his responsibilities, frequenting the gay quarters, and wasting his father's money. Surely he was not perfect, and he doubtless sampled the pleasures that were available. His early stories show a familiarity with the demimonde that must have been based on personal observation. As the young Akinari made deliveries of oil and paper to Sonezaki, he probably paused in his duties to exchange flirta-tious remarks with the girls and was invited to come back in the evening. As an old man, he specifically recalled visiting Kyoto's Shimabara amusement district in his youth and lamented how the courtesans of the present had deteriorated compared to those of his younger days.[28] But patronizing such establishments did not constitute abnormal behaviour for a young man of Akinari's circumstances, and in any case there was opportunity for more than just sensual debauchery to be found in the gay quarters. They served as a social gathering place, and courtesans, at least those of higher rank, were better educated and more refined in tastes and manners than the average young woman.[29]

Another indication that Akinari's youthful waywardness has been exaggerated is the role that he played when his sister (actually Mosuke's daughter by his first wife) ran away from home. Little is known about this girl, not even her name or age. Akinari never referred to her in any way except as "elder sister" and said virtually nothing about their home life. It is clear from his writings, however, that when he was twenty-two, this elder sister carried on a secret love affair with a man of whom her parents disapproved. Finally she left home and supported herself at some disreputable occupation—perhaps by running a tea house or a brothel. Enraged, Mosuke disinherited his daughter, but Akinari rose in her defence. He had no right, he told his father, to inherit the family estate in the place of a cast-off natural child. If Mosuke were to sever ties with his daughter, then he ought to do the same with his adopted son. Mosuke protested that blood ties were of minor importance, pointing out that the Chinese sages had taught that it was better to give inheritance to someone of upright heart even though he may not be a true relative. Akinari did not pursue the argument but continued to act as mediator between his father and sister and eventually was able to bring about a reconciliation. As Mosuke saw that his daughter was doing well at her business, he conceded that she at least deserved credit for being able to make her own way in the world, and he accepted her as his child once more.[30]

This incident provides our only real insight into Akinari's home situation. The father's behaviour displays both the strict moralism of a samurai and the pragmatism of a merchant, a combination that may be traced to his own background. Raised as a warrior, Mosuke had seen his own father accept a life of poverty for both himself and his family rather than compromise his principles. The man by whom he had later been adopted had been a habitual drunkard, so addicted to wine that it eventually cost him his sight, but like a true son or loyal retainer, Mosuke had continued to serve him faithfully. When the Shimaya and a wide surrounding area were destroyed by fire, he was able to prove his fidelity and resourcefulness even more. Looking for some footwear for his foster father, he had come upon a burned-out shop that had sold wooden clogs. Sensing an opportunity, he had bought up all the undamaged stock and sent to Tamba for his brother. Jizō had hurried to Osaka and helped Mosuke hawk the footwear in the streets, then rushed back to Tamba with the profits and reinvested them in tobacco leaves which he then brought back to Osaka to sell. With the capital thus raised, Mosuke had rebuilt the Shimaya and made a fresh start in business, accumulating two thousand *ryō* in gold within a few years.[31] Thus, having himself experienced numerous hardships which he had overcome through his own efforts, Mosuke could understand and perhaps even grudgingly admire his daughter for doing the same, even though he did not approve of her trade. Akinari made no mention of the mother's role in this trouble, but the scattered references to her found in his writings indicate that she was a kind and understanding woman who gave her step-children all the care and attention expected from a real mother. The young man with a stern father and a doting mother appears often enough in Akinari's fiction to suggest that his own home life was similar. Akinari himself, in this incident, does not come across as a dissipated youth, but as a man concerned for others' welfare and willing to make sacrifices in order to hold the family together. Considering Mosuke's treatment of his wayward daughter, it is hard to conceive of him being so kindly disposed toward an adopted son whose conduct had been less than pleasing. In fact, it is quite likely Akinari's close association with his sister at this time, when she was engaged in work of a questionable nature, that gave rise to the rumour that he himself had once been the proprietor of a brothel.[32]

From time to time he enjoyed travel excursions. These include a trip to Yamato with his father, in the course of which he may have met his relatives in the area. In his early twenties he seems to have spent a relatively long time at his uncle Jizō's home in Tamba, and he also visited the hot springs at Kinosaki on the west coast of Japan, and the nearby Amanohashidate, long celebrated as one of the most famous sights in Japan. He made frequent excursions to Kyoto and possibly may have once journeyed as far as the Kantō region, where he was able to view Mt. Fuji.[33] The liking for travel that he showed in middle and old age appears to have been born during his youth.

At the beginning of 1753 the poet, Kashima Hakuu, edited a new collection of *haikai* verse, that branch of Japanese poetry encompassing informal linked poems and the independent seventeen-syllable epigrams now known as haiku, with the title *Jogengin*. Among the numerous contributions was one by a poet called Gyoen:

> *Toshimori ya*   Guardians of the year,
> *Kitchūsen ka*   The old men in the tangerine,
> *Mochi mushiro*   Rice cakes on their mat.[34]

The verse appeared in a section headed "Year's End," and so was most likely composed towards the end of 1752 when its author, now known to be Akinari, was in his nineteenth year. Allusion is made to an old Chinese tale in which a man cuts open a large tangerine from his orchard to find inside two old men happily immersed in a game of *go*. The story has given rise to the saying,

"Pleasure within a tangerine" (*kitchū no tanoshimi*), usually a metaphoric reference to the game of *go*, but sometimes to the enjoyment of simple pleasures. Thus the above verse may evoke images of the legendary old men seeing the New Year in by playing *go*, with a good supply of festive rice cakes on hand, or it may refer to the poet himself enjoying the New Year season within the narrow confines of his humble home.

Kashima Hakuu belonged to the circle of the *haikai* master, Ono Shōren (d. 1761). In 1755, when Shōren's followers compiled *Utatane* in honour of his eightieth birthday, Gyoen made a contribution to the collection:

> *Katakare ya*   Be strong, you bamboo pins,
> *Haru yatsu hata no*   And hold fast the eightfold
> *Mekugidake*   Banners of springtime.

There was also a linked-verse sequence by Gyoen and three other poets. Later that same year, *Haikai jū-roku nichi*, compiled by Shōren's group in memory of the recently deceased Hakuu, carried an independent verse by Gyoen, but more significantly, Gyoen was given the honour of composing the opening stanza for the chain of elegiac poetry:

> *Kumo sabishi*   How lonely the clouds!
> *Fuyu wa arawa ni*   Winter plain to see
> *Kita no yama*   Upon the northern hills.[35]

Such are Akinari's earliest known poetic efforts. He was still only twenty-two years old, but to judge from the position of his verses in these collections he already ranked fairly high in the group. However, he did not limit himself to the circle of Ono Shōren; he associated also with Matsuki Tantan (1674–1761), Shiimoto Kushū (1704–80), and others, displaying even at this age the aloofness and independence that were to characterize him all his life. He gave no *haikai* master his undivided allegiance, and the only one to whom he referred as teacher was Takai Kikei (1687–1761) of Kyoto. Even in this case, the title was probably used only for respect, since it is doubtful whether Kikei served as Akinari's teacher in the true sense of the word. Akinari would get together with Kikei's followers in Osaka whenever Kikei came to visit, but these contacts would have been sporadic; nor did Kikei live for many years after their first meeting, about 1756.[36] Nevertheless, in 1758 Akinari was permitted to compose the opening stanza in a linked verse sequence produced by himself, Kikei, and one other poet, which implies that he sat high in Kikei's estimation.

> *Susuhaki no*   A wind comes blowing
> *Kaze ga fukinari*   For the house cleaning rites, as we
> *Koromogae*   Change into New Year garments.[37]

Akinari developed a true and long-lasting friendship with Kikei's son, Kitō (1741–89), who was later to describe him as a talented man who wrote good poetry, *waka* in the style of the *Man'yōshū*, the earliest collection of Japanese verse (comp. ca. 759), and *haikai* in the vein of Nishiyama Sōin (1605–82), Kamijima Onitsura (1661–1738), and Konishi Raizan (1654–1716), but who also lamented that he stayed aloof from society.[38] In time his friendship with Kitō would pave the way to association with Kitō's teacher, the renowned poet and painter, Yosa Buson (1716–84).

It was with *haikai* that Akinari made his debut in the literary world, and he retained his liking for the pursuit throughout his life, but his interests soon broadened to other areas that he considered more important. He did not consider *haikai* to be an art form and tended to be intolerant of those who took the pursuit too seriously. Nevertheless, activities in *haikai* circles may well have provided his introduction to men who helped mould his scholarly interests. Among such acquaintances he numbered Fujitani Nariakira (1738–79) of Kyoto,[39] who is generally remembered more as a philologist, *waka* poet, and student of Chinese and Japanese literature, not as a writer of *haikai*. Presumably Nariakira, like Akinari, composed *haikai* for recreation; perhaps they met at such a gathering but became friends because of their mutual interests in the more highly regarded activities of *waka* and classical studies. The same may be true of Akinari's friendship with Katsube Seigyo (d. 1789), a physician and *haikai* poet from Nishinomiya whom he met around 1759.[40] Seigyo had studied both classical and vernacular Chinese literature, and he may have been one of the first men to influence Akinari in that direction. Undoubtedly some influence also came from Goi Ranshū, who was a great admirer of Keichū (1640–1701), a monk whose studies of the Japanese classics had been largely responsible for generating a revival of interest in the past that came into full flower in Akinari's day. But it was to a man named Kojima Shigeie (d. 1760) that Akinari gave the most credit for guiding him into classical studies through examination of Keichū's works.[41] He said that he had been about thirty when he met Kojima, but he must have actually been a few years younger, for he was only twenty-seven the year Kojima died. Of Kojima himself very little is known aside from the fact that he lived in Kyoto, not far from the noted *waka* poet Ozawa Roan (1723–1801), of whom he was a close friend. Akinari's own association with Roan in their old age raises the possibility that he had heard of him through Shigeie even at this early date.

In 1760, Akinari married Ueyama Tama, then twenty-one years old. The daughter of a Kyoto farmer, she had been adopted at an early age by the Ueyama family and taken to live in Osaka. How the marriage came about is not clear, but whether it was a love match or one arranged for convenience, it was to prove a happy union for them both.[42] No children were ever born to them, and most of their life together was spent in poverty and uncertainty, but for the next thirty-seven years Akinari was to find in Tama a faithful and devoted companion who understood him and even shared many of his interests.

It may be that Akinari's wedding had a significance beyond the fact that he had reached a marriageable age. His sister died about this time, and her death made him the sole heir to the family estate. If she had indeed died before the wedding, then the marriage may be seen as an attempt by the parents to get Akinari settled and help prepare him for his future responsibilities. All that is known for certain, however, is that the daughter died not long before her father, and that Mosuke himself died in mid-1761.[43] Of course, if his father's health had been visibly failing, that in itself would have been reason enough to hasten plans for Akinari's marriage.

Whatever the actual circumstances of the marriage may have been, the death of his father marks a turning point in Akinari's life. Now aged twenty-eight, he found himself the owner of a business with the responsibility for supporting his new wife and widowed mother resting squarely upon his own shoulders.

2

The Beginnings of a Literary Career

As master of the Shimaya, Akinari proved to be a willing spirit encumbered by weak flesh. After the death of his father, he bowed to his mother's wishes and tended the shop, but he felt keenly his own lack of business acumen.[1] There is no concrete information on his commercial activities, but during his ten years as a merchant, he began to study and compose *waka* poetry, wrote at least two full-length collections of short stories, and became an accomplished student of both Chinese and Japanese classical literature. The attention he gave to the oil and paper trade must have been less than wholehearted, and it is doubtful whether the two thousand *ryō* that Ueda Mosuke had accumulated remained intact in the hands of his adopted son and heir.

Although Akinari said little of a specific nature about his studies during this period, when he was "about thirty," he met some Koreans with whom he was able to communicate in writing. This was probably early in 1764, when an embassy from Korea arrived in Osaka by ship, from whence its members travelled overland to Edo. When time permitted, students of Chinese were often allowed to test their language skills with such visitors from across the sea, and Akinari's success indicates that he had attained a fair degree of proficiency. Even so, Akinari noted that he found only two members of the group interesting. The others (there were about five hundred in the party), he said, merely wanted things. He apparently concluded that such foreigners, although viewed with curiosity by the masses, and with reverence by Japanese

Confucian scholars, were little different from the man in the street. As a sidelight to this experience, Akinari noted that later, after the Korean envoys had returned to Osaka and were preparing to leave Japan, a member of their party was murdered by a warrior from Tsushima. The criminal was shortly apprehended and put to death in front of the Korean ships. In his memoirs Akinari recalled seeing the condemned man paraded through the streets of Osaka en route to the place of execution and hearing the courtesans in the nearby gay quarter lamenting the fate of such a handsome young man. He also noted his belief that the culprit had been acting under his lord's orders and was punished as a scapegoat.[2] Although there is little in the way of political dissent in his later writings, sympathy for the underdog appears frequently.

He continued to enjoy travel and sometimes took time off from work to make sightseeing trips in the countryside. Apparently his interest in the literature of Japan had not extended to the travel diary, however, for he left no accounts of these early excursions. It is only his poetic descriptions of later journeys that permit speculation about travels in his younger days. For example, when he went to the Yamato area in 1782, he recalled having seen the same places some twenty years before. In 1799 he spoke of having once accompanied a group of pilgrims on an excursion of several days' duration to a number of famous and sacred spots in the mountains of Yoshino. This had been more than thirty years earlier, he said. And in 1803, when he wrote a postscript to a collection of scenic views of Waka-no-ura, painted by Kuwayama Gyokushū (1746–99), he spoke of having seen the actual place forty years before.[3] All of these outings appear to have been made during the 1760's, and since they are known today only because Akinari found occasion to remember them years after the events, it is virtually certain that they were not the only trips he took. He enjoyed seeing the natural wonders of his native land, and his heart was tuned to the traditions and sentiments associated with them. Eventually this would lead to expression in verse and lyrical prose, though at the time it was merely another distraction from his commercial duties.

He was also writing. Early in 1766 he published a collection of stories entitled *Shodō kikimimi sekenzaru* (The Ever Present, Eagerly Listening Monkey of Our Time). A similar work, *Seken tekake katagi* (Portraits of Mistresses in Our Time), appeared just a year later. Both works conformed to the standards of popular literature of the day. It is not surprising that Akinari chose this style for his literary debut, for he had grown up in the city where such writing had originated and flourished, and he was himself a member of the society which such works portrayed.

Popular literature had been a growing industry in Japan since the early Tokugawa period. As the long years of warfare gave way to peace, a general economic prosperity and a continually rising standard of living affected virtually everyone in the country to some degree. Literacy, which proved indispensable as government by the sword gave way to government by bureaucracy, and equally essential as business transactions grew increasingly complex, became widespread. And as people came to have more money to spend and more leisure time to enjoy, learning for its own sake became a luxury that many could afford to indulge in. Even the more prosperous farmers managed to get at least a basic education. As the number of people able to read increased, so did the demand for reading material. Printing had begun to prosper in the last decade of the sixteenth century and on into the seventeenth, in part as the result of patronage by the central government, the imperial court, and leading Buddhist temples, but credit must also be given to improved printing techniques brought back from Korea in the late sixteenth century by returning members of the Japanese invading forces. Before long, merchants saw their chance of printing and selling mass-produced books at a profit. Before the middle of the seventeenth century more than a hundred publishing businesses had been established; by the early eighteenth century, their number had risen to an estimated six hundred or more,[4] and stiff competition had already led them to form guilds in order to control their own numbers, regulate prices and production, and prevent piracy of their works. As the supply of books rose, their prices dropped, and with the rise in personal incomes, they were soon within the common man's reach. By the early eighteenth century, commoners formed a large segment of the reading public.

The first literary publications to be aimed at a mass audience were collections of medieval tales and narratives that had been handed down verbally or in manuscript form, but original works soon followed. This early popular literature covered a wide range of subject matter, including materials designed to educate or enlighten, as well as to entertain. Frequently these functions were combined. Didactic tracts, aimed at disseminating a particular viewpoint, sometimes had their readability enhanced by means of a story format. Guides to letter writing techniques sometimes took the form of epistolary tales. Travel guides often incorporated their geographical descriptions into a fictional narrative about a person making a journey. Being produced for an audience of limited education, works such as these were written primarily in the native *kana* syllabary, with only occasional use of Chinese characters, and for this reason, despite the variety of their contents, they are collectively known today by the generic name of *kana* books, or *kanazōshi*.[5]

As literature for popular consumption became firmly entrenched, its characters came to be drawn more and more from the ranks of the common people, and the stories, often based on actual events, increasingly came to depict realistic details of the contemporary world. In time a more sophisticated literature emerged, one directed specifically at townsmen, portraying the lives and surroundings of the merchants in the main commercial centres and usually written by members of the merchant class—a literature of the townsmen, for the townsmen, by the townsmen. These were the so-called *ukiyo-zōshi*. By the mid-seventeenth century the meaning of *ukiyo*, or "floating world" had broadened from its original reference to the transient world of Buddhist doctrine to include the current of life. Life itself was seen as a "floating world," in which one lived for the moment, leaving the future to the whims of fate. Life could end at any time, fortunes could be made or lost overnight, and the courtesan's fidelity lasted no longer than her patron's money. *Ukiyo-zōshi,* then, the "tales of the floating world," were stories about contemporary living. *Kōshoku ichidai otoko* (The Life of an Amorous Man), by Ihara Saikaku (1642–93), a recounting of a young rake's many and varied adventures in the ways of love, published in 1682, became the prototype of this genre, although in subsequent works Saikaku and others often played down or discarded the erotic theme in favour of depicting practical economic problems or difficulties related to one's station in life. Some were no more than collections of tales gleaned from all over the country. It was not long before a special variety of *ukiyo-zōshi,* the *katagimono,* appeared.[6]

The term *katagi* referred to human personality, or character, shared by persons of similar status, occupation, circumstances, and so forth; thus *katagimono* became the label affixed to stories about human characteristics. The genre was pioneered by Ejima Kiseki (1667–1736). By the time he appeared on the literary scene, *ukiyo-zōshi* had reached a state of stagnation, if not of decline, with most writers producing little more than insipid imitations of Saikaku's works. However, about 1699, when Kiseki became associated with Hachimonjiya Jishō (d. 1745), he was able to inject new life in the *ukiyo-zōshi,* making Jishō's publishing house, the Hachimonjiya, the "Figure Eight Shop," so famous that works of popular literature published in Japan from around 1700 through 1767 are commonly called *hachimonjiyabon,* whether actually printed there or not. The *katagimono* format was developed by Kiseki independently, during a period of estrangement from Jishō, but it became the hallmark of the Hachimonjiya after their reconciliation. A typical *katagimono* by Kiseki was a collection of stories about persons of similar type. Their personalities and idiosyncrasies would be portrayed in an exaggerated, often satirical fashion; humour would arise from the caricature and from the people doing things unbefitting their assigned roles in the feudal hierarchy. Usually a moral lesson (albeit often of doubtful sincerity) would be appended. Such was the formula used by Kiseki in *Seken musuko katagi* (Portraits of Sons in Our Time) (pub. 1715), *Seken musume katagi* (Portraits of Daughters in Our Time) (pub. 1717), and *Ukiyo oyaji katagi* (Portraits of Fathers in the Floating World) (pub. 1720). Meanwhile, contemporary authors published numerous imitations of these successes, and similar works continued to appear until late in the century.

When Akinari made his literary debut, poetry, prose, and drama were as profuse as they had ever been, but they had in large measure become stylized for commercial purposes. A dearth of fresh ideas had made them conventionalized and uninspired. Rather than experiment, authors preferred to stick with formulas that had proven successful in the past; there was little of the creativity and spontaneity that had characterized the earlier period. Even at their best, Kiseki's works had been divorced from the real world, his characters and plots lacking in vitality. He had never succeeded in portraying life's realities with the incisive satire and critical insight of Saikaku, nor had he created believable characters with whom the reader could empathize. The same was largely true of his successors. But even when advancing in new directions, literature draws on its antecedents, either by improving on the style of previous works or by reacting against it. Akinari chose the former course and succeeded in producing the last significant *ukiyo-zōshi* to be published.

Akinari's paper business may have helped him to get involved in the world of popular literature. Writer and publisher generally operated on a contract basis, so if Akinari supplied paper to publishing houses, he would have had ample opportunity to make the necessary contacts. Customers who knew of his literary interests may even have urged him to write for them. In any case, *Shodō kikimimi sekenzaru* was published early in 1766, though the record shows that it had apparently been completed more than a year before. When a publisher wished to print a new work, he would first send the manuscript, together with a request for permission to prepare the printing blocks, to the representatives of the publishers' guild. After determining that publication of the material would not violate any law or infringe on any existing published work, the representatives would normally give their approval and submit a request to the appropriate government officials for permission to print the work. Only after this permission had been granted could the printing begin. The publisher paid a fee, based on the number of pages to be printed, to the guild representatives and an additional fee to the authorities. When permission to publish was granted, the guild representatives would give the publisher a permit to market the work. A record of these proceedings would be kept on file by the guild for future reference.[7] The publisher's request for permission to print *Sekenzaru* dates from the end of 1764.[8] On this document the author's name was given as Sontoku-Sō (Old Man Profit and Loss) of Dōjima Era-chō, probably a reference to Akinari's commercial enterprises, but when the book appeared in print the pen name had been changed to Wayaku Tarō. Since delays in publication and changes of pen names were not uncommon, they are probably of no particular importance in this case.

"Wayaku Tarō," which might be rendered into English as "Jesting Tarō," "Tarō the Absurd," or "Tarō the Mischievous," was a fitting pseudonym for the author of the droll and satirical tales of the townsmen that make up

Sekenzaru. The generally playful and humorous tone is established at the outset. The brief preface seems to have been consciously designed to frustrate the reader who would grasp its true meaning; it is like a butterfly that allows itself to be approached and observed, but stays just out of reach of the collector's net. Akinari seems to be chuckling in the background as the reader tries to come to grips with its elusive phrases. The abstruseness may be related to the writer's desire to remain incognito, but the style is in keeping with the spirit of the whole work. The author implies in the preface that his book is a collection of gossip picked up here and there (a point also suggested by the title) and that he had in mind when he wrote it the well-known figure of the three monkeys who "speak no evil, see no evil, and hear no evil." In relation to these virtuous monkeys, Akinari's monkey stands in ostentatious defiance, his hands cupped not over his ears to shut out malicious gossip, but behind them, the better to hear it. And what he hears, he repeats. He is a metaphorical expression of mischief. Placing himself in the role of this monkey, Akinari proceeds to tell an assortment of tales about the townsmen of his day. But since he himself was also a townsman, he appropriately dubbed his stories a collection of *shiriwarai* (literally, "arse laughter"), a self-mocking reference to the monkey who laughs at his fellow simians' red posteriors, blissfully unaware of the colour of his own backside.[9]

    Sekenzaru has the flavour of Kiseki's *katagimono* in combination with the method of Saikaku's collections of tales from the provinces. Akinari drew his material from a variety of sources, but he took pains to conceal his debt, often drawing from more than one source for a single tale and so changing his material that the finished product bears little resemblance to what inspired it. Certain characters and events were drawn from real life—some of them have been identified with well-known persons and happenings of Akinari's day— and he may have used other, less obvious, live models as well. It would be in keeping with the spirit of the title and the preface for all of the stories to have some basis in fact, and such may well be the case. Still other material and inspiration seem to have been gleaned from earlier *ukiyo-zōshi*, a common practice among popular writers, but Akinari did not engage in wholesale borrowing. He drew from his sources only in fragments and usually adapted what he did borrow. Moreover, the Chinese characters that Akinari selected for his pen name (as commonly used, *wayaku* was generally written in the *kana* syllabary) suggest that his book may feature some translations from foreign works. It is unlikely that this was mere coincidence, for at least four of the fifteen *Sekenzaru* tales appear to have been partially drawn from Chinese sources. This is a further indication that Akinari had been reading not only Japanese popular fiction but Chinese works as well. While the name Wayaku Tarō basically refers to borrowing or adaptation rather than translation, it has further nuances of meaning.[10]

Sekenzaru probably reflects Akinari's degree of knowledge and his way of thinking at the time it was written. Numerous quotations, or parodies of quotations, from the Japanese classics and casual references to Chinese and Japanese works and authors show that he was well read, and the pedantic tone suggests that he was proud of the fact. The prose is often stiff and intricate and so adorned with allusion and unorthodox word usage that virtually every phrase requires careful reading. Akinari's knowledge must have been equal to that of nearly any other *ukiyo-zōshi* writer, but his use of such material conveys the impression that while he had acquired the learning, he had yet to digest it.[11]

Conventionally, *katagimono* were written in a light-hearted comic tone, the author taking a position of amused detachment in order to poke fun at human imperfections and the misfortunes that inevitably result. Akinari followed this pattern in *Sekenzaru*, but while the usual practice was to end on a cheerful note, laughing at the failure and ignoring its repercussions, Akinari often mingled pathos with his humour. He was not always unsympathetic toward his characters. Even in these early, non-serious writings there are signs of the pessimism that became so apparent in his later years. In the first tale of Book II, "Kōkō wa chikara aritake no sumōtori" (The Sumo Wrestler Who Practised Filial Piety With All His Might), for example, there is criticism of a social system which binds a son to support his undeserving family. The father is a drunkard and a gambler, the mother a stubborn and lazy woman, and the younger son an invalid as a result of syphilis that he contracted in the gay quarters. However, the elder son, Uranosuke, is a paragon of filial piety and works diligently to support his impoverished family even though they are singularly ungrateful. Feeling that such is no more than his duty, they are sparing with their thanks and complain bitterly when he falls short of their expectations. An amateur sumo wrestler, Uranosuke enters a contest in Osaka, but hard work and inadequate food have made him weak. He loses badly and returns home to be upbraided by his family, but, humbly enduring their insults, he goes out and finds employment as a fisherman's helper. The new job carries the fringe benefit of a high protein diet. His strength returns, and he wins decisively at a local sumo contest; buoyed up by his success, he starts out for the Capital to wrestle for higher stakes. En route, however, he encounters a decrepit old man who turns out to be the god of poverty, and he falls sick, his dreams of prosperity dashed. The story is told in a droll style, but the serious themes stand out nonetheless. Besides the implied social criticism, the role of luck or destiny in man's life is apparent. It is bad luck that condemns Uranosuke to striving to raise his family's fortunes; it is good luck that restores his strength and makes him a potential sumo champion; and it is bad luck once again, or perhaps the cynical working of fate, that brings him to cross paths with the god of poverty. Man's power is limited, Akinari seems to be saying. In large measure he is at the mercy of forces beyond his control.

This latter idea appears with more force in the third tale of Book III, "Suzume wa hyaku made maiko no toshiyori" (An Aged *Maiko* Tries to Copy the Sparrows and Dance Till She Is a Hundred). A former *maiko*, or dancing girl, now more than fifty years old, longs for her former popularity and spends her time trying to convince men that it is the state of the heart, not of the body, that is important. Growing old is inescapable, but her inability to accept the fact makes her pleas for affection all the more pathetic. As a further example of man's inability to control his destiny, her son is introduced, a handsome and talented lad who had the misfortune to be conceived as the result of a liaison on the night of *kanoe saru*, the cyclical sign of metal and the monkey. According to tradition, such a child grows up to be a kleptomaniac. The boy starts out well, being apprenticed to a rich man in Edo, but, just as was feared, he shows an uncontrollable penchant for stealing. Discharged by his master, and disinherited by his mother, he ends up as a catamite for the young braves of Edo, doomed, it would appear, not by any personal flaw, but by his horoscope.

Perhaps the most amusing of the fifteen tales is the first one of Book III, "Kiryō wa miru ni bonnō no amaydori" (A Man Beholds Beauty and His Refuge from the Rain is Fraught with Evil Passions). A samurai from the Capital is going about with his servant, seeing the sights of Edo. Caught in a sudden rainstorm, the two men seek shelter in a nearby Buddhist temple, where a young nun of striking beauty, her appearance marred only by a bandaged wound on her forehead, receives them. She invites them inside, feeds them, and even offers to let them spend the night if the rain persists. The warrior has a lascivious imagination, and the nun's considerate actions, together with her physical charms and the fact that she seems to be alone in the temple, convince him that she is not a nun at heart, but a young widow who has withdrawn behind a religious façade to indulge her unsatisfied passions. The facial sore is a venereal infection, he assumes, but he finds her so enchanting that he decides the risk is worth taking. So he awaits his chance, but when, feeling that the time is propitious, he starts to make advances, the nun responds with a challenge to a fencing contest. The man is taken aback. He denies his samurai status and insists that he is only a merchant travelling in the guise of a warrior. He is adept at all the gentle arts, he says—poetry writing, the tea ceremony, preparing incense, the courtly game of football, playing the samisen, painting in the Chinese style, and so on—but knows nothing of military prowess. In reply to his query, "How did a girl like you. . . ?" the nun answers that she has practised the martial arts from her childhood. Her family had long been distressed by her pugnacious disposition, and after a recent quarrel with a group of young men, in which she had felled four or five of her assailants but sustained the wound on her forehead, they had forced her to take the tonsure. She then proceeds to demonstrate her skill with the halberd, and when she threatens to attack the man for presenting a false front, he and his servant forget about the downpour outside and dash away in terror.

On first reading, this tale appears to be mocking the decay of martial skills among the military class, but the Japanese in the Kamigata area of Akinari's day would have seen it as poking fun at a real person. When the man in the story denies his samurai status, he gives his name as Yanagiya Gombei, otherwise known as Rikō. Considering the numerous arts at which he claims to be proficient, the name must be taken as a pun on that of Yanagi Rikyō (also called Yanagisawa Kien; 1706–58), a resident of Kyoto who was qualified as an instructor in sixteen different arts. As he had only recently died when Akinari wrote the story, the pun would have been obvious to his readers. The same is true of the nun's name, Jōkei. Readers would have recognized it as a play on the name of Shōkei, a nun who had recently created a scandal by taking a Kyoto physician as her lover and living with him at her temple.

The foregoing illustrates how Akinari selected his material for *Sekenzaru*. Yanagi Rikyō is portrayed as a dilettante, prone to put on airs, and an out and out lecher at heart. The caricature in which he is presented, along with the exposure of his disguise and the frustration of his lust, provides considerable humour, but in fact the man bears little resemblance to the real Rikyō, nor does the nun bear much similarity to the real Shōkei. Neither is there any record of an actual meeting between Rikyō and Shōkei. If the characters in the story were not given names, their models would be impossible to identify. The same is true for most of the characters in the other stories who were or may have been inspired by real persons.

Making fun of samurai decay was probably not Akinari's intention in the tale of the militant nun, but he does mock the breakdown of traditional values in the first story of Book I, "Yōgai wa ma ni awanu chōnin no jōkaku" (A Merchant's Stronghold Fails to Meet Its Purpose), showing a world in which the abacus has become mightier than the sword. The characters are stock opposing types. Konishi Sanjūrō is a merchant who wants to be a warrior; Yamamoto Kanroku is a warrior who wants to be a merchant. Yearning after the past glories of the military clan from which he traces his ancestry, Sanjūrō assiduously studies the martial arts, even going so far as to remodel his shop on the lines of a military stronghold. Kanroku, however, believes that the way of the warrior is no longer the way to success; he has given up his samurai status in order to learn how to carry on a commercial business. Sanjūrō cultivates Kanroku's friendship in hope of learning more of warlike skills, but Kanroku would rather talk about his own entrepreneurial ambitions. In time a certain daimyo, impressed with Kanroku's commercial knowledge, hires him to manage the financial affairs of his fief, while Sanjūrō, having neglected his business in order to study the arts of war, goes bankrupt. After failing in a number of attempts to make a living, Sanjūrō makes his way in rags and despair to Kanroku's new home. Moved to tears by his old friend's plight, Kanroku gives him a job selling goods to the daimyo's retainers, but this apparent kindness is really no more than the plot of a scheming merchant. After Sanjūrō has sold the goods, Kanroku claims such a large share of the profits for his services as middleman that Sanjūrō ends up taking a net loss. Sanjūrō vows to get even and lies in ambush for Kanroku, but Kanroku manages to evade him. Pursuing the way of the merchant has won a post in the service of a daimyo for one man, while pursuing the way of the warrior has led to ruin for another. It is an ironic twist, but there was no doubt a high degree of truth in it at a time when Japan's economy was becoming more and more commercialized.

In the second tale of Book II, "Shūshi wa ikkō me no mienu shinjinsha" (A Pure-Land Believer Is Unable to See), use of the ironic twist provides a wry look at extreme religious piety. A devout adherent to the True Pure Land, or *Ikkō* (Singleminded) Sect, whose members were noted for petitioning Amida Buddha with singleminded devotion (*ikkō isshin*) has two sons, the younger of whom shares his father's pious temperament, while the elder scorns such things and seeks a career on the kabuki stage. The younger son sets off on a religious pilgrimage but is waylaid by a band of robbers on the way and killed. When word of the tragedy comes to the father, he does not grieve; rather he rejoices that his son has been so favoured as to be taken into paradise in his youth, escaping a long existence amidst the cares of this transient world. Misfortune continues as the elder son's wife becomes sick and dies, and a fatal illness overtakes one of the grandchildren, but still the father only rejoices that his loved ones have found everlasting bliss. Even when the family cat falls down the well and drowns, his reaction is the same. But when his eldest son, the kabuki actor, loses his life in a stage accident, the father's piety is at last shown to have its limits. Perhaps feeling that his own turn is next, he petitions Amida Buddha with *ikkō isshin* that his personal salvation be delayed.

The ironic twist is a recurring device. In the second tale of Book I, "Bimbō wa kami todomarimasu urakashiya" (Poverty in a Back-Street Lodging House Wherein Dwells a God), an unscrupulous man marries the devout widow of a Shinto priest and persuades her to sell her daughter to a brothel. As time passes, the man turns into a kindly religious person, while his wife becomes greedy and devilish and finally drives him out of the house. In the third tale of Book II, "Nomikomi wa oni hitoguchi no irochaya (The Teahouse Demon Has a Gulp of Understanding), a brothel keeper goes to the home of a deadbeat customer only to find him gone and the house stripped of even the straw mats on the floor. When he finally tracks the man down, the object of his search is shivering in an underheated room clad only in a loincloth. Instead of collecting the bill, the brothel keeper gives money to his delinquent patron. In the second tale of Book III, "Misugi wa abunai kara-waza no kōjō" (Life Is Uncertain for an Acrobat's Barker), a young man who scorns working in his parents' apothecary shop leaves home, drifting from one mean occupation to another, leading travellers to an inn, or drawing crowds to acrobatic performances, until he is destitute. Then he chances to meet a fortuneteller who informs him that he has an innate talent to be an apothecary. The youth goes home to find that his parents have died, but he reopens their shop and becomes very prosperous.

In Book IV the first tale, "Kyōdai wa ki no awanu tanin no hajime" (Brothers Are Disunited and Grow Estranged), is interesting for its possibly autobiographical nature. It features two brothers, again opposite character types. The elder, a shrewd and stingy man, tends the family shop with an excess of diligence, refusing to leave his business affairs even to view the cherry blossoms once a year or to make an occasional visit to the theatre, nor will he take the time to attend festivals other than those honouring patron deities of commerce. The younger brother scorns the life of a tradesman, considering it an unworthy way to make a living. Scrupulously honest himself, he detests flattery and cultivates nobility of soul. He lives simply, feels deeply, seeks harmony with nature, and practises the arts of Noh drama and linked poetry. His preference for the quiet scholarly life outweighs even his respect for the code of filial piety. Despite his widowed mother's pleading, he refuses to become encumbered with a wife and family. When his mother dies and the business fails, he becomes a priest. Akinari must have felt some personal identification with this character. At the time he wrote the story, he himself was managing his own family's business, but probably spending as much, if not more, energy on the arts. The younger son's views, with some exaggeration, may well be an expression of Akinari's own.

The characters of *Sekenzaru* are well portrayed throughout. Perhaps the best example is a man from the first tale of Book V, "Mukashi wa makkō kemutakaranu yobanashi" (An Irreverent Evening Tale of Old), whose miserly nature provides considerable humour. In the western part of Kyoto, the house of Isōemon has become a stopping-off place for men on their way to and from the Shimabara pleasure quarter. Among the regular visitors is one Shichizaemon, a wealthy but incredibly stingy individual.

Loathing the expense of candles, he would come before it was completely dark, and when leaving would go home in the company of someone who had a lantern. He would depend on others for tobacco and for paper to wipe his nose. When a collection was taken for an evening snack, he would rush off saying that he had forgotten an important engagement, but if someone offered to treat the group, he would not refuse though the *sushi* be made from snake's flesh.[12]

Naturally, he incurs his companions' disfavour. One night, when only Isō-emon, Shichizaemon, and another friend, Sumigorō, are present, Isōemon drops a remark to Sumigorō about the fascinating exhibition of fox-catching that they had witnessed a few nights before, at no charge. Shichizaemon pricks up his ears at the mention of free entertainment and begs his friends to arrange for him to see this performance also. Isōemon and Sumigorō express doubt that the *rōnin*, or masterless warrior, who traps foxes will agree to a second demonstration, but promise to speak to him. A few days later they inform Shichizaemon that, since they are the *rōnin*'s special friends, he has agreed to exhibit his skill just one more time. Shichizaemon is so overjoyed that he insists on at least giving the man a bottle of wine for his pains. On the appointed night, the three men meet the *rōnin* and accompany him to the moors. The *rōnin* leaves them, saying that he is going to set his snare and warns them not to follow until he calls. Time passes. At last Isōemon, feigning impatience, goes to see if anything is wrong. When he does not return, Sumigorō and Shichizaemon at last go to search also and come upon the *rōnin* and Isōemon quarreling violently. The *rōnin* accuses the three of them of trying to spy out the secrets of his hereditary art. In order to placate him, the parsimonious Shichizaemon is forced to treat him to an expensive spree in the city's restaurants and theatres.

Sekenzaru's immediate success may be inferred from the publication of a similar work by the same author within a year of its first appearance, and the fact that it was reprinted at least twice after Akinari's death, in 1839 and 1849, is an indication of its enduring popularity. Of all Akinari's works, only *Ugetsu monogatari* would appear to have been more widely read.

A request for permission to publish Akinari's second *ukiyo-zōshi, Seken tekake katagi*, was submitted during the latter part of 1766, but it was refused, probably on account of deficiencies in the written application. A second request was sent out in the first month of the next year and approved. The addresses of those in charge of the publication, missing from the first application, were included in the second, and the name of one of them was changed. The author's name was also changed, from Wayaku Tarō to Shimaya Senjirō. Presumably Senjirō was one of Akinari's official names, as it was customary for a writer's real name to appear on a publication request (though failure to do so had caused no apparent difficulty in the case of *Sekenzaru*). Carving the printing plates for a work was not to be started until permission had been received, but *Tekake katagi* was published without delay, in the same month as the revised application was submitted.[13]

Tekake katagi is a collection of twelve tales or, more correctly, ten, since two of them are continuations of the story which precedes them. It was published in four volumes, a puzzling departure from the general rule that such works consist of five or six. Perhaps, as a result of the success of

Sekenzaru, the publisher was impatient to put out another work by the same author and so considered four volumes adequate. *Tekake katagi* does bear the marks of being tailor-made for the publisher. *Shodō kikimimi sekenzaru* was an unorthodox title that bespeaks its author's individuality, while *Seken tekake katagi* could easily be overlooked in a list of similar titles. The preface, in which Akinari freely acknowledged his debt to Kiseki, Jishō, and Saikaku, is straightforward and similar in tone to that of the typical *katagimono,* unlike the impertinently incomprehensible preface to *Sekenzaru.* The style of the text is also more orthodox and more polished than that of *Sekenzaru,* but it lacks the freshness of its predecessor's free and novel expressions. Akinari had probably been asked by his publisher to follow the accepted *katagimono* style more closely.

Still, certain aspects of *Tekake katagi* may be seen as reflecting a greater degree of maturity on the part of its author, which is only to be expected if he had written *Sekenzaru* three years earlier and continued to widen his field of knowledge in the interval. The ostentatiously pedantic style of *Sekenzaru* is softened in *Tekake katagi,* and the direct references to Chinese and Japanese classics are fewer in number. Probably Akinari was now more confident of his own ability and did not feel the need to show off so much—a natural stage in a writer's development. At times, however, there are apparent attempts to echo the style of certain classical works, which might be considered a more refined sort of pedantry. This classical style is interwoven with, and modifies, the colloquial style of the *ukiyo-zōshi. Waka* poetry is used to a greater degree than in *Sekenzaru.* An appropriate verse, either an original composition or a parody from an old collection, appears at the beginning of each tale, and in places *waka* are fitted smoothly into the narrative. This may be a further reflection of the degree to which Akinari had been influenced by Chinese literature, for it was characteristic of Chinese vernacular fiction to commence each tale or chapter with a poem. For reasons such as these, *Tekake katagi* can be seen as a transitional piece moving toward *Ugetsu monogatari.*[14]

As the title suggests, *Tekake katagi* presents contemporary portraits of mistresses, but the field is not confined to women living in unnatural seclusion such as the modern-day term *mekake* (*tekake* is an obsolete reading of the same Chinese character) connotes. In Akinari's day, being a mistress was simply one of the few lines of work open to a woman, and society recognized the role along with that of the wife. Indeed, two of the ten tales are about real wives, and mistresses become proper spouses in four others. Strictly speaking, they are stories of relationships between men and women, not necessarily of illicit love. As in *Sekenzaru,* Akinari portrayed his characters' frailties, often drawing laughs as a result, but there is an undercurrent of sympathetic understanding. He was not merely telling stories about stock characters; he also recognized the pathos in their lives. Born out of wedlock, abandoned by his real mother, separated by death from his first foster mother, and left deformed by a debilitating illness, Akinari was too aware of the pain in the world to take the position of a sneering, completely detached observer.

Some of the *Tekake katagi* tales are thought-provoking; others merely offer amusement. Of the latter variety, perhaps the most entertaining is the story comprised by the second and third sections of Book I, "Yaara medetaya ganjitsu no hiroiko ga fukuriki" (How Auspicious! The Health and Wealth of a New Year's Foundling) and "Orihime no hottori mono wa torite oki no tamatebako" (The Object of the Weaver Maid's Affection Is the Jewelled Box on the Shelf). Akinari made no attempt to conceal his debt to the legend of Urashima Tarō, a Rip-Van-Winkle-like character of Japanese folklore. Indeed the heroine's father, Jusai, is identified as Urashima's descendant. As the story begins, Jusai is on the verge of despair because he has no child to carry on the family name. Now an old man, there is nothing he can do except appeal to the gods for a miracle, and so, on the last night of the year, he stands on the seashore in prayer. Two messengers from the realm of the Dragon King appear to him. They tell him that he will be granted his heart's desire, and that if he will but refrain from opening the jewelled box that they entrust to him, the child will live forever. Jusai returns home to discover a baby girl beside his door. He names her O-Haru, since it is now the first day of the lunar spring, and brings her up as his own daughter. When O-Haru becomes eighteen Jusai adopts a young physician as a husband for her, and then dies, satisfied that the family name will endure. But things do not turn out as foreseen. Before long, O-Haru's husband also dies. Still young, she promptly remarries, but her new husband, Denzaburō by name, is a sailor, and shortly he leaves on a voyage from which he does not return. O-Haru waits for three years, but then gives her husband up for dead and marries once again, this time to a blind masseur named Rokuemon. Then Denzaburō, who had been stranded in China and Korea on account of shipwreck, comes home to find his wife married to another man. Bloodshed is forestalled only by the intervention of a mutual friend who proposes that, circumstances being what they are, Denzaburō be reinstated as the proper husband, but that Rokuemon be permitted to live in the neighbouring house as O-Haru's male concubine. This proves acceptable to all parties, and the triangular arrangement continues harmoniously until the two men both die in old age. O-Haru, meanwhile, remains to all appearances a young woman in her mid-twenties.

In the second half of the story, O-Haru, still outwardly young, marries her fourth husband, a scholar named Tamon. This husband proves to have a roving eye, however, and his infidelities soon leave him caught between a demanding mistress and a jealous wife. One evening, as he ponders over his dilemma, Tamon hears the sound of rats gnawing in the darkness. He has a sudden flash of inspiration. He makes his way home, confesses his infidelity to his wife and promises to see his mistress no more. O-Haru goes to bed greatly relieved, but after she has fallen asleep, Tamon stealthily places some sweetmeats, which he had purchased on his way home, upon the jewelled box that the Dragon King's messengers had entrusted to O-Haru's father many years before. By the third morning thereafter, rats have chewed holes in the box, and O'Haru awakens to find herself transformed into a shrivelled old hag. Unaware of her husband's treachery, O-Haru spends the rest of her life waging a personal feud against rats. The villagers call her Neko-Irazu Nezumi-Tori Baba, or Granny Rat Catcher Who Needs No Cat, and after she dies, they give her the posthumous name of O-Neko-sama, or Madame Cat, and revere her as the patron deity of rat extermination. A pebble from her grave mound, if kept in the house, will drive all rats away, so powerful is her spirit—which proves a boon to the people in the area who make their living from sericulture.

Like *Sekenzaru, Tekake katagi* also takes a satirical look at religion. In the third tale of Book II, "Waka goke no teramairi wa tekkiri shitatemonoya no yadogae" (A Young Widow's Piety Is In Fact the Scheme of a Tailor on the Move), Ginshichi, a tailor, and his beautiful wife, O-Ito, open a shop in the Capital, pretending to be brother and widowed elder sister. O-Ito gives every appearance of being devoutly religious. She faithfully tends the household altar and makes frequent visits to the local temple. In due time she acquires six priestly admirers, whose interest in her has nothing to do with religion. When a quarrel develops over which of the six will be privileged to enjoy her favours, Ginshichi intercedes, proposing that each priest spend two months of the year with his "sister", the order to be determined by drawing lots, using the six Chinese characters in the well-known invocation to Amida Buddha. The priests hail this as a brilliant suggestion. They send appropriate gifts and gladly rent a separate house in deference to Ginshichi's plea that the neighbours will be offended by the arrangement. At the appointed time the six priests arrive at the house, wearing festive attire over their robes, it being the season of *O-Bon*. Ginshichi and O-Ito are waiting for them with a group from the neighbourhood, but not, it turns out, as a welcoming committee. Falling on the priests, they beat them, strip them of their clothes, and drive them away. Using the booty as a start, Ginshichi and his wife open a secondhand-clothing shop.

Clever schemes are a feature of other tales as well. In the first story of Book IV, "Musuko no kokoro wa terifuri shirenu kitsune no yomeiri" (A Son, His Heart Unfathomable, Marries a Fox), an elderly lady is passing through a secluded place when she is accosted by an attractive young woman who introduces herself as a fox who has taken human form, the better to search for her child, who has been captured and sold. She begs the old woman to help her and, if possible, to buy the young fox from its captor and set it free. Touched to learn that even animals have tender maternal feelings, the old woman sends her servant to the market place, where he finds the fox pup and purchases it. The old woman returns it to its mother, who is overcome with gratitude and asks how she can ever repay the favour. The old woman makes a motherly request of her own. She has a son, she says, Wasaburō by name, who has divorced his wife and gone to live with a former courtesan whom he has ransomed, and she begs the fox to use her magical power to bring him to his senses. The magic appears to work, for not long afterwards her son indeed does come home, announces that he has broken off with his mistress, and begs his mother's pardon for the pain he has caused her. Thereafter he behaves like a truly reformed man. After some time has passed, the old woman is approached by a matchmaker who wishes to arrange a marriage between Wasaburō and the daughter of a certain *rōnin*. Overjoyed that her son will be able to marry a respectable girl and convinced that the grateful fox has brought all this about, she gives her consent. And so the marriage takes place, but after the nuptial ceremony is over the bride lifts her veil to reveal herself as the "fox". In reality, she is the son's mistress. It has all been a trick to enable Wasaburō to secure his mother's consent to their marriage.

The first tale of Book I, "Hitogokoro kumite shirarenu oboroyo no shuen" (Delving into the Unfathomable Heart of Man on a Misty Moonlit Night), also features a clever scheme. Hanazono, the mistress of a Kyoto aristocrat, loses her heart to an impecunious townsman named Hampei, but her love has its limits. She has grown accustomed to luxuries; detesting the thought of working for a living, she cannot bring herself to abscond with her lover until he tells her of his plan to steal fifty *ryō* that have been entrusted to him. When he shows her the bag containing the money, she agrees to run away with him. So they set out, but once they are clear of the Capital, Hampei confesses that in reality there is no money in the bag, only broken pieces of tile. Hanazono realizes that she has been deceived, but it is too late to return to her former paramour. Since there is nothing else she can do, she changes her name to the more plebian sounding O-Sono, and makes her living with Hampei, operating a teahouse at the Ausaka Barrier.

Coming to grief on account of greed is a theme in other stories as well. In the second tale of Book II, "Shikigane no nihyaku ryō wa aita kuchi e yakimochiya" (A Two-Hundred-*Ryō* Dowry Is Stuffed into an Open Mouth Like Toasted Rice Cakes), Saburōshichi, a prosperous merchant of Edo, requests assistance from Densuke, who sells rice cakes at the neighbouring shop. He must spend the coming year in Nagasaki, he says, and since he must make some arrangement for his concubine, O-Sumi, he proposes to marry her off to his lazy clerk, Hachizaemon. He plans to provide an ample dowry for O-Sumi, and promises to reward Densuke handsomely if he will act as go-between. Densuke readily agrees. O-Sumi protests the arrangement at first, swearing undying fidelity, but at last gives in. Thus Saburōshichi departs, and the wedding takes place. At the marriage feast, Densuke rises to announce the reading of Saburōshichi's list of the items he has provided for O-Sumi's dowry. But, to the consternation of all concerned, the supposed list turns out to be a declaration from Saburōshichi to the effect that he had known that O-Sumi had been untrue, granting her favours to Hachizaemon. He has permitted her to marry her lover, but the dowry, he now admits, was a false promise, and O-Sumi must now spend her life married to a penniless clerk. Since Densuke had assisted in arranging their meetings, Saburōshichi says, he likewise will receive no reward.

The second tale of Book IV, "Hitori musume no ogori wa sue no kareta kogane take" (An Only Daughter's Pride Ends Up Like a Withered Bamboo), presents another variation on the same theme. Despairing of finding a husband worthy of their beautiful daughter in their rural home, a *rōnin* and his wife move to the Capital, hoping to place her in the mansion of a nobleman. But the pampered daughter has become even more fastidious than her parents. She refuses all offers, and at length, discouraged by his failure to find a suitable position for her, her father dies. The daughter then sets out on her own to find a wealthy patron and indeed does succeed in becoming the mistress of a man to her liking, but she demands so many luxuries and services that he finally leaves her. At last she ends up as the wife of a shopkeeper.

The stories described above are typical of *Tekake katagi*, but there is one that stands out in contrast. This is the tale of Fujino, in the second and third sections of Book III, "Komeichi wa Nihon-ichi no ōminato ni kaizumi no omoiire" (Speculation on the Rice Market in Japan's Foremost Port Town) and "Nido no tsutome wa sadamenaki yo no Shijimigawa no fuchise" (Re-employment in the Depths and Shallows of the Floating World of Shijimi-gawa). It lacks the scorn and satire, the jesting and exaggeration of the other stories, being a simple and straightforward tale of love and duty. Saitarō, a wealthy farmer, tries speculation on the Osaka rice exchange and loses everything he owns. Shunned by his family, he lives an aimless life in Osaka with Fujino, a former courtesan whose contract he had purchased. When, in despair, he begs Fujino to leave him for her own sake, she refuses, proposing instead that she return to the brothel where she was formerly indentured and let him make a fresh start with the money she receives. Saitarō gratefully agrees. Eigorō, the master of the brothel, provides fifty *ryō* as a lump sum, and Saitarō journeys to Hachijō Island where he uses his capital to buy local fabrics, expecting to sell them in Osaka at a high profit. But on the way back to the mainland, his boat is attacked by pirates. He escapes with his life, but his purchases are all stolen. Once again he is destitute.

The action now shifts to the brothel in Osaka where Fujino is working, awaiting word from her man. One morning her master unexpectedly calls her to his room and informs her that Saitarō is dead. He reads to her the letter that

Saitarō has sent him, telling of his misfortune and of his determination to put an end to his life. In the letter, Saitarō begs Eigorō not to allow Fujino to follow him in death or to take religious vows, but to encourage her to serve out her time in her present situation and live for the future. Kind and understanding, Eigorō releases Fujino for forty-nine days to observe the rituals of mourning and even summons a priest to read Buddhist scriptures on every seventh day. On the fiftieth day, Fujino returns to work and thereafter serves her master with impeccable fidelity. Numerous admirers try to ransom her, but Eigorō refuses all offers, no matter how high, saying that the decision must rest with Fujino. Fujino also declines their offers, and when her term of service ends, she makes her living as a hairdresser. She remains unmarried and continues to observe faithfully the proper memorial services for Saitarō. Fidelity such as this can come only from her heart, for it is more than the social conventions of the time demanded. Here we see the earliest example of Akinari's feminine ideal—the faithful, loving, long-suffering woman, later epitomized by Miyagi in the "Asaji ga yado" tale of *Ugetsu monogatari*, and given further dimensions in his old age through another character of the same name, the heroine of "Miyagi ga tsuka", in his last work of fiction, *Harusame monogatari*.

At the back of the last volume of *Sekenzaru* there had been an advertisement for two forthcoming works by the same author—*Seken tekake katagi* and *Shokoku kaisen dayori* (A Cargo Vessel's Tidings from the Provinces). When *Tekake katagi* appeared in print, it carried a further advertisement for *Kaisen dayori* and for another title, *Saigyō hanashi uta makura someburoshiki* (Saigyō's Tales from Places Celebrated in Poetry). However, in this announcement the *Shokoku kaisen dayori* title had been expanded to *Sekenzaru kōhen shokoku kaisen dayori* (The Monkey of Our Time, Part Two: A Cargo Vessel's Tidings from the Provinces), suggesting that Akinari had first planned the work as an independent composition, but later decided to style it as a sequel to his first *ukiyo-zōshi*. Akinari's publisher may have been behind the change. It was sound business practice to publish a "sequel" to a successful literary venture, and there were numerous precedents for so doing. Whether Akinari ever completed or even commenced writing these intended works is unknown. They never appeared in published editions, nor are any manuscripts known to exist. Indeed nothing more of any description was ever published under the name of Wayaku Tarō, and from this point on, as far as can be determined, Akinari's literary activities moved in a different direction. Perhaps he had rebelled against the prospect of becoming a hack for his publisher; perhaps too he had been distressed when forced to reveal his true identity. But it is true that Akinari's *ukiyo-zō*shi had been ill-timed. Few similar works were then being published, and in the same month that *Tekake katagi* appeared, the Hachimonjiya, in a state of near bankruptcy, sold its printing materials to an Osaka firm and went out of business. This was tantamount to a death knell for *ukiyo-zōshi* and must have been a shock to Akinari, enjoying his first literary success. Perhaps he saw the handwriting on the wall and decided to abandon this kind of writing immediately.

The *ukiyo-zōshi* as a genre fell into disrepute. Scholars have generally conceded that *Sekenzaru* and *Tekake katagi* are historically significant as the last noteworthy examples of such works, but otherwise they have tended to dismiss them as merely early efforts by the author of *Ugetsu monogatari*. Until recent years, few have been willing to say that they have any literary value in their own right. Yet both works are able to stand on their own merits. They are not pedestrian tales for an undiscriminating audience, but stories which can be understood and appreciated only by readers whose level of knowledge approaches that of Akinari himself. They display a degree of maturity surprising for an author's first offerings, and above all, reveal the young Akinari as an irrepressible storyteller, of infinite variety.

Another factor, perhaps the most important one, in Akinari's decision to give up light fiction was his increasing involvement in classical scholarship. Information is inadequate and contradictory, making reconstruction of exactly how he became a *kokugakusha*, or student of the national learning, impossible, but even though he himself mentioned no dates, the decade of the 1760's was no doubt a crucial time.

According to Akinari's own description of his scholarly progress, until he was nearly forty he was engrossed in the study of *haikai*. His teachers praised his talent, but persons who regarded *haikai* as a plebian pursuit urged him to shift his efforts to the more respectable art of *waka*. Having always thought *waka* to be the prerogative of court nobles, Akinari was reluctant to commit himself, but in the end he enrolled in the Shimo no Reizeike school, which traced its line back to Fujiwara Tamesuke (1263-1328) and which advocated a style of poetry relatively free from conventions. Again Akinari found himself praised for his talent, but he seems to have wanted to delve into literary theory rather than to obediently follow his teacher's advice on how to compose *waka*. Discouraged at getting nothing else but evasive answers to his questions, he left his teacher and turned to private study of the works of Keichū. Still many questions remained unanswered. He sought instruction from the scholar and writer Takebe Ayatari (1719-74), but found his knowledge unsatisfactory. Apparently realizing his own inadequacy, Ayatari introduced him to Katō Umaki (1721-77), as a result of which, in Akinari's words, "the road to the ancient learning was opened up."[15]

But when did all this happen? One of Akinari's associates stated that Akinari and Umaki met for the first time in the autumn of 1766,[16] but either this date, or the report that Takebe Ayatari suplied the introduction must be rejected, since Ayatari did not come to the Kamigata region until the spring of

1767. It is possible, though by no means certain, that Umaki was in Osaka during part of 1765 and 1766,[17] but Akinari's account of Ayatari's role in his meeting with Umaki is too straightforward to be taken lightly. Akinari once stated that he corresponded with Umaki over a period of seven years,[18] and since Umaki died in 1777, one might assume that their first encounter took place in 1770. This is possible. Umaki was in Kyoto from mid-1768 until at least the tenth month of 1769 and very likely stayed even longer. It is even possible that he spent some time in Osaka in 1770. But it is not necessary to assume that Akinari met Umaki *exactly* in 1770. He did not say that he *knew* Umaki for seven years, but that he *corresponded* with him for that length of time. Nor is it essential to place Umaki in Osaka at the time of their meeting, as a brief look at the careers of Umaki and Takebe Ayatari will show.

Originally from Hirosaki, in northeastern Japan, Ayatari had left home in disgrace in 1738, following an affair with his brother's wife. Eventually he made his way to Kyoto, where he took the tonsure, but he soon began to practise *haikai* with various teachers in the region. In 1747 he went to Edo, where he turned to more scholarly pursuits, eventually enrolling with Kamo Mabuchi (1697–1769) in 1762 to study the Japanese classics. From 1767 until 1771, when he returned to Edo, he was in Kyoto, giving lectures and engaging in the two pursuits for which he is best remembered, painting and story writing. Umaki, who was one of Mabuchi's leading disciples, had become a *rōnin* around 1762 and purchased *go-kenin* status, which made him a low-ranking direct retainer of the shogun, a year or two later. His new position involved spending each third year on official duties at either the Osaka Castle or the Nijō Castle in Kyoto, and it must have been on one such assignment that he met Akinari.

By 1767 Ayatari had become a well-known man of letters, so it is reasonable to assume that when he came to the Capital, Akinari, attracted by his reputation, took the trouble to attend some of his lectures and seek his advice on studying the classics. Akinari was probably making occasional trips to Kyoto then anyway, in order to visit his *haikai* associates. Ayatari probably went to Osaka from time to time as well, but since his relationship with Akinari was one of teacher to pupil, it is most likely that their contacts were primarily in Kyoto. Umaki is only specified as being "in the castle" when Akinari met him, not in any particular city.[19] Thus Akinari could have met Umaki in Kyoto as early as 1768 with Ayatari, who had become acquainted with Umaki through their mutual studies with Mabuchi, acting as the intermediary, and associated with him until his return to Edo, probably in 1770, and then corresponded with him until he died in 1777. Umaki may have been on duty at the Osaka Castle in 1771, and almost definitely was there in 1774, so the seven year period probably included some personal contact, but this may mean that their relationship was primarily by correspondence rather than entirely so. In the final analysis, Akinari's first meeting with Umaki cannot be dated precisely. More important than the chronology of their association is the effect that it had on Akinari's subsequent activities.[20]

In any case, Akinari's statement that he first began to study *waka* when about forty years old must be wrong. By Japanese reckoning he would have been forty in 1773. Even supposing that by "about forty" he actually meant, say, thirty-six or thirty-seven, if he had commenced the study of *waka* at that age, then privately studied Keichū's works for, as he said in one source, "two or three years,"[21] then received instruction for a time from Takebe Ayatari, and only after that met Katō Umaki, he would not have had seven years before Umaki's death in which to correspond with him. "About forty" was probably an error, or a deliberate fabrication, for "about thirty."[22]

There is no substantial information available on the nature of Akinari's association with Ayatari, but however cordial their relationship may have been at the start, it went sour. Akinari later described Ayatari as "a clod who couldn't read Chinese characters at all," who was taken aback every time he was asked a question. When writing his own account of the incident on which Ayatari had based his *Nishiyama monogatari* (A Tale of the Western Hills), Akinari called the work "a useless tale that misunderstands a good man."[23] Considering Ayatari less intelligent than himself, Akinari was envious of his fame and came to regard him as a rival.

There is little of a concrete nature about Akinari's relationship with Umaki either.[24] Since Umaki spent most of his time in Edo, their personal contacts were limited, but they became very close even so. The tone of Umaki's letters implies that he considered Akinari more a friend than a disciple, and to his death Akinari remained loyal to the memory of Umaki and conscious of his own position as an intellectual descendant of Mabuchi. One of the strongest indications of his high regard is that after Umaki passed away, Akinari made no effort to find another teacher, but turned once again to private study. Umaki had left an indelible impression on the younger man; he could not be replaced. Still, Akinari did not become a classical scholar only because he studied with Umaki. On the contrary, he sought Umaki's guidance because he was already deeply involved with the classics, but even so, it was under Umaki's influence that his own views began to take shape. No doubt he experienced a growing desire to emulate his teacher. Perhaps this is why he seemed more willing to talk about himself after he met Umaki, while remaining secretive and apparently ashamed regarding his earlier life and activities. His introduction to Umaki was the turning point in Akinari's life. He felt that he had been reborn, and he rejected his former self.

In 1802, at the request of Ōta Nampo, who had recently become friendly with Akinari, a man named Tamiya Yoshizō called on Akinari and asked him some questions about *Sekenzaru*. Nampo had probably realized that Akinari was sensitive about the matter and so decided to make inquiries through a third party. Just what questions Tamiya asked is not certain, but Akinari flew into a rage and refused to have anything more to do with him.[25] Even as an old man it pained Akinari to be reminded of his early writings or to have others learn about them. Such was the impact that Umaki had made, and such was the magnitude of the rift that Akinari felt with his past. In his own view, he had attained enlightenment, and his *ukiyo-zōshi* were an embarrassing blemish on the record of the classical scholar he had striven to become. Like the repentant man who forsakes the evils of this world to strive for rebirth in paradise, so Akinari, after experimenting with the fashionable novels of the street, left them to seek the beauty of ancient times in the classics.

3

Kashima-Mura

About noon one day in the spring of 1768 fire broke out in a teahouse in Sonezaki. The flames spread, leaped across the river into Dōjima, and created a blaze that lasted until nearly six o'clock the following morning. Thirteen lives were lost and about 6,500 buildings destroyed in the disaster.[1] The Ueda family's home and business, the Shimaya, was located in the burned-over area, but judging from Akinari's silence on the matter, the shop must have escaped serious damage.

Ironically, it was a smaller fire three years later that robbed him of his property and changed the course of his life. The only major conflagration of record in Dōjima in 1771 occurred on the seventeenth day of the first month, and if the description is accurate, the flames stopped well short of Akinari's home. But even so, Akinari stated in three independent writings that he was thirty-eight at the time of the disaster, so the year must be accepted.[2] Perhaps flying sparks from the main blaze descended upon the Shimaya, or, just as likely, the shop fell prey to a local fire which caused such insignificant damage to the neighbourhood as a whole that no record survives.

Akinari's house and his means of livelihood had gone up in smoke. To compound the misfortune, looters made off with what little property the flames spared, leaving the Ueda family destitute. Two years were to pass before they were again settled in permanent lodgings; in the meantime they drifted from one temporary abode to another, changing their residence more than ten times in all.[3]

Akinari probably had mixed feelings about his loss. On the one hand, he may well have felt a sense of relief. Normally a burned-out merchant would at least be expected to attempt a fresh start, but there is no evidence whatever that Akinari tried to re-establish his business. On the contrary, he apparently determined to use the fire as an avenue of escape from a way of life in which he had never felt comfortable. As long as the business that his father had left him remained in his hands, he had felt duty bound to operate it, but its loss seems to have given him the excuse he was searching for in his desire to leave the merchant life. On the other hand, however, the shop that had been such a burden had also been a source of income, and another means of livelihood was not readily available. However much he had felt out of his element as a merchant, this was the first period of want that he had ever experienced, and as head of the family he felt the burden of responsibility. It was no doubt a trying time for him. The frequency with which he mentioned the fire in his later writings suggests the degree to which the loss upset him. Any sense of liberation that he may have immediately felt was surely tempered by trepidation and regret.

It is uncertain just what Akinari did for the next two years. At least part of his income seems to have come from giving lectures on the classics, as is implied by the existence of a student's collection of notes from such lessons, dated Meiwa Era, 9th year (1772), 12th month, 3rd day, and signed "Fuji Teibu, disciple of Ueda Akinari."[4] Teibu was a son of the family that had presided over the Kashima Inari Shrine since the late Kamakura period and continues to do so to the present day. Akinari's supposedly miraculous recovery from smallpox in his childhood, and his consequent long years of patronage of this shrine, had given him an intimate relationship with the Fuji clan. In addition to the genuine friendship which they held for each other, Akinari's gratitude to the deity naturally extended to the priests of the shrine, and the priests were surely pleased to see in Akinari living proof of the power of the god they served. Teibu, thirteen years younger than Akinari, was already prominent in his neighbourhood, noted for his keen mind and for his paintings and comic *waka* verses (*kyōka*). He regarded Akinari both with respect for seniority and superior learning and with genuine affection as a friend of the family, and he no doubt received special consideration among Akinari's students, of whom there were several in the Kashima area. The Kashima Inari Shrine may even have been the Ueda family's residence for part of the first two years after the loss of the Shimaya, but Akinari's record indicates that their more permanent move to this area came later. For much of the period they lived from day to day, going here and there in search of whatever means of livelihood was offered. *Sono yuki kage*, a *haiku* collection prepared by Takai Kitō to commemorate the thirteenth anniversary of his father's death, published in late 1772, carried a verse by Gyoen—as one would normally expect, since Akinari had once belonged to Kikei's circle—but this contribution was not a new composition, but the same "How lonely the clouds!" verse that had appeared in *Haikai jū-roku nichi* seventeen years before. It may well be that Akinari could not be contacted since he was continually moving from place to place, and so Kitō arbitrarily selected one of his old compositions.[5]

It is indeed possible that in the years immediately following the fire Akinari tried to set himself up as a professional scholar, privately studying to advance his own knowledge while living off the revenue received from teaching and writing. He could have been living for short periods with a number of different students or friends between 1771 and 1773, which might explain his unsettled existence during those years. But teaching and writing would have been a poor source of income for all but the most established man of letters and certainly a premature step for Akinari to take at that time. Stringent living soon convinced him of the need to establish himself in a remunerative line of work. And so, sometime in 1773, Akinari settled with his wife and mother in a small cottage not far from the Inari Shrine in Kashima-mura and began to study medicine.[6]

Sumitsukishi	Should you seek what remains
Mukashi no io no	Of the hut where I dwelt
Ato toeba	In years gone by,
Suzuna hana saku	Look below the river bank
Kishi no shita ne ni[7]	Where the spring flowers bloom.

Thus Akinari wrote about his home beneath the dike on the Mikuni River.[8] It was a peaceful environment, but by no means isolated from civilization, and the Fuji family, who had probably assisted with the move, kept a protective and watchful eye over him and his family.

Perhaps Akinari's study of medicine had actually begun before he moved to Kashima-mura. In one reference to this activity he indicated that it began only after he had moved to the countryside, but in another he implied that this undertaking preceded the move and that he merely intensified his efforts at Kashima. It does seem improbable that he spent two aimless years deciding what to do, and delving into medical lore might well have occupied a part of his time during that period. Be that as it may, Akinari studied diligently at Kashima, "not sleeping at night, and working even harder during the day," as he hyperbolically described his activities.[9]

In deciding to become a physician, Akinari was not necessarily sacrificing his dreams of a literary career, for there was ample precedent for combining the two roles. Among his friends at the time he counted the haiku poet Katsube Seigyo and Kawai Rissai, a disciple of Goi Ranshū and scholar of the national learning, both of whom were physicians. Very likely acquaintances such as these had encouraged him to study medicine. In addition there was Tsuga Teishō (1718?–95?), who is widely believed to have been Akinari's medical instructor. No definite proof that Teishō did fill this role survives, but Akinari was personally acquainted with him, and decidedly influenced by his writings. Finally, there was Motoori Norinaga (1730–1801), whose commentaries on the *Kojiki*, the oldest extant account of Japan's mythical origins, were then making him a leader in the *kokugaku* field. Although it is uncertain whether he and Akinari had yet heard of each other, Norinaga was at that time the outstanding example of the successful scholar-physician.

Akinari's other activities while studying medicine are a further indication that the pursuit was not incompatible with literary scholarship. He continued to pursue the classics, and he remained active in literary circles, making occasional trips to Osaka in order to give lectures[10] and presumably to meet with his colleagues. Most likely he continued to visit Kyoto from time to time as well. He either wrote or extensively revised *Ugetsu monogatari* during this period, and the Kaguwashi Shrine preserves a number of unpublished manuscripts that date from that time, including a lengthy commentary on the ancient poem-tale collection, *Ise monogatari*.[11] Moreover, he continued to conduct study sessions for a group of students in the vicinity. Perhaps it was activities such as these, in addition to study of the healing arts, that left him no time to sleep at night.

In the ninth month of 1773 a request was submitted asking for permission to publish a work called *Yasaishō* (A Commentary on *Ya* and *Kana*).[12] The author was listed as Ueda Tōsaku, which was Akinari's real personal name, but it is not certain whether he actually did the writing. Three of his students supplied a preface to the published edition in which they claimed that they themselves had written it as a record of his lectures on *haikai* theory. They confessed that, harbouring doubts concerning the validity of Akinari's teachings, which sometimes differed from more respected traditions, they had secretly gone to the Capital, shown their notes to Yosa Buson, and asked his opinion. Buson, it turned out, was very much impressed with Akinari's ideas and strongly urged the three to make them public. Thus encouraged, the students said, they had made arrangements with the publisher and had had everything ready when Akinari became aware of their actions. Having an innate aversion to fame, he upbraided them severely and ordered the publication to be suspended. Not until 1787 did he finally relent and allow the work to go to press, the students said.

Yasaishō was indeed not published until 1787, though the printing blocks had been prepared by early 1774.[13] In his own preface, which also was written early in 1774, Buson confirmed the students' visit to him and his reaction to Akinari's views on *haikai* as contained in their notes. Akinari's refusal to allow the manuscript to be published also supports Buson's and the students' accounts. Had he written it himself, he must have intended it for circulation. Still, it seems strange that three of Akinari's students would rewrite their lecture notes as a formal treatise, sign his name to it, and proceed with the business of getting it published while keeping the whole matter a secret from him. An alternative view is that Akinari did write *Yasaishō* and went ahead with plans to publish it, but had second thoughts before the printing was carried out and withdrew the manuscript. It was only years later, probably under pressure from his colleagues, that he relented, and then only on condition that it be made to appear as someone else's work. This is plausible. Denying authorship of one's own works was a measure which protected one against both accusations of pride or pedantry if the work succeeded or of incompetence if it failed, and the practice was not uncommon among writers of Akinari's day. Nevertheless, there is no real consensus among Japanese scholars as to whether Akinari was the real author of *Yasaishō* or not, and a definite answer to the question appears to be impossible. Whoever may have done the actual writing, however, the views expressed are undoubtedly Akinari's.

Just three months before the publication request for *Yasaishō* was submitted, Akinari's friend Fujitani Nariakira had completed *Ayuishō*, a philological work in which he tried to explain the meanings and usages of certain particles, auxiliary verbs, interjections, and suffixes, with illustrative examples from old *waka*. The author of *Yasaishō* appears to have first read *Ayuishō* and then written his own work, making a deliberate effort to emulate the style of the earlier piece.[14] In a similar format, *Yasaishō* discusses the role of *kireji*, or "cutting words", those words conventionally employed as a kind of verbal punctuation in the writing of *haikai*. The author begins by deploring the lack of new studies and developments among *haikai* poets, criticizing their reliance on the old explanations of the *renga* schools and calling his own work an attempt to instruct and enlighten. What follows amounts to a summary of Akinari's views on the two common *kireji, ya* and *kana* (read *sai* in Sino-Japanese). An exhaustive treatment of their meanings and usage is given, and numerous haiku by the recognized masters are quoted as illustrations. Improper uses of these words are also pointed out and condemned. *Yasaishō* is a purely philological work, not an apology for *haikai* poetry. Although many of its points require revision when viewed by present-day grammarians, it was, at the time it was written, the most detailed and authoritative work on its subject that had appeared. Nevertheless, Akinari found it embarrassing. A *kokugaku* scholar, which he considered himself to be, was supposed to study ancient and medieval writings, not contemporary material, and this was why he resisted having the work published. If he had considered *haikai* to be a legitimate art form, he might have overcome his hesitation much earlier, but his view of *haikai* remained that it was nothing more than a pleasant way to enjoy one's leisure time.

In his preface to *Yasaishō*, Buson referred to Akinari as his friend. Just how long they had been acquainted is uncertain, but since Buson belonged to the same line of *haikai* poets as Takai Kikei, Akinari had probably at least heard his name from Kikei in the course of their lessons together, fifteen or more years earlier. It is even conceivable that Akinari and Buson met then for the first time, when Buson was about forty and Akinari in his early twenties. Even if this is so, however, their actual association took place only later, when Akinari had established more of a reputation. Indeed, it may be that *Yasaishō* marked the beginning of their real friendship. While Akinari was living at Kashima he was in contact with Takai Kitō, and since Kitō, like his father, was active in the same circle as Buson, some of Buson's ideas may have passed through Kitō to Akinari and thus onto the pages of *Yasaishō*. That could be one reason why Buson found the work so much to his liking. Perhaps, impressed with *Yasaishō*, he even took the initiative in arranging an introduction to Akinari and wrote his preface in order to place his own prestigious stamp of approval on the work and thus ensure its favourable reception. All this is speculative, but some months after Akinari had moved back to Osaka, Buson still referred to him as "the man of Kashima,"[15] implying that it was the image of Akinari at Kashima-mura that remained uppermost in his mind.

Buson's preface described Akinari as "my friend Muchō the Hermit" who "lives in seclusion in the village of Kashima in the province of Tsu, refusing visitors, and not mingling with the common crowd." This was surely an exaggeration, but it was an image of Akinari that other acquaintances would also express. It is not necessary to suppose that he completely shunned human society at this time, but certainly his life was much quieter than it had been at Dōjima. No longer was he a tradesman, and presumably it was to proclaim the break with his past that he shaved his head in the style of a Buddhist monk. Such was a common practice in his society. It was forbidden, at least in theory, to move from one social class to another, so when a man retired, or otherwise ceased to be an active member of the group to which he belonged, and wished to make the fact clear, he frequently shaved his head, as does the central character in the *Ugetsu* tale "Buppōsō."[16] Of course shaving their heads was a practice common among physicians of the day,[17] and Akinari's action may have initially had no more meaning than that, but pictures and clay figurines of him, even those made after he had given up the medical profession, invariably show him with his head shaven, so his withdrawal—at least his psychological withdrawal—appears to have been unwavering.

The name "Muchō" by which Buson called him, and which subsequently became perhaps his most popular cognomen (rivalled only by Yosai, a name he used especially when writing *waka* verse), apparently came into use about this time. As stated earlier, the name means "crab" and was a self-mocking reference to his deformed hands, but Akinari also used it to point out the relative seclusion in which he was then living.

Tsuki ni asobu	Playing in the moon,
Ono ga yo wa ari	He finds a world of his own,
Minashi gani[18]	The poor orphan crab.

So he had written when he moved to the countryside. Moreover, as a crab has a soft body beneath its hard exterior, so the name was supposed to refer to Akinari's outwardly stern but inwardly gentle disposition.[19] Also revealing is this verse of Akinari's:

Tsu no kuni no	In the province of Tsu,
Naniwa ni tsukete	Whatever thing he does
Utomaruru	The world rejects him—
Ashiwara gani no	The crab, scuttling sideways through
Yoko hashiru mi wa[20]	The reed plains of Naniwa.

Also dating from this time, or at least from no later, is Akinari's companionship with Kimura Kenkadō. The congeniality of the two men was probably enhanced by certain common factors in their backgrounds. The eldest son of an Osaka *sake* brewer, Kenkadō, like Akinari, had been plagued from early childhood by poor health. When he was fifteen, his father had died, and he had attempted to assume responsibility for the business, but lacked the physical energy and, like Akinari in similar circumstances, the inclination to take an active part. Having long been interested in botany and Japanese antiquity, he devoted himself to the study of such things, eventually becoming well-known as a compiler of all sorts of unusual information. He was a top-ranking authority on medicinal herbs, an accomplished student of art, and a painter in his own right, and he was also an authority on the tea ceremony, and well-versed in things Chinese. At the height of his career, his companionship was very much sought by writers, painters, and scholars of the Kamigata region. Akinari often called on him for advice on medicinal plants.[21] It is not known whether they became acquainted in time for Kenkadō to influence Akinari's decision to become a physician, but they had become good friends by no later than 1774.[22] Their relationship continued until Kenkadō's death and must have been intimate, to judge from the frequency of their visits to each other. Akinari once invited Katō Umaki to join him, along with Kimura and Hosoai Hansei, on a boating excursion,[23] which also suggests that he considered Kimura a friend and not just a fellow scholar.

Thus, studying medicine and literature, teaching and writing, Akinari continued his quiet existence at Kashima, until tragedy intervened. In the last month of 1775, Fuji Iehide, the head of the family and the twenty-first priest of the Kashima Inari Shrine, died at the age of sixty-two. Teibu took over his father's duties, but only a month later death struck him down as well.[24] The deaths of father and son in such quick succession suggests that a contagious disease was the cause, and Akinari, now a qualified physician, probably attended at their sickbeds.

The role of family head and chief priest now fell to Utsuna, then aged twenty-six. Of course, he continued to visit Akinari and render whatever assistance he could, but with Iehide and Teibu gone Akinari could hardly have found Kashima the same. There were now painful memories attached to the place, and it was a convenient time to move on. He may have been content with the life he had been living, but his mother was urging him to return to Osaka.[25] He felt obliged to raise his personal income and provide for his wife and mother a standard of living more to their liking. And so, with the poetic reflection,

> *Dare ka mata*   Perhaps one day
> *Sumikawaruran* Another will dwell in my place,
> *U ni taeshi*   Here in this borrowed lodging
> *Toshi no mitose no* Where I bore my sorrows
> *Kari no yadori wo*[26] For the space of three years,

Akinari, sometime in 1776, took his family back to Osaka[27] and opened a medical practice in Amagasaki-chō, not far from their old home in Dōjima.

4

Ugetsu Monogatari

Shortly after returning to Osaka, Akinari published the collection of nine tales of the supernatural that he called *Ugetsu monogatari* (Tales of Moonlight and Rain).[1] Based in large measure on Chinese sources, but so adapted to the Japanese scene as to make them a unique blending of both cultures, the *Ugetsu* tales have come to rank among the representative works of Japanese literature. Scholars are almost unanimous in calling them Akinari's masterpiece.

Although the tales defy characterization, *Ugetsu* must be seen as an early example of *yomihon*, a variety of prose literature that had begun to appear by mid-century. The term *yomihon* (literally, "reading books") originally referred simply to books where written content was more important than the pictures, and in that context it was applied to the *hachimonjiyabon* to distinguish them from the liberally illustrated books that were popular at the same time. Today, however, as a technical term in Japanese literary history, the word denotes a category of books that appeared from the mid-eighteenth century to the mid-nineteenth, often quite lengthy, written in a blend of elegant and colloquial styles, their intricate plots generally borrowed from Chinese sources but combined with Japanese history and legend. Books of this variety, represented by the works of Santō Kyōden (1761–1816) and Takizawa Bakin (1767–1848) came out in profusion in Edo during the Bunka

(1804–17) and Bunsei (1818–30) Eras, but their early predecessors, most of which appeared in the Kamigata region, shared many of the same qualities. These include Tsuga Teishō's *Hanabusa sōshi* (pub. 1749) and *Shigeshige yawa* (pub. 1766), Takebe Ayatari's *Nishiyama monogatari* (pub. 1768) and *Honchō suikoden* (pub. 1773), and Akinari's *Ugetsu monogatari*. Books such as these laid the groundwork for what was to follow. Most of the early *yomihon* were relatively short works or collections of stories; with the exception of *Honchō suikoden*, few were of conspicuous length, but they do possess all the other recognized characteristics of the later *yomihon*, including a more serious quality that sets them apart from the *ukiyo-zōshi*.

Effectively, the year 1767, when the Hachimonjiya ceased operations and sold its printing materials, marks the end of the *ukiyo-zōshi* genre. No works of enduring merit were published after that date, and it was about the same time that the *yomihon* began to appear. *Yomihon* were not so much the offspring of the *ukiyo-zōshi* as a reaction against them—a conscious effort to create something better. Actually, translations and adaptations of Chinese literary works had been common among the *kanazōshi* and *ukiyo-zōshi*, but around the beginning of the eighteenth century, a category of Chinese fiction known as *pai hua*, or vernacular, stories started to come into Japan. Books of this kind, dating largely from the Yuan and Ming dynasties, and written in a style much like the spoken language of their day, proved most influential in the development of the *yomihon*. Their elaborate plots often featured bizarre or supernatural themes or heroic deeds, and they were frequently interrupted with intellectual asides by the characters or with comments by the author on historical or cultural matters. An overt stress on ethical principles was common. Although the market for such novels in Japan was at first limited to those who could read Chinese, their admirers soon began to produce annotated editions and translations into Japanese. Thanks to the efforts of men like Okajima Kanzan (1674–1728), who began work on the first edition of *Shui hu chuan* (Water Margin) to be annotated for reading with Japanese pronunciation and word order, Chinese vernacular fiction had become quite popular in Japan by mid-century. Credit must also be given to the central government's emphasis on Confucian teachings, as well as to the general trend towards education during the Tokugawa Period. It was only a matter of time before men who were searching for a new direction to take from the *ukiyo-zōshi* style of literature began to try their hands at adaptations from the Chinese.

One such man was Tsuga Teishō. From reading widely in Chinese works, he had acquired an abundance of material that he could transpose with relatively minor revisions into a Japanese setting. His works sometimes bore the signs of immaturity, however, for he was so faithful to his sources that his adaptations sometimes appear more like translations. Aside from giving Japanese names to the places and characters, and a more local flavour to the conversation, he added little that was original. The characters' thoughts and actions are sometimes quite un-Japanese. Frequently Teishō even took the original Chinese language directly into his Japanese version, a move which in some instances helped to preserve the Chinese mood, but more often just seemed unnatural. Such weaknesses were most apparent in *Hanabusa sōshi*. In subsequent works, such as *Shigeshige yawa* and *Hitsuji gusa* (pub. 1786), he improved his technique, making his stories less conspicuously Chinese in origin, and his language more purely Japanese. Unlike the *hachimonjiyabon*, which portrayed the contemporary world, Teishō's adaptations were of supernatural tales. Such foreign-flavoured, sometimes even bizarre stories had a refreshing newness which many readers found fascinating and worthy of emulation.

   Still, one must not assume Akinari's supernatural tales to be indebted only to eerie stories from China, for there was also a long indigenous tradition from which he could draw. Numerous tales with supernatural elements may be found in the *Nihon ryōiki* of the ninth century, the *Konjaku monogatari shū* of the twelfth century, or in similar collections of the middle ages. During the Tokugawa period an abundance of such stories appeared among the *kanazō-shi*, and to some extent these can be seen as bypassing the *ukiyo-zōshi* and contributing directly to the development of the early *yomihon*.[2] Many of these tales were drawn from earlier Japanese narratives or from Chinese stories. *Kii zōdan shū*, for example, which was written in the sixteenth century, though not published until 1687, borrowed liberally from such works as the *Konjaku monogatari shū* and the thirteenth-century collection, *Uji shūi monogatari*, but also contained translations of three tales from the Chinese collection *Chien teng hsin hua*. Later, Asai Ryōi (ca. 1612–91) published adaptations from the same title in his *Otogi bōko* (pub. 1666) and its sequel, *Inu hariko* (pub. 1692), and other authors produced similar collections. When Akinari wrote *Ugetsu*, then, both adaptations of Chinese tales and the indigenous material in collections like those mentioned above were available to him. He may also have made his way back to the Chinese originals.[3]

   But in the writing of *Ugetsu*, Akinari was directly indebted more to Tsuga Teishō than to any other author. Even the five-volume, nine-tale format was copied from Teishō's collections. Like Teishō, he adapted most of the tales from Chinese sources, though unlike the older author he fully digested his material and embellished it with details from Japanese history and classical literature. Akinari's flair for literary style also made his stories literary works in their own right, sometimes superior to their models. They were in no sense plagiarisms. But Akinari's personal relationship with Teishō is not at all clear. Ōta Nampo said that Akinari had learned from Teishō, and it has been widely assumed that what he learned was medicine,[4] but the only basis for this conjecture is that he was studying to become a physician at the time Teishō's influence on his writings is most evident. The only firm proof that they knew each other is the fact that Teishō wrote a preface for Akinari's *Yasumigoto* in 1792.[5] Even if Teishō did serve as his teacher, Akinari never indicated a regard for him comparable to his respect for Umaki. Teishō was not a true scholar; rather he used his ability to read popular Chinese novels in order to adapt them to the tastes of the book-buying public. He was not the man to study under if one's concern was for academic purity. Having studied Chinese in his youth, Akinari very likely did not feel the need for further instruction. He may have sought companionship with Teishō as a popular author whose name would be good advertising for his own writings, but he probably learned more from Teishō's works than from Teishō himself, at least as far as literary matters go.

Takebe Ayatari, whose *Nishiyama monogatari* had combined a romantic plot with a scholar's knowledge of the native classics, must also be considered among those who helped set the stage for *Ugetsu*. While basing his story upon a contemporary event, he had employed an elegant form of Japanese, the so-called *gabun* style, reminiscent of the language of court romances of the Heian period, (794–1185) to tell the tale. It was to some extent an artificial creation; Ayatari deliberately used expressions taken directly from the great classics and even went so far as to note the sources in the text of the story. But *Nishiyama* sparked considerable discussion in literary circles in spite of its pedantry. As a purely Japanese tale it was, in a sense, a reaction against the popular translations and adaptations from the Chinese and so suggested new directions in which Japanese literature might move. Subsequently Ayatari wrote *Honchō suikoden* (The Japanese Water Margin), which was, as the title indicates, inspired by the Chinese tale *Shui hu chuan* (Sino-Japanese reading, *Suikoden*), but he managed to break free from his source and adapt the story smoothly to a Japanese setting. This work also created great interest among literati, and Takizawa Bakin even went so far as to call it the first *yomihon*.[6] In their efforts to remove themselves from *ukiyo-zōshi* conventions and break new ground, the early *yomihon* authors came to look to the Japanese classics for inspiration. The classics were seen as absolutes, and the ideal goal, therefore, was not to modernize them, but to go back to them and emulate their style. Even Teishō's works, despite their commercial orientation and lack of originality, had such a revolutionary aim. In his preface to *Hanabusa sōshi*, Teishō called his book a work unlike the popular literature of the day, having aims in common with those of *Tsurezuregusa* and *The Tale of Genji*.[7] Ayatari's *Nishiyama* was a still more obvious attempt to go back to the classics. Even the use of *monogatari* in the title indicates that intention.

Akinari signed *Ugetsu* with the pseudonym Senshi Kijin, the only time he used the name, which seems fitting, for, as a reference to his deformed hands, it was derived from the experience that had given him an enduring belief the supernatural. Nevertheless, one should be wary of accounting for *Ugetsu* simply in the light of its author's acceptance of such things. True, it is beyond dispute that Akinari did believe in a world beyond the one he lived in, but in this respect he was no different from the average person of his time. Not every believer in the supernatural produces a masterpiece of literature about it—not even every believer with literary talent. Nor should an actual belief in ghosts and demons even be necessary in order to write vivid stories about them. A keen imagination and a gift for expression are far more important. Moreover, it is only in *Ugetsu*, of all Akinari's writings, that the supernatural takes on dominant proportions. It does appear in some of his other fiction, but on nowhere near the same scale—none of those works can be called ghost stories. Yet *Ugetsu* has overshadowed all of Akinari's other work to such a degree that he has come to be known, in the popular mind, as a confirmed romantic absorbed in the occult. Just how obsessed with metaphysical things was he?

Akinari did believe in supernatural manifestations, and he took issue with those who denied their occurrence. In response to certain rationalists who maintained that so-called fox possession was nothing more than the symptoms of disease, for example, he countered that there were numerous cases of such possession on record. He noted the experience of Hosoai Hansei who, while visiting a certain temple in Kyoto, had seen the sun apparently go down in the middle of the day. Stating his conviction that Hansei had been deceived by a fox or a badger, Akinari went on to relate a personal experience. When he was an old man, living in Kyoto, he said, he had once set out to visit a temple in the northeastern part of the city. Although the path was clear and wide, he inexplicably went astray and ended up far off the mark. After correcting his error, he reached his intended destination and related what had happened to the abbot, who told him that his mistake was a sign of illness and advised him to take special care. But even though he took the utmost pains to follow the right path on the return journey, he lost his way once again. He concluded that a fox had bewitched him.

On another occasion, also after he had moved to Kyoto, he set out to visit a shrine at which it was his custom to pay his respects each month, the enshrined deity being the tutelary god of his birthplace in Osaka. He reached the shrine, completed his worship, and started home before noon. En route he was caught in a rain shower. Suffering from fatigue and troubled by his eyes—he was then nearly blind—he stopped at the home of a friend and ate the mid-day meal with him. The host offered to call a palanquin or let him stay the night, but the rain had eased, home was no more than a mile away, and he was quite familiar with the route, so he decided to start out on foot once again. The rain intensified, but the road was wide, so Akinari kept on, thinking there was no chance of mistaking the way, yet he did get lost, and even went astray again while trying to correct his error. Night was falling by the time he reached home. Experiences such as these, said Akinari, proved that foxes and badgers really do cast spells over men, and he ridiculed Nakai Riken, who maintained that such things never happened. Riken could make such statements, Akinari said, only because he stayed shut up in his school and never ventured into the real world to see for himself.[8]

Nevertheless, aside from these experiences and a few remarks on the supernatural here and there in his writings, Akinari on the whole maintained a rational view of life. He realized that some things could not be explained scientifically, but even so, his citing of what were, to him, factual examples of fox possession in order to counter Riken's arguments illustrates his fundamentally rational position. These supposed experiences with the supernatural occurred long after the appearance of *Ugetsu*, and thus were not necessarily connected with it. Nor is there any evidence that Akinari's belief in the supernatural extended to all of its manifestations that appear in his work. It is probably better to explain his authorship of *Ugetsu* in the light of the ghostly element in the Chinese and Japanese stories that he read and the desire, common at the time, to emulate the style of the classics. Augmenting his sources with his own imagination and weaving his plots together with an elegantly poetic style, Akinari produced a work of eerie beauty that represents the highest artistic level reached by the supernatural tale in Japan. His actual belief in the other world, though perhaps helpful, was surely not the decisive factor.

The *Ugetsu* preface is dated late spring, 1768, yet the tales were not published until 1776. One naturally wonders why there was such a long delay, and some scholars have speculated that Akinari wrote the preface before he wrote the book, while others have suggested that he had some reason for falsifying the actual date of completion. The first explanation of the reason for the gap between completion and publication is unlikely, for the preface speaks of the tales as being already finished. The established practice was to write the preface after the work itself had been completed, and in any case, it is unnatural to do otherwise. The other explanation for the delay, however, has been the subject of considerable discussion.

However high the literary merit of Akinari's *ukiyo-zōshi* may be, they are quite unlike *Ugetsu* in content and literary style. It is hard to imagine their author turning out a work so different in only a year's time. Talent requires time to mature, especially when moving in new directions. Common sense indicates that Akinari would have needed more than a year in which to broaden and deepen his artistic sense to the point where a work of *Ugetsu's* stature became possible. But if the tales were not complete by 1768, why did Akinari affix that date to his preface? One possible answer is his feelings of jealousy toward Takebe Ayatari. Ayatari's *Nishiyama monogatari* had been based on a real event, but written in imitation of the classical style; his *Honchō suikoden* had been based on a Chinese source, but skilfully adapted to a Japanese setting. Thus by 1776, when *Ugetsu* was published, the qualities of which it could boast had already been introduced by Ayatari. Akinari did not like Ayatari and considered himself the better man. Perhaps he even felt that he had made his own literary developments independently, but realized that if he dated *Ugetsu* correctly he would be considered indebted to Ayatari. Such a debt he refused to acknowledge, and so he falsified the date of *Ugetsu* to make it appear contemporary with *Nishiyama*.

This view seems plausible. But it is easy to overestimate Akinari's scorn for *Nishiyama*. Granted, he already had acrimonious feelings toward its author, but he did not openly condemn the work itself until 1806, when he met the protagonist of the incident on which it was based, learned this man's version of the facts, and was outraged at Ayatari's distortion of them. Still, this outrage did not deter him from writing his own fictionalized version of the incident, which he included in his *Harusame monogatari*. Furthermore, if Akinari had really wanted to avoid any appearance of indebtedness to Ayatari, why did he not make *Ugetsu* seem to antedate *Nishiyama* unmistakably? *Nishiyama* had appeared in the second month of 1768. The "late spring" date given in the *Ugetsu* preface suggests that it was completed a bit later. If the date was a fabrication designed to upstage Ayatari, it was a careless one.

It appears more likely that *Ugetsu*, or at least the first draft, was indeed finished in the spring of 1768, but for reasons that are not clear the publication was delayed for eight years. This is not to say that the *Ugetsu* of 1768 was the same work that was finally published in 1776. The shift from the everyday world of *Sekenzaru* and *Tekake katagi* to the transcendence of reality found in *Ugetsu* could not be accomplished overnight. More likely the original draft of *Ugetsu* was in the *ukiyo-zōshi* vein. The published edition of *Tekake katagi* had carried an advertisement for a forthcoming work by the same author, entitled *Saigyō hanashi uta makura someburoshiki*, and the first tale in the *Ugetsu* collection has the poet-priest Saigyō as its central character. Quite likely the final version of *Ugetsu* grew out of stories that were written earlier, at least some of which were originally intended for *Someburoshiki*. To be sure, this remains a reasoned guess, but Akinari apparently wrote more around that time than he published. In his preface to *Tekake katagi*, he implied that its ten tales had been selected from over twenty he had composed. Presumably then, when he wrote *Ugetsu* he first made use of material that he had intended for *Kaisen dayori* and *Someburoshiki*. Then, before the manuscript went to press he saw the wisdom of abandoning the *ukiyo-zōshi* style, but unwilling to discard what he had written, he kept it, revising it over the years until he was satisfied. The period of rewriting was a time of considerable intellectual and artistic development for Akinari, and he incorporated into the work the new knowledge that he had gained from his studies. Part of it was also a time of economic hardship, which probably made him think more seriously about life and sobered his general outlook.

The above is likely what happened, but in the final analysis it is impossible to say just when *Ugetsu* was written. The problem of dating it remains another of the intriguing, but as yet insoluble, mysteries of Akinari's career. Early in 1771 a notice appeared for a soon-to-be-published five-volume collection of supernatural stories, called *Ugetsu monogatari* and written by one Senshi Sanjin,[9] very nearly the same pen name. By 1771, therefore, *Ugetsu* was close enough to its present form to be identifiable as a collection of ghostly tales in five volumes, although the advertisement does not necessarily mean that the work was complete. Indeed, there is no record of the publication of *Ugetsu*, the date of 1776 merely being that on the oldest extant copy. Perhaps it was published primarily at the author's own expense.[10] If so, a further possible reason for delay comes to mind. Around the time that the notice of forthcoming publication appeared, Akinari was burned out of his home and business and left in penury. Not only may this disaster have left him unable to finance the publication, but if he had not yet turned the manuscript over to the publisher, it may have been destroyed in the fire, necessitating further rewriting from memory.

Novels that had been produced by the courtly society of the Heian period were regarded with near reverence in Akinari's time, but contemporary fiction, which was generally aimed at pleasing the masses for commercial purposes, tended to be dismissed as light literature. Even popular works of discernible literary merit suffered this neglect, and consequently it was hard for a writer of fiction to be taken seriously. Akinari himself had come to see the literature of his day as being in a sorry state. As his acquaintance with the masterpieces of the past broadened, it was natural that he feel a yearning for the glories of a bygone age and a desire to elevate contemporary literature to a similar plane. In his preface to *Ugetsu*, Akinari compared his work to *Shui hu chuan* and *The Tale of Genji*. It is doubtful whether he really expected it to prove equally monumental, but it represented his conscious attempt to revive the spirit of the Heian classics, and he had polished it meticulously. He must have been proud of *Ugetsu*. Notwithstanding the humble terms in which he described his own work in the preface, the fact that he chose such outstanding works against which to judge it suggests a degree of conceit.

Akinari wrote his preface in Chinese, perhaps as a gesture toward the Chinese stories from which he had drawn inspiration, or maybe as a display of his ability, or possibly because a Chinese introduction was a precedent that Teishō and Ayatari had established. The preface is short. Akinari begins by saluting the artistic achievement reached by the authors of *Shui hu chuan* and *Genji*, despite the tradition that both received divine chastisement for publishing falsehoods. He assures his own readers that his tales are not true, and no one should be deceived by them. In closing, he describes how he had completed the stories on a night when the moon shone dimly through the clouds after the rain, and so had chosen the title *Ugetsu monogatari*, which means "Tales of Moonlight and Rain," or perhaps more accurately, "Tales of a Clouded Moon." This may or may not have been true; the title was in fact taken from the Noh drama *Ugetsu*, in which Saigyō appears as the secondary character.[11]

Ugetsu was to be Akinari's only venture into the literature of the supernatural, yet it has proved superior to all of its predecessors and followers in the genre in Japan. Like no other work, it combines a vivid ghostly atmosphere with a poetic style that is a delight to read. Into the world of the classics, which was a dream world, one not to be known, but rather to be felt, Akinari blended fantasy, imagination, and a supernatural element which suggests mystery and a kind of twisted beauty. While striving to emulate the spirit of the Heian classics, he drew much plot material from China—no contradiction, for he recognized that Japan was indebted to China for many aspects of its own culture. This awareness is implicit in his parallel consideration of *Shui hu chuan* and *The Tale of Genji* in the preface.

Throughout *Ugetsu*, Akinari retains control over his ghosts, never letting them get the better of him, using them not to convey terror for its own sake, but to enhance the ideas and sensibility that he wished to stress. In the first tale, "Shiramine" (White Peak), for example, the ghost's ghoulish form is terrifying, but of secondary importance nonetheless. The opening lines carry no hint of the nether world, merely setting an appropriate mood for the story. The reader accompanies the protagonist on a journey from the Capital region up to the Kantō and Tōhoku areas, then back down through Osaka and on to the island of Shikoku, passing through places whose names are imbued with tradition and tinged with emotion in the Japanese mind. This, together with the aura of sweet sadness that so often accompanies a journey in Japan—the beauties of the landscape tempered by the fatigue of travel and the hardships of the journey, the changing of the seasons that gives the viewer a renewed awareness of his own mortality, the implied sorrow of separation from beloved persons and places, intensified by the uncertainty of ever seeing them again—serve to transfer the reader from the present into an unreal world of long ago. With the mood thus established, Akinari proceeds to construct the setting. It is night in early winter. The thick vegetation that makes the site dim and gloomy even on a clear day intensifies the darkness, and the mists that rise from the deep gorge below add their own sombreness to the scene.

In this lonely and deserted place, the once proud Emperor Sutoku (r. 1123–1141) now lies buried in an insignificant grave, and here the poet-priest Saigyō (1118–1190) sorrowfully prays for the departed monarch's soul. In this manner the atmosphere for the ghost's appearance is created, yet the spirit of

Sutoku does not come in any frightening guise, and the main body of the tale is not a ghost story at all, but a debate between opposing views of history and political action—a confrontation between Menicus' doctrine of the right to revolt and Saigyō's view that rebellion to satisfy personal ambition is not appropriate for Japan.

Akinari in effect uses Saigyō as his alter ego. The political and historical ideas put forth by Saigyō are those of Akinari, who rejects the continental philosophy in favour of the Japanese tradition of an unbroken imperial line. But the tale amounts to more than an intellectual discourse, for through the mood that has been established, Akinari manages to give a kind of tragic beauty to Sutoku's fall. Moreover, here is the first instance of a recurring theme in *Ugetsu*—the idea that human feelings can carry over from this life into the next and even affect the course of history. It is to underline this point that, toward the end of the story, Sutoku transfigures himself into the form of the demon that he had become. Only then does he emerge as a terrifying figure, and before long he passes out of sight, but his fearsome appearance and the subsequent fulfilment of his dire prophecies leave the reader awed by his power. But here, as in the other tales, cheap sensationalism is avoided. Throughout *Ugetsu*, the apparitions' function is nearly always to stress the author's ethical views, either acting as his mouthpiece or, as in the case of Sutoku and others, emphasizing his views by standing in opposition to them. An ethical theme pervades the whole of the work, but it is not simply the "reward virtue and punish vice" of Confucian morality, which became standard fare in the later *yomihon*. Rather it is a call for the cultivation of the innate goodness of man, of the pure Japanese spirit that is expressed in the classics.

The ethical focus is even more apparent in the second tale, "Kikuka no chigiri" (Chrysanthemum Tryst), considered by some to be the most nearly perfect of the nine stories. Like "Shiramine," its mood is established at the beginning, though with a moral discourse, not a travel scene.

> Green, green grows the spring willow. But never a plant in your garden. Never pick a falsehearted man for a friend. Although the willow may bud early, does it hold up when autumn's first wind blows? A false-hearted man makes friends easily, but he is fickle. Whereas the willow for many springs takes on a new colour, a falsehearted man will break off with you and never call again.

The next sentence introduces the hero and the setting in straightforward prose: "In the province of Harima in the town of Kako there dwelt a scholar whose name was Hasebe Samon,"[12] but the reader has already been transported out of his real world by the lyrical parallel passages of the opening homily. These lines, and those of the conclusion, which are a simple restatement of the introduction, reveal Akinari's intention in "Kikuka." He extols those who live lives of sincerity in a world of fickleness and dishonesty; those whose fidelity and devotion to duty transcend any attachment to life and self-interest. The faithfulness of Samon and Akana stands out in contrast to the fickle man, against whose inconstancy Akinari warns.

Samon lives in the manner of the ideal scholar, unconcerned about material things, leading a simple and honest life, concentrating on his studies and shunning all frivolity. His mother, who is likened in her maternal devotion to the mother of Mencius, supports him in his chosen profession and may be a reflection of Akinari's own mother, who endured considerable discomfort and anxiety for the sake of his scholarly pursuits. When Samon encounters the ailing Akana, he dismisses warnings that the disease may attack him as well, and selflessly nurses the man back to health. After he has recovered, Akana's duty as a warrior forces him to leave, notwithstanding the vow of brotherhood that he and Samon have sworn, but through all the vicissitudes of his journey, he remembers his promise to return on the appointed day. He must keep the pledge at the expense of his honour, so when, having been placed under arrest, he finds it beyond his power to fulfil his word, he takes his own life. Now, freed from mortal bonds, he makes the journey to Samon's house as a spirit. Upon learning what has happened, Samon fulfils his duty to Akana by avenging his death. It is a vivid portrayal of loyalty in the Japanese tradition; Samon and Akana are truly the antithesis of the falsehearted man, against whom the reader is warned once again as the story ends.

Besides being a great moral tale, "Kikuka" is also an outstanding example of Akinari's talents as a storyteller. In this, as in all of the *Ugetsu* tales, his key technique is to keep himself out of the action, saying no more about it than is necessary. The reader is thus unable to play the role of detached observer and is forced to become an active participant with the hero. Knowing no more than the protagonist, the reader has no choice but to follow him—in effect, to identify with him. Reader and hero have an intimate relationship, acting and feeling together. As the events unfold, the reader reacts in his real world as the central character does in his imaginary one. "Kikuka" is told entirely from Samon's point of view, and thus when Akana departs for Izumo, the reader stays behind with Samon and like him, knows nothing of Akana's fate. There is no indication of what is going to happen. Like Samon, the reader can only wait and see. Nevertheless, just like Samon's mother, the reader cannot help feeling some misgivings when her son, doubting nothing, begins to prepare for his friend's return. His unquestioning trust seems excessive, almost naïve. The day passes, and the travellers who go by on the highway, none of them Akana, serve to intensify the mood of mounting impatience. Now the reader's uneasiness increases. Perhaps Akana will not come. Perhaps he is dead. Perhaps he is the falsehearted man who was mentioned in the opening lines. But though the reader may begin to waver, Samon stands firm, and at last his trust is vindicated. Before this, however, Akinari arranges the appropriate setting:

> The Milky Way shimmered with a pale light. The moon's icy wheel shed its glow on him, aggravating his loneliness. A watchdog's bark rang out through the clear air, and the sound of the waves in the bay seemed as if surging round the very place where he stood. The moon presently disappeared behind the mountain peaks, and about to give up, Samon decided to go back in and close the door, when he happened to take a last look.[13]

And so Akana arrives. The reader, having been kept in ignorance of what has transpired in Izumo, naturally rejoices along with Samon. While he quickly senses from Akana's demeanour that all is not as it should be, he is only slightly ahead of Samon in realizing that the visitor is a ghost. This is the high point of the story. Samon's journey to Izumo to avenge Akana and Tsunehisa's decision not to pursue such a shining example of loyalty are necessary to give the tale a satisfactory conclusion, but they are anticlimactic nevertheless.

The same storytelling method is skillfully employed in the third tale. Unlike the two that precede it, "Asaji ga yado" (The House Amid the Thickets), has no lyrical passage of introduction to set the mood. In a matter-of-fact way the scene is placed in the village of Mama, district of Katsushika, province of Shimōsa. This is appropriate, for at the outset the story appears to be about the prosaic subject of commerce. Attracted by prospects of easy and substantial profit, Katsushirō, the hero, has invested everything he owns in fabrics and is about to depart for the Capital, where he intends to market them. It has already been noted in the opening sentences that Katsushirō is an impractical man whose poor judgment and lack of diligence have already cost him much of his property. His wife, Miyagi, recognizes his weakness and feels uneasy about this risky venture but, like the devoted wife she is, she conceals her misgivings. Thus she bids farewell to her husband, to whom the possibility of failure seems never to have occurred. The reader accompanies Katsushirō to the Capital. He is told only that Miyagi is caught in the midst of warring armies and that, although her safety is threatened by neighbours whose hearts have succumbed to the moral decay that accompanies famine and hardship, she stays on while others flee, faithfully awaiting her husband's return.

But Akinari gives only this small glimpse of Miyagi in her home village. Then, leaving the reader in suspense, he moves on to join Katsushirō in the Capital. Katsushirō and the reader both remain ignorant of Miyagi's fate. The story follows Katsushirō as he sells his wares for the expected high sum, only to have the profits taken by robbers, and while he is detained, first by illness, and then by reports that the fighting has made it impossible for him to return home. During the seven years he is away, neither he nor the reader hears anything about Miyagi. Thus, when he finally does begin the journey back to Mama,[14] the reader shares his anticipation and trepidation; when he finds his house undamaged, and Miyagi waiting for him, the reader shares his joy and relief. To be sure, there are warnings that all is not as it appears. It is after sundown when Katsushirō arrives, and lowering clouds intensify the gloom. Adding to this foreboding atmosphere, the village is in a shambles, the fields untilled, and everything so changed that Katsushirō can scarcely find his way. Strange indeed that only his house remains as of old. Miyagi's voice has changed; she is dirty and emaciated, and her hair disheveled, quite unlike her former self. Yet so subtly are these points expressed that the reader, like Katsushirō, is inclined to attribute them to coincidence and to Miyagi's age and the trying conditions under which she has been living. Thus the reader shares Katsushirō's shock and dismay when he awakens the next morning to find his house collapsed and overgrown with weeds and his wife gone, and he realizes that he has spent the night with a ghost. The tale ends not at this climax, but in an extended decrescendo of sadness as Katsushirō learns all that has befallen Miyagi and offers prayers for her spirit.

Like "Kikuka no chigiri," "Asaji ga yado" is a tale of fidelity, in this case a wife's fidelity to her husband. The epitome of the traditional Japanese woman, Miyagi is perhaps Akinari's most skilfully portrayed character. Her husband, however, is not a very satisfying hero. It is hard to sympathize with his failure to return home for so long. While it is true that he has little hope of finding his wife alive, he could at least have made an attempt to go to her. He accepts the hopelessness too readily; his attitude strikes the reader as more of the carelessness and irresponsibility that has caused him grief before the story opened. Yet Katsushirō's very weakness serves to emphasize Miyagi's strength. While there is little in Katsushirō to inspire undying fidelity, Miyagi nevertheless faithfully waits for him as her world collapses about her. Such devotion is, it would appear, strong enough to transcend the bonds of death, so that even though she has left the world, she is on hand to welcome Katsushirō when he arrives home. Then, her duty carried out and her fidelity proven, she dissolves into the dawn with the morning dew. There is a beauty in this kind of feminine devotion that Akinari took very much to heart. Perhaps Miyagi reflected something of Tama's devotion to him. In any case, Miyagi was by no means a new character for him, but a direct outgrowth of Fujino, the outstanding heroine of the *Tekake katagi* tales. Having introduced his feminine ideal in his earlier work, Akinari brought her to perfection in *Ugetsu*,[14] likening her to the legendary Mama no Tegona from Katsushirō's native village, remembered in song by *Man'yōshū* poets, who drowned herself in despair over her inability to please all of her many lovers.[15]

In "Muō no rigyo" (The Carp that Came to My Dream), unlike the preceding tales, the supernatural functions not to awe or frighten the reader, but to delight him. A gentle humour pervades the story. There are elements of the eerie and the bizarre, but none of terror. Although the reader is as ignorant as anyone in the story as to why Kōgi the priest is able, immediately after his return to life, to describe events in the Vice-Governor's mansion in such detail, the prose is cast in such a way that the reader does not share the characters' wonder and discomfiture, but is entertained by it. The reader is also amused by the deliberations of Kōgi, transformed into a hungry carp, as he weighs the consequences of taking or leaving the fishermen's bait, and after he has been caught, by his vain efforts to attract his captor's attention. It is the standard comedy device of pain or distress becoming funny when too unreal to be taken seriously. Like the clown scenes in Shakespearean tragedy or the farces peformed between Noh plays, "Muō no rigyo" provides *Ugetsu* with a note of comic relief. But even more than the humour, it is the fantasy that gives this tale its appeal. Anyone who has dreamed of performing feats beyond his natural abilities can identify with Kōgi, who realizes his desire to swim like a fish. Technically, the story could have occurred around any body of water, but since Akinari chose as his protagonist the historical Kōgi, who was a monk at the Mii Temple, the water had to be that of Lake Biwa. Conversely, he may have chosen Kōgi as the hero because he wanted to write about the locality of Lake Biwa. Whatever the case, he used the setting to great advantage, taking the reader on a tour around the lake and showing him its various beauty spots from a fish's eye view. Again, in his poetic description of these natural wonders, all of them famed in poetry, his legacy from the national learning appears.

"Buppōsō" (Bird of Paradise) again utilizes the technique of setting the mood with a poetic opening passage:

> Japan, the Land of Peace and Calm, had long been true to its name. Its people rejoiced in their labour and still found time to relax underneath the cherry-blossoms in spring and to visit the many-coloured groves of trees in autumn. Those who wished might take long trips by sea with the tiller as their pillow and visit the strange shores of Tsukushi. Yet others could set their hearts on the pleasure of climbing such peaks as Mt. Fuji and Tsukuba.[16]

The implied praise of the Tokugawa shogunate, which had brought this era of tranquility to the land, should not be overlooked. Although Akinari was sharply critical of his society, he did not see political reform as the way to change things for the better. Later, in 1789, he even wrote a short piece in praise of the Edo government and the peace enjoyed under its adminis-tration.[17]

As a story, "Buppōsō" is quite simple. While spending the night on Mt. Kōya, the haiku poet Muzen and his son encounter the ghostly retinue of Toyotomi Hidetsugu and his retainers, who years before had taken their own lives on the mountain. The spectral visitors hold a nighttime drinking party, during which they discuss the meaning of a poem and finally call upon the mortal Muzen, who has been cowering in the background, to join them and compose the opening stanza for a linked-verse sequence. Like "Shiramine," "Buppōsō" is as much a discourse as a story. Akinari uses the narrative format to convey reverence for the traditions of Mt. Kōya, to present his own views on certain historical persons and events, and to discuss poetry. Nevertheless, the setting is expertly portrayed; the atmosphere of Mt. Kōya, both sacred and eerie, pervades the tale. Here in the silence of the night, broken only by the sound of running water and the occasional cry of the unseen bird, the stage is set for the appearance of Hidetsugu and his followers. As the spot where these warriors committed suicide, as the site of the Tamagawa River, which is the subject of the debated verse, and as the home of the bird called *buppōsō*,[18] whose cry sounds in the background, Mt. Kōya is indispensable as the setting.

Still, "Buppōsō" is too simple to make a very satisfying story. Not much really happens, and the abrupt digression from the action to a lengthy discussion on the correct interpretation of a poem which has no connection with the events of the story is distracting. The discourse itself has little meaning for readers other than those possessing specialized knowledge. This detracts from the story, but it may be a reflection of Akinari's desire to appeal to a different kind of audience than he had in the past. Remembering his lighter works, he may have wanted to stress to the reader (and to himself as well) how much he had changed his views and come to appreciate a higher degree of learning.

For readers dissatisfied with "Buppōsō," "Kibitsu no kama" (The Caldron of Kibitsu), offers more than adequate compensation. Like "Asaji ga yado," this is a tale of a foresaken wife, but whereas Akinari presented Miyagi as his ideal of the patient and long-suffering woman, in Isora he portrays the epitome of the woman scorned. As Miyagi's love and devotion transcend even the grave, so does Isora's bitterness. Miyagi faithfully waits for her husband and returns after death to welcome him home, whereas Isora dies in vexation and comes back from the grave to wreak a bloody vengeance. Miyagi is Akinari's most endearing character; Isora, his most terrifying one. While Miyagi's gentleness and fidelity may remind us of Yūgao in *The Tale of Genji,* Isora's vengeful spirit evokes memories of Lady Rokujō in the same book.

Women of Akinari's time were bound by conventions set by men and had few rights. The *sanjū*, or "three subordinations," required a woman to obey her parents while single, her husband while married, and her eldest son while widowed, while the *shichi kyo,* the "seven separations", set down the seven reasons—unfilial conduct, infertility, infidelity, jealousy, gossiping, stealing, and poor health—for which she could be divorced. Even if her husband transferred his affection to another woman or abandoned her altogether, as Shōtarō does in "Kibitsu," her duty was to continue in her responsibilities as wife of the house, marriage being a union not of individuals but of families. This Isora does, while she lives. In a society where polygamy and male infidelity were not necessarily grounds for censure, jealousy was surely a passion that many wives were forced to contend with. There is no indication that Akinari meant to attack the system which bred such jealousy, but he called for wisdom and restraint on the part of men. The tale begins with a short discourse on the perils of a jealous wife, arguing that a man must protect himself against this jealousy by disciplining his own conduct and extending guidance to his mate. Jealousy, Akinari implies, is an inborn fault of women against which men must be on guard. Shōtarō fails to do so and suffers the fearsome consequences.

The conduct of Isora's ghost reflects Akinari's view of non-humans. Living, she displays the self-denial of the ideal wife; dead, she exhibits the self-interest of a beast. As a mortal she appears to accept her husband's philandering with resignation, but the fires of jealousy arise and consume her. Once out of this world, she is free from law and convention. No longer a person, she may vent her primitive passions at will. Akinari saw in non-humans a fidelity to the self, noting with keen interest that animals respond to a different kind of logic than do people. One day, he recorded, while walking down a street, he saw a dog steal a fish from a fishmonger's basket. He called the man's attention to the theft and watched as the fishmonger put down his basket, beat the dog with a rod, retrieved his fish, and continued on his way. But the dog, Akinari observed, followed after the man, with an expression and demeanour suggesting that it considered itself not the justly punished thief, but the victim of the crime. Akinari also recalled the story of the maidservant who had unwittingly poured a tub of dirty water over a sleeping fox and had at once been possessed by the beast. For the fox, the reaction was a natural one. The maid had committed her mistake without malice, but the fox, with his simple animal nature, could not see her moral innocence. It could only understand that it had been wronged, and so took a simple and direct kind of revenge.[19] Elsewhere, Akinari told of a maiden who, since her lover had been forbidden to visit her, would secretly make her way to his lodgings by night over a mountain pathway. On one such journey she met a hungry wolf. She begged the beast to allow her one last visit to her lover, promising to return and surrender herself to him if he would grant her this one favour. The wolf let her go, and later that night when she returned to the place, expecting to be devoured on the spot, the beast was nowhere to be seen. On her next journey she left some food beside the path, at the spot where she had met the wolf, and found when she returned that it had all been eaten. On subsequent visits she would leave similar offerings. In time a certain highwayman learned of her nocturnal excursions and lay in wait beside the path to apprehend her, but when he accosted the girl, the wolf sprang out of the darkness and killed him. In the same vein, Akinari recalled the story of Hada no Ōtsuchi from the *Nihongi*. Ōtsuchi had come upon two wolves fighting and had begged them to desist. Having restrained them, he cleansed their wounds and sent them away, thus saving their lives. In gratitude, the wolves appeared in a dream to the emperor, and advised him to take Ōtsuchi into his service. In this way Ōtsuchi rose from being a humble merchant to keeper of the imperial treasury.[20]

On the basis of such reports, Akinari contended that foxes, badgers, and other animals, unlike people, have no moral sense of right and wrong, but merely reward what is good for them and punish what is bad. The deities of Japan were of the same nature, he believed, blessing those who serve them and cursing those who neglect them, unlike Buddhas and sages, who have human bodies and feelings.[21] In animals and supernatural beings Akinari saw a quality that rose above considerations of good and evil—a simple, pure, amoral instinct, beyond normal logic, to protect one's self and one's personal interests. Such is the behaviour of Isora the ghost as opposed to Isora the mortal.

"Kibitsu" is a tale of events rather than of setting or atmosphere. Except for its proximity to the Kibitsu Shrine, with its famed divining caldron, the location is of minor importance. It is what actually transpires that gives the story its stunning finality. Akinari heightens the terror of the supernatural by describing it only vaguely. Thus, after Shōtarō has deceived Isora and absconded with Sode, the reader senses a suspicious nature in the illness from which Sode begins to suffer, but he can only suspect that Isora's jealousy is the cause. Nor is there anything unusual about the girl whom Shōtarō finds tending the new grave near Sode's and who takes him to meet her grieving mistress. Like Shōtarō, the reader is prepared to accept everything as genuine until the pale and emaciated Isora suddenly appears. Only then does he learn that she is really dead, her spirit thirsting for revenge. As Shōtarō takes refuge in his house, the doors and windows sealed with charms, and the story approaches the climax, Isora is now represented only as a voice, more terrifying than any tangible form. Suspense mounts as the days pass until, as Shōtarō and the reader believe, the danger period is over. But as he prematurely opens the door, Shōtarō emits a bloodcurdling scream—and simply vanishes. More than any detailed account, the topknot of her hair and the blood trickling down the wall—all that remain—attest to the awful fury of the specter and the thoroughness of Shōtarō's destruction.

"Jasei no in" (The Lust of the White Serpent), the longest of the nine tales, repeats the theme of lax behaviour and its consequences, though with a different emphasis. While Toyoo's behaviour is not immoral, he spends his time at effeminate pursuits and fails to live in a steadfast and disciplined manner, thus becoming an easy target for the serpent Manago. Even so, he is sympathetically portrayed. Perhaps Akinari identified with him, attributing to Toyoo some of his own perceived faults. At the time he was writing *Ugetsu*, Akinari's artistic interests were conflicting with hard economic reality, and even Toyoo's home, with its strict father and indulgent mother, bears comparison with the author's own childhood environment.

Akinari again places the reader in the participant's role. One goes through the tale knowing little more than Toyoo himself, for Akinari as usual drops only subtle hints that things are not all they seem to be. By this time the reader knows that he is reading a ghost story and is therefore alert for suspicious details, but he never gets enough information to remove the shock from the events when they occur. It is strange that Toyoo could have failed to know of such a conspicuous figure as Manago if she really had, as she tells him, been living in his village for some years, yet the reader becomes truly suspicious only when, searching for Manago's home, Toyoo can find no one who has ever heard of her, and when he at last does locate the house, he discovers it to be identical to the mansion in his dream of the previous night. But these and subsequent developments do not really prepare for the revelation that Manago's stately dwelling is really a ruin overgrown with weeds, nor for her dramatic disappearance in a clap of thunder. With a growing awareness of her true nature, the reader accompanies Toyoo with a sense of foreboding to his sister's home in Yamato. True to expectations, Manago reappears, and Toyoo again reveals his weakness of character by accepting her patently flimsy explanation and taking her in as his bride once more. But indeed the reader himself is tempted to believe her, so earnest are her entreaties.

Even so, the reader is again forcibly reminded of her demon nature when she suddenly disappears into a waterfall, a cloudburst following in her wake. This will not be the last of her, and yet her next appearance, where it is least expected—in the person of Tomiko, Toyoo's new bride—comes as still another shock. The serpent's tenacity and guile are astounding. Like Toyoo, the reader is inclined to despair. No one, it seems, can subdue Manago. It is significant that Toyoo succeeds in escaping from her clutches only after he ceases to flee from her and determines to sacrifice himself in order to protect others. Paradoxically, when he submits to Manago, in full knowledge of what she is, and pleads for Tomiko's life, he shakes off his passive nature and acts like a strong man. Significant too is the fact that Toyoo himself must accomplish the task of overcoming Manago, pinioning her beneath the charmed cloth and forcing himself to ignore her feminine appeals for mercy.

"Jasei no in" is a masterfully woven tale, and Manago deserves to be ranked alongside Miyagi as one of Akinari's best drawn characters. Although she is not really human, she is skilfully portrayed as a person—as a sensuous woman currying favour according to her present whim. If there is any dissatisfying element, it is the final scene. The subjugation of Manago is too easy. In view of the power that she has heretofore demonstrated, a more dramatic confrontation might be expected. But the very simplicity of the task emphasizes the efficacy of the abbot's sincere efforts as opposed to the pompous overconfidence of the priest who lost his life in the first attempt to subdue Manago. Also, it emphasizes how the exorcism is mainly accomplished by Toyoo's disciplining himself and confronting his problem head on, thus pointing up Akinari's view that if one lives steadfastly all will be well, but if one is careless the consequences may be severe. Some readers will no doubt be dissatisfied with Tomiko's fate, for it seems unjust that an innocent party must be the one to die. But her death illustrates that the results of lax behaviour affect not only the guilty but extend to others as well.

The consequences of unrestrained behaviour are shown once again in "Aozukin" (The Blue Hood). "A slothful mind creates a monster, a rigorous one enjoys the fruit of the Buddha,"[22] says the main character, and the tale is essentially an illustration of this idea. As he seeks for lodging for the night, the itinerant priest, Kaian Zenji, is told the story of the abbot of a local temple who has allowed himself to be overpowered by sorrow and frustration. In an excess of grief over the death of a youth whom he had loved beyond the bounds of propriety, the abbot has turned into a fearsome being who now terrorizes the neighbourhood. Determined to bring the demon monk to his senses, Zenji makes his way to the temple. As in other tales, the setting is suitably eerie. It is autumn, and night is approaching. Long shunned by everyone but its lone ghoulish inhabitant, the temple yard is overgrown with brambles and moss; spider webs are stretched between the images, and bird droppings cover the altar. Now the monk appears, though not in his demon form. He merely receives his visitor and gives him permission to spend the night, then leaves his guest alone. Total darkness falls, broken only by a crescent moon, while only the sound of running water disturbs the silence. The scene is indeed similar to that on Mt. Kōya in "Buppōsō."

Later that night the abbot returns, apparently intending to devour his guest, but Zenji has been rendered invisible to his eyes. Not until dawn breaks can the monk see him. Now convinced of his visitor's virtue, the abbot listens willingly to his remonstrations. Having established the demon priest's desire to reform, Zenji takes his own blue hood and places it upon the monk's head, gives him a Zen problem to meditate upon, and leaves him seated on a flat rock. Not until a year later does he return. He finds the temple yard completely overgrown, the buildings beginning to collapse, but the demon monk, to all appearances, has not moved. Oblivious to the decay around him, he still sits in meditation, his body emaciated, his hair and beard long and disheveled. Zenji observes the scene; then, abruptly he strikes the monk on the head and demands the solution to the problem. Thus stimulated, the monk suddenly attains enlightenment and dissolves into thin air, leaving only the blue hood and a pile of bones. Thus the story ends, a simple tale but a strong statement of Akinari's belief that human nature is neither irrevocably good nor irrevocably evil. A bad environment or personal carelessness may cause moral deterioration in a man, but the same person, given instruction and self-discipline, may progress even to Buddhahood.

Finally there is the tale "Himpukuron" (Wealth and Poverty). Here the supernatural is manifested in the form of a tiny smiling old man, the spirit of the gold that the hero possesses. There is nothing frightening about him. Only his size and his self-introduction indicate that he is more than mortal. There is no dramatic action, no ghostly atmosphere. Thus "Himpukuron" is of little interest as a ghost story; in fact, it is of little interest as any kind of story, for it amounts to no more than a logical discourse on the capricious nature of fortune. As a discourse, however, it comes to grips with a universal question, one that, in Japan, neither Confucian nor Buddhist doctrines had been able to explain: Why is the morally upright man seldom rich, and why is the wicked man so often prosperous? A degree of cynicism is apparent. The spirit attacks the official ethic that branded the pursuit of wealth a social evil and condemns Confucian doctrine that one can be happy without wealth. Such an idea, he says, leads scholars astray and may even cause the warriors to forget that wealth is the basis of a strong state, leading them to scorn money and crave glory won on the battlefield, to the sorrow of all concerned. To seek gold is as honourable as to desire fame, the spirit says. Contrary to what the Buddhists say, one's abundance or lack of wealth in this life has nothing to do with one's good or bad conduct in a former existence. As a spirit, the little man says of himself, he has no sense of human society's standards of right and wrong. Like animals and Shinto deities, he is motivated by a simpler, more selfish interest. Thus he rewards those who honour and serve him and ignores those who do not.

Akinari had found his own half-hearted efforts in commerce unrewarding financially and his wholehearted efforts in letters even less so. All around him he saw bad men who were wealthy and good men who were impoverished. It was evident to his logical mind that wealth is not a divine reward given to the righteous, but something which comes only to those who forsake other gods to follow Mammon. But to say so directly would have been to contradict the official code of his society, so he found it prudent to present this idea in a story format. He could then, if necessary, deny that his intention had been serious. He had already stressed in his preface that his tales were pure fiction, and the proponent of the heresy was the spirit of the gold, voicing precisely the kind of ideas that one might expect from such a being. Protecting himself against possible censure may also have been Akinari's reason for closing the story, which is set during the administration of Hideyoshi, with a prophecy of the coming ascendency of Tokugawa Ieyasu, who would at last bring peace to the land. Akinari may have intended this complimentary reference to the Edo government, with the accompanying condemnation of Nobunaga and Hideyoshi, to allay any suspicions of subversive intent.

Such is the content of *Ugetsu monogatari*. A superb combination of originality and adaptation, its characters and events never fail to fit naturally into the Japanese scene; in some of the tales of the Japanese setting even becomes an essential part of the story. The reader who has not been told of the book's foreign antecedents finds no direct reference to them in the text. The prose is elegantly constructed; to read it is an aesthetic experience. The tales conform to the highest traditions of the storyteller's art. They demand to be read. The reader shares the hopes and fears, joys and sorrows, wonder and amazement of the characters as the events unfold. Underlying each of the stories is the theme of man and his fate. All of the characters, mortal and immortal, are memorable in their own right, each having his or her own distinctive and clearly defined qualities. For such reasons, *Ugetsu* has become a classic. It went through successive printings during the author's lifetime, and today holds a place in Japanese literature no less secure than that of *The Tale of Genji*.

5

The Scholar-Physician of Osaka

It was unfortunate, in a sense, that *Ugetsu monogatari* was such a success, for it has so eclipsed everything else Akinari wrote as to become his only work that is widely known today. It is now more than synonymous with his name—indeed, while most present-day Japanese are at least familiar with the *Ugetsu* title, there are many who have never heard of Ueda Akinari. Perhaps this was inevitable. Yet *Ugetsu* does not mark the culmination of Akinari's literary career, but only a crucial turning point. After his attempt to recreate the spirit of the classics in his own fiction, Akinari shifted his efforts toward explicating this spirit in scholarly terms. Although he never again wrote fiction for its own sake, he produced learned writings in profusion. His diversified interests and the wide range of his talents are most evident in the latter half of his life.

Nevertheless, when Akinari returned to Osaka, he concentrated first on practical matters. His wife and aging mother were dependent upon him, and Akinari felt obliged to make up to them for the privation they had endured since the loss of the family business. Moreover, he felt the responsibility he had assumed in becoming a physician, and he approached his new duties seriously and with determination. Medical practitioners of the day frequently supplemented their earnings by engaging in sidelines such as moneylending, arranging marriages, acting as agents for vendors, or by cultivating wealthy patrons, but Akinari considered activities such as these to be a disgrace to the medical profession, and resolved from the beginning to take no part in them. Determined to compensate for his lack of experience through consideration and diligence, he would visit a patient several times a day if the ailment seemed to require such attention, and he made no pretence of possessing knowledge that he did not have. Pride would not deter him from calling in a more experienced physician if his own skills were taxed, but even when he did so he retained interest in the case and continued to visit the patient himself. In time such kindness and concern won him a large clientele. The resultant financial prosperity provided some compensation for the fact that the work kept him "running east, west, south, and north every day."[1]

While Akinari was still in the process of learning the healing arts, one of his fellow students became ill, and no one in the group was able to ease his suffering. At length the patient's elder brother arrived from the family home in Ise. He thanked the attending physicians for their efforts but then dismissed them and applied his own techniques. Stripping his brother naked, he cooled him with a fan, fed him at intervals on a thin gruel, and administered a medical concoction prepared from a bear's liver. Within two days the fever broke, and the patient was able to eat normally. Before long he recovered completely, whereupon he returned home with his brother, apparently convinced of the superiority of the local brand of medicine. The incident impressed Akinari. He stated that he was very close to agreement with a physician from the brothers' native village, who advocated light clothing and moderate eating as to the way to avoid sickness, saying, "What you think is enough is too much." Such an approach to medicine suited Akinari's own temperament. He himself believed in simple living and he had no faith in extravagant remedies or flamboyant cures, believing that genuine concern and conscientious attention were the keys to effective healing. "Medicine," he once wrote, "is the heart."[2]

By the end of 1780, Akinari was able to purchase a house in Awaji-chō, about six hundred yards west of the quarters he had been renting in Amaga-saki. During the winter the house was renovated, and when spring came the Uedas at last were once again able to move into a permanent home of their own. "For the first time, my mother showed a smiling face," Akinari said of the occasion. The house cost sixteen *kamme*, or 270 *ryō*, probably a difficult sum to obtain in so short a period for a physician who refused to supplement his income by engaging in sidelines. Akinari just said that he "managed it somehow," implying that some of the money was borrowed. Thus it would appear that he had become prosperous enough to be considered a good credit risk. Now, as a man of property, his standing in the community no doubt rose even higher. Subsequently he purchased another house nearby, which he rented to a fishmonger.[3] Materially, this was the high point of his life.

Yet, Akinari's heart was not solely devoted to his official occupation. There is no question that he worked hard at it and that, initially at least, he restricted his literary activities to do so, but the evidence does not indicate a complete curtailment of his outside interests. It is known that he went to Kyoto and stayed at the home of Takai Kitō early in 1776,[4] probably about the same time that he was moving back to Osaka. He apparently saw Buson as well on this visit and gave him, or at least discussed with him, some verses,[5] most likely those for *Zoku Akegarasu,* the *haikai* collection that was published later that year to commemorate the seventeenth anniversary of Kitō's father's death. The seven verses that Akinari contributed to the anthology include these:

> *Sakura zakura*   Cherry blossoms fall,
> *Chirite kajin no*   Entering into the dreams
> *Yume ni iru*   Of lovely women
>
> *Asagao ni*   In the morning glories,
> *Shimabara mono no*   Water for the tea
> *Cha no yu kana*   Of the ladies of Shimabara.[6]

His name appears often in Buson's letters around this time, indicating that he was very much in Buson's thoughts,[7] but usually Buson simply asked the recipient to convey his regards to Akinari. Probably these comments support the evidence that in the early days of his medical practice Akinari concentrated on establishing himself. It appears he enjoyed contact with Buson's acquaintances in Osaka but had little time for socializing with friends in Kyoto. Even so, early in 1777 he published a collection of 113 haiku verses by Nishiyama Sōin,[8] whose combination of poetic spirit with relaxed expression closely paralleled, and had no doubt influenced, his own ideal of poetry. And later he did find more time to visit the Capital and participate with Buson and Kitō in their *haikai* circle.

He was barely settled in his new life when he experienced another turning point in his literary career. He had spent part of his time at Kashima-mura preparing for publication Katō Umaki's commentary on the well-known section in the second chapter of *The Tale of Genji* in which Genji and his friends pass a rainy evening discussing their concepts of the ideal woman and comparing the virtues and shortcomings of women they have loved. Umaki had completed this work in 1769. Akinari's preface to it was dated 1775, and the publication was carried out in the fourth month of 1777.[9] Little did Akinari suspect that this would be his parting gift to his teacher. Just two months later, Umaki died suddenly in Kyoto while on duty at the Nijō Castle.[10]

As soon as word reached him, Akinari hurried to the Capital to oversee funeral arrangements. As Umaki's senior disciple, this was his duty, but it was more than a sense of responsibility that drew him to the scene. His relationship with Umaki had developed beyond that of the ordinary master–disciple connection. He respected Umaki for his knowledge, but also loved him as a friend, and the loss left a scar on his mind that never really healed. Years later, near the end of his own life, he copied in his manuscript the message that Umaki's widow had sent him after receiving the hair that he had shaved from the corpse, and added, "Even as I copy this down, my heart is crushed with memories of long ago."[11] For Akinari, his teacher's death had an air of finality. Umaki was irreplaceable; Akinari could not conceive of anyone being able to equal the man, and so he continued in the scholarly world on his own. It was now a matter of standing on his own feet or not standing at all.

Among Umaki's effects Akinari discovered some pages from *Kojiki den*, the monumental commentary on the *Kojiki* that Motoori Norinaga was then working on. As both of them had been disciples of Kamo Mabuchi, Norinaga permitted Umaki to examine a portion of the manuscript. An associate of Norinaga's, Tonami Imamichi, attended the funeral, and Akinari entrusted the pages to him for return to their owner. Norinaga was pleased and expressed his gratitude to Imamichi in a *waka* verse.[12] Norinaga's gratitude surely extended to Akinari as well, and it is ironic that this first known instance of contact (albeit indirect) between them should have been so amicable since an acrimonious dispute between them was only a few years away.

In the autumn of 1779 Akinari took time off from his work to make an excursion to the hot springs at Kinosaki. Ostensibly the trip was for his health. He had been suffering from pains in his legs for the past three years, and, medicine having proven ineffective, a colleague had suggested that he try the healing baths at Kinosaki. Tama had been in low spirits for some time, and at his mother's urging, Akinari decided to take her along.[13] It appears, however, that the excursion was taken as much for pleasure as for his health, for both Akinari and his wife enjoyed it immensely. A fair portion of the journey seems to have been made on foot, so despite Akinari's complaints, his legs could not have been extremely painful. The trip also reflects his improved financial situation. An excursion such as this, of approximately six weeks' duration, surely entailed much expense, to say nothing of the cost in lost earnings. That Akinari was able to take the time off and still go ahead with the purchase of a home a year later bespeaks his new-found prosperity.

This was Akinari's second visit to Kinosaki. He had gone there for his health once before in his younger days,[14] and reminiscing to Tama about the familiar sights no doubt made the journey even more enjoyable for him. They started their journey in the early morning chill of the twelfth day of the ninth month, with friends accompanying them as far as Nishinomiya. In good time they made their way as far as Sumiyoshi, where they spent the night. Next day, blessed with fine weather, they walked along the shoreline of Suma, enjoying the sight of boats going to and fro on the calm sea, fishermen plying their trade, and the mountains overlooking the scene. The setting called to Tama's mind Prince Genji's exile to Suma, and she expressed wonder that a sea so placid could ever have raged so violently as depicted in the tale. Where, she asked, was the exact place where Genji had dwelt? According to Akinari's written account, an itinerant priest who happened to be nearby overheard her question and volunteered an answer. *The Tale of Genji*, he said, should not be regarded as the truth, for it was merely a story that Murasaki Shikibu had made up. Indeed, he continued, Murasaki had been condemned to eternal suffering for writing such a collection of lies, much as Lo Kuan-chung had paid the penalty for writing *Shui hu chuan* by having three generations of his posterity born deaf and dumb.[15]

Since the priest was following the same route as Akinari and Tama, he fell into step with them and expanded his statement as they went along. By the time their paths diverged, he had made a lengthy critical discourse on *The Tale of Genji*, rejecting commonly held views such as those which called the tale an allegorical presentation of Buddhist teachings or Murasaki a Buddha in disguise, or which held that, being a mere woman, Murasaki could not have produced such a masterpiece on her own and so must have been assisted by her father. He praised Genji's character as being in no way inferior to that of the Chinese sages, but concluded that while the tale does portray the glories of the past, it depicts a world that was fated to break up in disorder. Thus, he said, *The Tale of Genji* should be read strictly for entertainment; it is useless to see it as anything more than a source of pleasure.

Of course, this episode probably never occurred, at least not in the manner in which it was related. As Tama was by no means uneducated, and shared her husband's interest in literature to a degree, she very likely did speak of *The Tale of Genji* while passing through Suma, but the priest's appearance is too apropos to be credible, and his discourse too formal to have been impromptu. Probably what really happened was that when Akinari was writing his account of the journey, he felt that Suma was the logical place to include some of his own opinions on *Genji*—indeed, he and his wife may actually have discussed some similar points as they walked along—and so he introduced the priest to act as his mouthpiece. To state the views as his own would have appeared pedantic and detracted from the story format of his diary, but masked as the ideas of a chance acquaintance, they fit smoothly into the narrative as talk heard on the way. Yet by introducing such a fictional episode into his record, Akinari was doing no more than following precedent. Convention did not require the literary diary to be absolutely faithful to reality, but rather to improve on it. Material could be added or deleted as necessary in order to fulfil this purpose. The passage deserves special attention, however, because the priest's views foreshadow those expressed in *Nubatama no maki*, Akinari's more ambitious criticism of *Genji*, which was also connected with his trip to Kinosaki.

Akinari and Tama spent that night at Ōkuradani (now a part of Akashi-shi) and enjoyed watching the moon on the beach, it being the night of *nochi no tsuki*, the thirteenth evening of the ninth month, when tradition called for the moon to be viewed instead of on the fifteenth night, as was the custom in other months. Next day they pushed on with their journey, ignoring most of the opportunities for sightseeing, although they did visit a certain Sonezaki Shrine where a festival was taking place. Here they witnessed a large-scale tug-of-war by country folk, though Akinari confessed he was quite unimpressed with it all. They slept that night at a place called Mamezaki. Next morning, the fifteenth day of the month, they set out before dawn, passing over a moor in the province of Harima, enjoying the variety of flowers in bloom along the way and watching birds catch fish in the marshes. A light rain began to fall, but Akinari was more impressed by the beauty of the mountains half shrouded in mist than he was troubled by getting wet. They were now in an isolated section of the country; few human beings besides themselves were in evidence. At length they stopped at a village to rest and eat and found that the sun was inclining toward the west by the time they started out again. Awed by the rapids, and by the mountains which towered on either side, they followed the upper reaches of the Ichikawa River to a village called Yakata. It was a miserable-looking place, but for lack of anywhere better, they stopped there for the night.

The record is not entirely clear for the next three days. On the sixteenth, they appear to have pushed on over the provincial boundary into Tajima and lodged at the village of Takeda, famous for its lacquer ware, though Akinari also mentioned a visit to the nearby village of Awaga to sample its tea. He was later to achieve some recognition as an authority on the tea ceremony and seems to have been interested in the pursuit even at this date. From Wadayama, he said, the country became more and more familiar, and he recalled with nostalgia the sights that he had come to know twenty years before. Descending the river by boat on the last leg of their journey, they arrived at Kinosaki on the nineteenth day of the month. The inn where he had stayed on his previous visit was little changed, but he recognized few familiar faces. Children he had once known were now mature adults. Occasionally people would ask him whether he remembered them, and only then would he recognize an old acquaintance. His former host was now old and retired, and his son, whom Akinari remembered as a young boy, had taken over the management of the inn.

The weather was rainy most of the time in Kinosaki, and generally they remained indoors, passing the hours with other guests or with acquaintances in the district and enjoying the natural hot-spring baths. Nearly a full month went by in this manner. By then their planned period of stay had elapsed, and Akinari's mother would be expecting them to return. But before going back to the realities of everyday life in Osaka, Akinari wanted to make an excursion to Amanohashidate. Twenty years before, he had seen this celebrated beauty spot, which is ranked with Matsushima and Miyajima as one of the "Three Views of Japan," and now he wished to relive the experience and share it with his wife.

On the morning of the sixteenth day of the tenth month, Akinari and Tama left the inn and made their way to the inlet of Kumi. They had considered taking a boat along the coastline, but fearing the weather would not hold, they decided to make the trip overland. Thus, they journeyed to Iwataki, enjoying the autumn colours on the way. At Iwataki they hired a small boat to take them to Amanohashidate on the opposite shore, and while the sand bar came into view overgrown with pine trees twisted into weird shapes Akinari related to his wife the legends surrounding the place. Amanohashidate was said to be the remnant of the Floating Bridge of Heaven, upon which the deities Izanami and Izanagi had stood when they stirred up the ocean and created the islands of Japan. Nevertheless, although Akinari appreciated the tradition, he was too much of a realist not to be sceptical. He did not think the scene really looked as though it had fallen from heaven, and he decried people who lead others astray with ill-founded tales.

After passing the night at Miyazu, Akinari and Tama rose while it was still dark and commenced the homeward journey, making their way over the Fukō Pass and on to Fukuchiyama, where they secured lodgings. Next morning they found the landscape shrouded in frost. As they travelled along through the Hikami district of Tamba, they passed the village of Kuroi, which was the home of Ueda Jizō, Akinari's foster father's brother. Akinari would have liked to stop and visit his uncle, but he was worried about his mother, and as both he and his wife were beginning to feel the pangs of homesickness, they passed the village by. Next morning the frost was heavy again; winter was clearly on the way. Osaka was now only one or two days' journey, but they felt that even one more night spent on the road would seem like an eternity, so eager were they to be home. But Akinari ended his narrative on that note. He did not say just when they reached Osaka, and his readers can only guess at his mother's joy and relief to see them safely back.

For Akinari, the time had been well spent. It appears to have had the desired effect on his health, and it was apparently the first time that he had been able to make an excursion with his wife. Indeed, it is rather surprising that he did so, for it was hardly socially approved for a married couple to travel together as Akinari and Tama had done. The fact that they chose to ignore convention attests to the depth of their mutual affection and independence of spirit. As a "second honeymoon," the trip gave them time to be together, away from the interferences of others and free from the cares of daily life. Surely it served to strengthen their already close relationship.

Moreover, the trip provided the material for two literary travel records. Akinari appears to have written the first of these, *Akiyama no ki* (A Record of Autumn Mountains), shortly after getting back to Osaka; the second *Kozo no shiori* (The Trail Blazed Last Year), the next autumn, as can be inferred from its title and from the preamble, which speaks of wild geese flying by under a wintry moon.[16] Each account mentions certain things that the other omits, and there are a few apparent departures from the truth for the sake of literary effect. On the whole, however, both accounts refer to the same events, and the dates generally agree, so they can be considered reasonably accurate as history. Both were written in the conventional style of the travel diary, the events being subordinated to the sights and sentiments of the journey, with numerous literary allusions and the prose narrative interspersed with poems. *Akiyama no ki* especially abounds with descriptions of natural beauty, but the most obvious difference between the two accounts is that the poems in *Akiyama no ki* are *waka*, while those in *Kozo no shiori* are haiku.

A further indication that Akinari found the trip to Kinosaki unforgettable is that he used it for the background setting of *Nubatama no maki*. According to his preface to *Nubatama*,[17] while he was staying at the inn at Kinosaki in the autumn of 1779, he became acquainted with the guest in a neighbouring room, who had a manuscript in his possession. Since the manuscript was written in a style too abstruse for his understanding, the man begged Akinari to rewrite the work for him in a simpler, more readily comprehensible form. Akinari obliged, and since the manuscript bore no title, he called his version *Nubatama no maki*, the opening line of the text being *Nubatama no yoru wa sugara ni*, or "All through the dark night." Thus, Akinari accounted for the work. The story need not be taken seriously, of course, though it is quite possible that Akinari did write *Nubatama*, or at least a draft of it, at Kinosaki. The task could have occupied much of his time during the rainy weather.

Nubatama no maki is on one hand Akinari's criticism of *The Tale of Genji*, of which he was a great admirer,[18] and on the other, an expression of his general views on the role of fiction in society. More than any of his other works, it reveals what Akinari saw as the purpose of the novel. Although a serious literary essay, it is couched in story form, revealing the penchant for fiction that Akinari retained even after he stopped writing it as such. The progatonist of *Nubatama* is a man called Sōchin, who lived during the last years of the Ashikaga shogunate (1333–1573), a time of incessant warfare. Grieved by the suffering and corruption around him, but feeling powerless to fight against it and doubting his ability to live up to monastic vows if he tried to retire from the world, Sōchin turned for solace to *The Tale of Genji*.

Sincerely believing it to be equal to the combined teachings of Buddhism and Confucianism, he devoted his life to copying the manuscript, hoping to serve mankind by making it available to others.[19] As Akinari's acount opens, Sōchin is an old man. He has copied the entire *Genji* manuscript a total of twenty-four times and is still hard at work. One night he falls asleep over his task and, in a dream, finds himself walking on the shore of Akashi Bay. He is not alone, for there is a man who looks about fifty years old seated beneath some pine trees nearby, gazing at the moon.[20] He invites Sōchin to join him. Struck by the beauty of the moon shining upon placid water, Sōchin becomes lost in reminiscences of Genji's exile to Akashi. He rambles on, talking more to himself than to his companion, when the man interrupts his reverie and tells him that *The Tale of Genji*, however skilfully it is written, or however much it may delight the reader, is of no value. It is foolish to believe that it can be a source of moral instruction for the world.

His interest thus aroused, Sōchin begins to ask questions. Why, he asks the man, does he speak so disparagingly of the tale, when for years learned men have regarded it as an allegorical explication of Buddhist and Confucian teachings, and thus a moral document of immeasurable value? By way of reply, the stranger launches into a discourse on the nature of fiction, and the story format abruptly gives way to didacticism. Fiction, he says, should exist for its own sake. It should be an artistic creation that brings joy to those who read it, but its proper function ends there. It should portray people and events realistically, neither as totally good nor as altogether evil, but just as they are. Being no more than a means of amusement, its role is not to encourage virtue nor decry vice. But nevertheless, he says in a more affirmative tone, even though fiction is pure falsehood, a note of truth may be found therein, for the author may, obliquely and in a manner that the casual reader might fail to discern, inject his own observations about contemporary society into his work and, by so doing, take on the role of social, or even political, critic. The matters that trouble the writer will be reflected in his stories, in a veiled fashion of course, lest he incur the displeasure of society or the holders of political power, but nevertheless in a fashion easily discernible to readers of like mind. Fiction, then, is a portrayal of the drama in contemporary human life. To disguise his true intentions, the author may set his story in the distant past, but his thoughts remain in the present.

Such is the principal message of *Nubatama*, though its narrator goes on to discuss fiction in general, and *Genji* in particular, to great theoretical lengths. It would appear that Akinari, like other intellectuals of his day, had reacted against the view of fiction as a moralistic tool. Fiction was falsehood; therefore its function was to entertain, not to instruct. Accordingly, literary masterpieces should be interpreted as works of art and no more. Yet even so, such an apparently useless thing as fiction was really of social value, for through the medium of prose the author could convey to the reader the truths that he had perceived; that is to say, in fiction, through the vehicle of untruth, truth may be transmitted.

Nubatama no maki apparently was never published. A request for permission to print a work written by one Sōchin, called *Genji nomatama no maki*, was submitted in late 1781, which must have been Akinari's *Nubatama no maki*, considering the author's name, the similar title, and the connection with *The Tale of Genji*.[21] Permission to publish was quickly granted, but no printed edition of *Nubatama* is known to exist.

The character by whom Sōchin is instructed in *Nubatama* is identified as the *Man'yōshū* poet Kakinomoto Hitomaro, and Akinari's choice of him as his mouthpiece probably reflects the interest that he was taking in the poet around this time. It was either shortly before or shortly after this that he wrote his study of Hitomaro's life, *Kaseiden* (The Life of the Saint of Poetry). A piece of biographical research, *Kaseiden* consists mainly of quotations from sources referring to Hitomaro, together with Akinari's comments on them. His intention apparently was to assemble as much information on his topic as possible, and the result is probably the most exhaustive treatise on Hitomaro written up to that time. Mostly a collection of data, it does not read smoothly, but it does display the author's remarkably wide knowledge of source materials and his painstakingly thorough investigation.[22] Akinari must have developed his interest in the *Man'yōshū* early in life, certainly no later than his study of Keichū's works, and this interest was surely nurtured by Katō Umaki.[23] But *Kaseiden* was his first actual writing about the *Man'yōshū* and may be regarded as the springboard for his subsequent *Manyōshū* scholarship.[24]

Akinari may have tried to make autumn pleasure excursions a regular practice. His trip to Kinosaki was one such outing, and during the tenth month of the following year, 1780, he visited the Shūgakuin Detached Palace in the northeastern hills of Kyoto, going by way of the Minase River and enjoying the scenery there on the way. He wrote two brief accounts describing this excursion.[25] Two years later, again in the tenth month, he made a five-day sightseeing trip to Nara with three friends, and wrote a travel diary that describes the events of this trip in some detail.[26]

In his role as an intellectual descendent of Kamo Mabuchi through Katō Umaki, Akinari spent some time during the 1780's editing a collection of notes about Mabuchi's lectures on the *Kokin waka shū*. A certain Nomura Tomohiko, who had received instruction from Mabuchi, had planned with her husband, Nomura Magahira, to prepare her notes for publication, but both husband and wife had died before completing the task. Nagahira's younger brother, Nobumoto, was a practising physician in Osaka. Knowing Akinari, and being aware of his interest in the Japanese classics and of his indirect connection with Mabuchi, Nobumoto requested Akinari to take over the editing of the manuscripts. Akinari agreed, but he carried out the task over an extended period, apparently in snatches of leisure time. He left the notes largely as Tomohiko had written them, merely inserting statements of Mabuchi and Umaki, as well as some of his own, into the text, and gave the finished product the title *Kokin waka shū uchigiki*. A request for permission to publish the first seven volumes was submitted late in 1784. Akinari finished editing the rest of the twenty volumes about a year later, but the publication request was not submitted until another year had elapsed, and the actual publication was delayed until 1789,[27] after Akinari had retired from medical practice and moved out of Osaka.

Early in 1787, by the Western calendar (Temmei Era, sixth year, twelfth month), the forthcoming publication of a work with the title *Kakizome kigen no umi* was announced. When it appeared in print the following month, the *no* had been deleted, making the title *Kakizome kigenkai*.[28] The author's name was given as Rakugai Hankyōjin, or "Half-Mad Man on the Outskirts of the Capital." If the pen name was chosen in order to preserve the writer's anonymity it succeeded quite well, for it was not until the twentieth century that *Kakizome* was discovered to be the work of Akinari.[29]

The word *kakizome* refers to the calligraphy that was traditionally practiced to usher in the New Year; *kigenkai* ("sea of feelings") is a pun on *kigenkae* ("the changing of feelings"). The title *Kakizome kigenkai*, then, calls attention to the changing, or easily changeable, feelings that people may experience when an old year gives way to a new one.[30] Akinari admitted that he had conceived the main theme of *Kakizome* from Saikaku's *Seken mune zan'yō*.[31] Both works are about events of the New Year, the dissimilarity being that Saikaku's stories are about the last day of the old year, while Akinari's are about the first day of the new.

A short piece, *Kakizome* consists of three sections, one for each of the three main urban centres of the day—Kyoto, Edo, and Osaka. Two of the sections have a story format, but both are preceded by introductory remarks of almost equivalent length, which describe, and speak critically of contemporary social conditions. The third section has no story at all. Thus it is doubtful that Akinari saw *Kakizome* as a work of fiction. The three sections, in effect, form a series of sketches about Japan in his time. He took the position of observer, looking down on the scene with a bemused, sometimes regretful, sometimes sharply critical expression. Although there is little overt didacticism, the tone is unmistakably present throughout. But the message is not presented successfully, and the work did not sell well. Akinari himself admitted this, saying that his advancing age had made him too logical, no longer able to write works with popular appeal.[32] To date, few appear to have disagreed with this assessment. *Kakizome* had attracted little notice among modern-day scholars until it was known to be the work of Akinari, and its chief claim to attention remains the identity of its author.

Even though *Kakizome kigenkai* may have been a failure, by the early 1780's Akinari had become a well-known man of letters. He had won the admiration of fellow participants in the leading *haikai* circles of the day. His fiction had been well received by the reading public, and he counted some of the top literary figures in Japan among his friends. A leading disciple of Kamo Mabuchi had taken him as a pupil but had ended up treating him almost as an equal. Moreover, he was now financially successful as well; no longer was it necessary to rely on others for his livelihood. In both the literary and the workaday worlds he was independent. His talents had been weighed in the balance and not found wanting. It was natural that he experience a surge of self-confidence; natural too that he be less willing to remain silent when he disagreed with a colleague. The only surprising thing is the stature of the opponent with whom he chose to do battle.

Born in 1730, Motoori Norinaga was only four years older than Akinari. Though his native home of Matsuzaka in Ise was a far more rural environment than Osaka, he, like Akinari, had been raised in a merchant family. His father had died when he was eleven, and eight years later, he was adopted into a family in nearby Yamada. His real family tried to carry on their trade after the father's death, but the business fell into a slow though steady decline, and when Norinaga returned to his own house at the age of twenty-two, his mother sent him to Kyoto to study to become a physician. Like Akinari, however, he combined classical studies with his medical training, being especially stimulated by the writings of Keichū and Kamo Mabuchi. He returned to Matsuzaka in 1757 and set himself up as a physician, but in his spare time he continued his efforts to master the Japanese classics, giving lectures on them and writing works of literary criticism. In 1762 he had an audience with Kamo Mabuchi. It was their first and only meeting, but from this encounter Norinaga was inspired to write his commentary on the *Kojiki*. Begun in 1764, *Kojiki den* occupied much of Norinaga's time until 1796, and it was not printed in its entirety until 1822. Norinaga's reputation, therefore, was still being made at the time Akinari squared off against him, but he was a formidable opponent even then.

Akinari and Norinaga had pursued the same line of scholarship. Norinaga's meeting with Mabuchi antedated Akinari's meeting with Umaki by just a few years. Their ages, their upbringing in merchant households, and even the manner in which they became involved in *kokugaku* studies were all similar. But there were differences, too. Matsuzaka was the commercial centre of Ise, it is true, but it was rustic in comparison to Osaka, then the commercial centre for all Japan. Norinaga's only prolonged experience with a real urban environment had been the five years he spent in Kyoto. Akinari considered Norinaga a country bumpkin and he spoke of him as such.[33] No doubt he resented the recognition that had come to such a man, when he himself lived in the economic and cultural heart of the nation, with access to all the best in the scholarly and literary worlds. Moreover, while it is surely an oversimplification to account for their different viewpoints in the light of their native homes, it would be a mistake to ignore the point. Growing up in the spiritual centre of Japan may have contributed to Norinaga's tendency to accept the Japanese myths naïvely, which led him to make frequent irrational statements, while Akinari's insistence on logic and reasoned interpretation may have been in part a legacy of the severe economic competition he had experienced in Osaka. Whatever the true influences may have been, their different backgrounds symbolize their respective positions in their quarrel. The Akinari-Norinaga confrontation may be seen as a clash between the rustic's blind faith and the urbanite's critical scepticism.

Akinari and Norinaga, it would appear, never met face to face. All intercourse between them was carried on through a go-between named Kikuya Hyōbe (also known as Arakida Suetomo; 1735-1801). A priest at the Ise Shrine, Kikuya had been an associate, perhaps a student of sorts, of Akinari, but in 1784 he formally entered Norinaga's school. He is first mentioned in Akinari's writings in 1782, though there is no concrete evidence as to just when they first met, nor of the true nature of their relationship. Possibly they became acquainted at a *haikai* gathering, for Kikuya is known to have engaged in such pursuits. The distance between their homes must have ruled out frequent contact, but a letter from Akinari to Kikuya that has been preserved implies that Kikuya did occasionally come to Osaka and call on Akinari. Still, this letter begins with Akinari's apologies for having taken so long to reply, which suggests that even correspondence between them was infrequent. But for the matter at hand, the most important fact about Kikuya is that while Akinari and Norinaga grew to despise each other, he was able to maintain a cordial relationship with both men. Norinaga trusted Kikuya sufficiently to lend him manuscripts, which Kikuya in turn would lend to Akinari, indicating trust between them as well. Akinari felt free to speak critically of Norinaga to Kikuya, apparently without fear of giving offence. Thus, it was largely through Kikuya that Akinari was able to become familiar with Norinaga's works and prepare his case against them.[34]

The Akinari-Norinaga dispute took place sporadically over a period of years; it is not clear precisely just when it began or ended. In the autumn of 1783, for instance, Akinari wrote *Asama no kemuri* (The Smoke of Asama) about the disastrous eruption of Mr. Asama in the summer of that year. He looked at the calamity from a scientific point of view and derided "a certain person" who was given to expounding on Japanese antiquity and who would explain such catastrophes as violent acts of the malevolent deities, or *magatsui no kami*.[35] Akinari avoided naming the object of his scorn, but Japanese scholars have seen his remarks as a reference to Norinaga's 1771 work, *Naobi no mitama*,[36] in which Norinaga argued that if the Japanese people would cast off corrupting foreign practices and adhere faithfully to the virtues of ancient times, the nation would be protected, for the *magatsui no kami* would be rendered powerless by their benevolent counterparts, the *naobi no kami*. And in 1784, Akinari wrote a short piece in which he clearly quoted from Norinaga's *Kara osame no uretamigoto*.[37] Definitely, then, Akinari had started to read Norinaga's writings no later than 1783 or 1784. These ultimately included the above-mentioned *Kara osame*, the twelfth and thirteenth scrolls of *Kojiki den*, and *Temakura*, which he returned all together, as is apparent from his letter to Suetomo,[38] but there is every reason to believe that he was able to read others as well. In the letter, Akinari noted that he had found some of Norinaga's conclusions hard to agree with, and he wrote a criticism of *Kara osame* under the title of *Ōō shōkai*, which he apparently sent to Norinaga by way of Suetomo. Unfortunately, no manuscript of this work has ever been discovered, nor is it even known precisely when it was written. The title and the nature of its contents are included in a letter from Norinaga to Suetomo,[39] but that is the extent of present information.

Accepting that it is impossible to reconstruct a precise chronology of the quarrel, one must turn to its nature. The principal record that has survived is *Kakaika*, which presents the dispute in the form of a debate, with Akinari first stating his position, and Norinaga then offering his rebuttal. But *Kakaika* is not an original record and Akinari played no part in its compilation. It was prepared by Norinaga in order to uphold the verity of his own conclusions, so he took pains to present himself as the wise and learned authority who was called upon to silence the upstart. Verbal fencing with his critics was nothing new for Norinaga. In 1780 he had written *Kuzubana* as a rebuttal to the attacks made by Ichikawa Tatsumaro (d. 1795) in *Maga no hire*, and not long afterward he wrote *Shinreki fushin kō ben* in response to Kawabe Hyakushō's *Shinreki fushin kō*. Norinaga had studied the classics since his youth, and had commenced writing *Kojiki den* at the age of thirty-five. Attacks on the conclusions that he had reached, coming as he was approaching old age, were in effect assaults on what he had devoted his life to proving. He was not prepared to admit defeat. Thus, for all that is known, he may have omitted, when editing *Kakaika*, some of the arguments that he found more difficult to refute. If the original manuscripts were available, Akinari's position might conceivably emerge in a more favourable light.

The Akinari-Norinaga dispute covered two distinct topics which are best considered separately. The first was concerned with phonetics in the old

Japanese language, and especially with the question of whether the syllabic nasal—the "n" sound occurring independently, not followed by a vowel—had existed in the ancient tongue. Norinaga's stand was that the "n" was a corrupt sound, and since old Japanese had been a pure language, the ancients had not used it. He stated that the sound did not appear in any of the old classics, and that fact, he contended, proved that it had not occurred in people's speech until Chinese influence had brought it into use. Akinari conceded that representations of that particular sound could not be found in ancient texts, but he maintained that it had occurred in the spoken language nevertheless. Moreover, he noted that there were words in the *Man'yōshū* that did end in the syllabic nasal: words such as *miten, tsugeken, yukuran, wakarenan*, and others. In the *Man'yōshū* script, *miten* was written with two Chinese characters that were pronounced "mi" and "ten" in Sino-Japanese, *tsugeken* with two that were pronounced "tsuge" and "ken"; the other words that Akinari cited as examples were written similarly. The "n" sound was never represented individually but even so, said Akinari, it was clear from such examples that the sound had indeed occurred. People had naturally used it when speaking, but since there was no Chinese character pronounced "n", there had been no way of expressing the sound in writing until a phonetic script had been developed. Therefore, he said, the "n" sound had been represented by means of a variety of characters that were ordinarily pronounced "mu", but people had nevertheless said "n" when speaking if the sound sequence made it the more natural choice. To insist on reading such characters "mu" in every case would be to sacrifice the niceties of speech for the sake of the written word.[40]

Norinaga countered with the dogmatic assertion that, without question, such sounds as "ten", "ken", "ran", and "nan" had in ancient times been pronounced, respectively, "temu," "kemu", "ramu", and "namu". Because "n" was phonetically not far removed from "mu", he said, such words had been written with single characters pronounced "ten", "ken", and so forth, for simple convenience. He noted that in ancient times the "nami" portion of the geographical name Kannami, had sometimes been written with the same character as that used to represent the "nan" portion of *wakarenan*, which Akinari had used as an example. Did this mean, he sarcastically inquired, that in ancient times Kannami had been called "Kannan"? He noted also that the "nan" portion of Akinari's *wakarenan* had alternatively been represented by a character that was still pronounced "namu" in the present day. The province of Tanba (Tamba), he asserted, had originally been called "Taniwa", and had been called by that name until medieval times, when the corrupted form had come into general use. There were many more examples to be found, said Norinaga, and he invited Akinari to consult the writings of old and discover them for himself.[41]

In essence, Akinari was saying that, depending on what sounds precede and follow a given utterance, there are times when it is natural to say "n" and times when it is natural to say "mu". Since this was just as true in ancient times as in his own day, he contended, it stood to reason that the men of old also had used both "n" and "mu", depending on which was the more natural sound in the particular situation. He argued that conclusions should be drawn from rational deduction, not from the inadequacies of the ancient writing system. To Norinaga, however, the Japanese classics were sources of absolute authority. The fact that the "n" sound was not seen in them amounted to proof that it had not existed in Japanese at the time they were committed to writing. By the same token, neither had the "p" sound occurred in ancient Japanese, he maintained. Norinaga's faith in the classics (or in his own interpretation of them) rendered him deaf to reason. To Akinari's contention that people would naturally have said "n" for ease in speaking, Norinaga could only reply that natural speech is what one is accustomed to hearing. "Mu" had been natural for the ancients because they were accustomed to it; "n" was natural in his own day for the same reason.

Akinari and Norinaga continued their debate to a much greater extent, and in much more detail, than can be related here, but their respective positions should already be clear to the reader. Norinaga's arguments were supported by his unshakable confidence, which was based on a great store of knowledge about the classics and the ancient language. His learning in those fields greatly surpassed Akinari's, and in this part of their quarrel he was able to present the stronger case (and modern-day phonologists are generally in agreement that the syllabic nasal was not a feature of early Japanese).[42] The weakness of Norinaga's position lay in his uncompromising view of the classics as gospel, which made him unable even to consider alternative explanations. This quality of Norinaga's was precisely what Akinari took exception to. He did not object to Norinaga's convictions so much as to his way of propounding them. Akinari felt that Norinaga's reputation was undeserved, and he could not remain silent while a man whom he considered his inferior came to surpass him in the public eye. The factor of envy cannot be ignored in accounting for Akinari's animosity.[43]

The other part of Akinari's quarrel with Norinaga centred on ancient Japanese legends and on Japan's position in the world vis à vis other nations. The genesis of this phase of the dispute may be identified as the appearance in 1781 of a work called *Shōkōhatsu*. Written by Fuji Teikan, who was both a Buddhist priest and a student of archaeology, this treatise argued that the traditional Japanese chronology would have to be shortened by six hundred years to make it coincide with the chronology of Chinese and Korean histories. Teikan also maintained that the language, customs, and traditional institutions of the Japanese, and even the imperial line itself, had all originated in Korea. He cast doubt on the value of the *Kojiki* and *Nihongi* as historical documents, pointing out contradictions between their chronology and that of continental records. Teikan's arguments were not unassailable, but they were nevertheless based on a growing knowledge of the ancient languages, cultures, and histories of China, Korea, and Japan. But to Motoori Norinaga, who saw the Japanese legends as historical facts and who regarded the *Kojiki* as virtually a sacred scripture, Teikan's conclusions were those of a lunatic. In 1785 he wrote *Kenkyōjin* (Bridling the Madman) as a reply to *Shōkōhatsu*. Like Teikan, Norinaga based his conclusions on a wide-ranging knowledge of the subject, but where Teikan had brought scepticism, Norinaga came with unshakeable faith in the Ancient Way.

Kenkyōjin was not published until 1821, but it circulated in manuscript form among Norinaga's associates and in time found its way to Akinari, who had apparently managed to read *Shōkōhatsu* as well. Although motivated not so much by admiration for Teikan's argument as by inability to stomach Norinaga's blind faith and his dogmatic and often patronizing manner of propounding his convictions, sometime in 1786 Akinari wrote a defence of Teikan's views.[44] Norinaga took this as an attack on himself and responded accordingly. Thus, the second phase of their quarrel arose, a dispute rooted in Norinaga's uncompromising assertion that Japan, as the land of the gods, was supreme over all other nations and that the sun goddess, Amaterasu-Ō-Mi-Kami, reigned over the whole world. In Norinaga's view, the sun goddess of the *Kojiki* and the *Nihongi* was none other than the sun itself. Being the land of her birth, he said, Japan, as illuminator of all the earth, deserved homage from every other country in the world.

Akinari urged a more rational approach. The Japanese people should not try to make their native legends apply to the whole world, he believed, for the sun goddess of Japan was not necessarily identical to the sun in the heavens. For example, he said, in the well known legend in which Amaterasu retires in anger to the Heavenly Rock Cave, the record states only that Japan, the "Central Land of the Reed Plains", was plunged into darkness; it says nothing about the rest of the world.

Castigating Akinari for his foolish refusal to accept the obvious, Norinaga countered by pointing out that the *Nihongi* clearly identified the sun goddess with the sun on high, and that this deity "shone looking over heaven and earth." Do China, India, and other lands, he asked rhetorically, have different heavens and earths than Japan? Do they have different suns and moons? Certainly not. Moreover, if it were not the sun itself that went to hide in the Rock Cave, why should darkness have resulted? But it *was* the sun, he insisted, and the same sun that shines over China and India as well as Japan. Therefore there was no question that the sun goddess' action had brought darkness upon the whole world.[45]

Akinari's intention seems to have been more to start a discussion than to score debating points. He was merely pointing out that the written record of the Heavenly Rock Cave incident spoke only of events within Japan. There was no mention of what had happened elsewhere, and in any case, the record's authenticity could not be proven. Akinari, who enjoyed intellectual activity for its own sake, did not insist on reaching firm conclusions in his studies. His own position was that if the meaning of a passage was not clear, one should let the matter stand unresolved, rather than force an interpretation that might prove incorrect. He acknowledged the diversity of mankind, whereas Norinaga insisted on the universality of the human race. Norinaga could not agree that Akinari had a point worthy of discussion; he could only say that Akinari was wrong. His rebuttal to Akinari's statement on the sun goddess and the Rock Cave was more than three times as long as Akinari's remarks, giving the impression that he felt threatened and overreacted, trying to smother his opponent with an excess of verbiage.

In Akinari's view, Japan should be seen in relation to the rest of the world. Since every country had its own traditions, those of Japan could not be regarded as true, and all others false, unless there were supporting evidence. One should recognize empirical facts, rather than place blind faith in tradition. Referring to the maps used by Dutch navigators, he noted that nations of the Asian cultural sphere were heavily outnumbered by other countries, many of which the Japanese were completely ignorant. In relation to these lands, Japan was extremely small, appearing on the maps like a solitary leaf floating on the surface of a pond. Suppose, he said, the Japanese were to go to foreign lands and demand homage and tribute on the grounds that their nation had been created before all others, and was the birthplace of the sun and moon, that give light to the whole world. The peoples of these other lands, having traditions of their own, would only rebuff the Japanese with the assertion that the sun and moon had appeared long ago in their own lands. And who would be qualified to judge whose tradition was correct?

Norinaga replied that it was hardly news that Japan's size was unimpressive when compared to other countries, but that quality had nothing to do with bigness. A great boulder could not compare with a tiny jewel, he said, nor were cows and horses the equals of men. In the same way, Japan, despite its modest size, was the suzerain of all other nations. To Norinaga this was self-evident. Japan's unbroken imperial line, its natural beauty, the fertility of its soil, its great numbers of people, its wealth and prosperity, and the fact that it had never been violated by a foreign invader all attested that for some unknown reason Japan was specially favoured by the gods. Unfortunately, generations of Japanese had lost sight of their nation's superlative qualities, impressed by the supposed grandeur of China. In the wake of cultural influences that had consequently poured into Japan from the Asian mainland, there had come, like a plague, a "Chinese spirit" that had warped the pure nature of old Japan, making the people self-seeking and blind to their true role in the world. Akinari was an outstanding example of a man so affected.

Granted, said Norinaga, all nations have their own traditions, but these traditions are not correct. It is the ancient traditions of Japan that are true and authentic. Norinaga offered no proof; he apparently saw no need to. Akinari too would be able to discern the truth if he could only escape from his "Chinese spirit." But until then, it was useless to argue. There were, said Norinaga, perhaps ten persons who claimed to possess the original manuscript of a poetry collection by Fujiwara Teika (1162–1241). Of course only one of the ten manuscripts could be genuine. But Akinari's statements on the ancient traditions were akin to dismissing all ten as forgeries, refusing to accept that one was truly the original manuscript. To Norinaga, this was thoughtless. There was nothing wise about being wary of fabrications because one cannot recognize the genuine object. To discern the one true manuscript and believe in it—that, said Norinaga, is wisdom.[46]

Although Norinaga here devoted the better part of his response to defending Japan's intrinsic greatness despite its small size, a careful reading of Akinari's remarks confirms that it was not his intention to call Japan an insignificant country. He meant only to illustrate that since Japan looked insignificant to the peoples of foreign lands, those people would not be inclined to accept the Japanese traditions without question. It appears that an excess of zeal led Norinaga to misunderstand and conclude that Akinari was equating Japan's unremarkable size with its worth as a nation. He seized on the issue to uphold Japan's supremacy in the world, but he was trying to refute a point that had never been made. In this portion of the debate, Norinaga's words are more like a sermon than an argument; he simply tries to tell Akinari what is right. He appeals to the ancient legends to support his own position as though he had failed to realize that it was those very legends that were in question. He could not understand how anyone could doubt them; he could not tolerate any viewpoint other than total acceptance of his own. Norinaga was not unlike the fundamentalist who sees the Bible as absolutely correct and to be interpreted literally, while Akinari in some ways resembled the rational critic who maintains that contemporary secular knowledge calls for reexamination of the Scriptures. He did not believe that legends could be taken as proof of the actual circumstances of former days. But Norinaga did not consider the ancient traditions to be legendary and he refused to allow any conjecture about them. While Akinari merely wanted the Japanese traditions to be examined rationally, Norinaga could see him only as a misguided heretic who needed to be led back to the truth. Moreover, Norinaga truly believed that the unsullied character of the ancient Japanese people could be revived in his own day by expunging the corrupting "Chinese spirit." To Akinari, however, returning to the past was too idealistic a goal, impossible however desirable. One could not escape the present, he believed; rather one should endeavour in a realistic fashion to bring the spirit of the past into the contemporary world.[47]

To leave his own version of the quarrel for posterity, Norinaga completed a record of their clash on ancient phonology early in 1787,[48] and one on their conflict on the ancient traditions probably about the same time, although the precise date is uncertain.[49] Subsequently the two manuscripts were published together under the title of *Kakaika*. This literally means "Reproving the Reed Cutter", and is a derogatory reference to Osaka, where Akinari lived, the area having traditionally been associated with reeds since earliest times. The characters with which the title is written may also be read *Ashi kari yoshi*, however, and in this reading there is a play on the word *ashi*, which may be interpreted as "wickedness" as well as "reeds"—the implication being that Norinaga saw himself as the good man (*yoshi*) cutting down the evil one.

The quarrel ended at this point, for Akinari never made a formal response to Norinaga's rebuttal. In a letter to Suetomo he restated his position that the past could not be restored, but only learned from, and he indicated that he was giving up further reading of Norinaga's writings and calling off the dispute. He was too busy, he said, to carry things further.[50] He apparently saw it as pointless to go on trying to reason with a man whose mind was closed, and so he withdrew from the fray, settling for less than a clear victory. Norinaga seems to have interpreted Akinari's silence as capitulation and so was content to let the affair rest. Thus overt hostilities came to an end, but there was no formal armistice, only an uneasy ceasefire. For the rest of his life, Akinari remained antagonistic toward Norinaga, never missing an opportunity to hurl verbal barbs his way. Even seven years after Norinaga died, Akinari set down the following:

A certain man said, "To strain to know the unknowable is ignorance indeed." Thinking this well stated, I do not add my own opinion to things that I do not know. However, there is a man who does recklessly interpret the things of old. There is a man who, calling his students the children of his teaching, gathers to him those who come from far and wide. Truly his self-interest is great. He is a man from the province of Ise. With the *Kojiki* as his source, he believes that he has succeeded in teaching the things of antiquity. I humbly submit:

Higa goto wo	Even though he says
Iute nari tomo	The most utter nonsense
Deshi hoshi ya	He still wants pupils—
Kojiki Dembei to	Even though people call him
Hito wa iu tomo[51]	Dembei the Kojiki beggar.

Besides disagreeing with many of Norinaga's statements, Akinari considered his desire for fame and followers unbecoming a true scholar. In another part of the same document he took pains to restate his own conclusions in his dispute with Norinaga.[52] Such was the depth of feeling that accompanied their quarrel.

The dispute attracts interest today more for what it reveals of the workings of the two scholars' minds than for its subject matter, but in Akinari's and Norinaga's own time it amounted to a contest of world views. It remains one of the famous intellectual confrontations of early modern Japan.[53]

6

The Quail's Abode

In the spring of 1787, at the invitation of a friend named Hirase Sukemichi, Akinari went to enjoy the cherry blossoms at Arashiyama, near Kyoto. He had gone there the previous summer, staying at the quarters of a monk from the Tenryūji Temple, and he lodged there with Sukemichi on this visit as well. The mountains and the river were virtually in their host's garden, Akinari said, and they spent three or four pleasant and relaxing days there, learning more of the local traditions, viewing the cherry blossoms during the day, and listening to the sound of the wind and water and the cries of plovers and frogs at night. As a sort of bonus, as he was passing through Kyoto on his way home, on the first day of the third month, Akinari was able to witness the ceremonial procession of a newly appointed high court official, Takatsukasa by name.[1] But more interesting than his account of the trip is his statement that it was taken during a period of respite from illness. Less than two months later, he gave up his medical practice and moved out of Osaka, giving as reasons the need to care for his ailing body and to find a place to dispose of his corpse when he died.[2] It would appear that his health had begun to fail during the previous year, and he felt that his life was nearing its end.

Although the nature of his malady is unclear, poor health may well have been Akinari's immediate reason for leaving the medical profession, but even though his physical condition subsequently improved, his decision to retire was final. In spite of financial embarrassment, he never again practised medicine as a means of earning his livelihood, so he was doubtless not sorry to give it up. In a day when medical science was undeveloped, a diligent physician surely found his work frustrating and often heartbreaking, and Akinari had been such a person. He had earnestly tried to help his patients, and his failures had brought him anguish and cause for reflection. Repeatedly he spoke of his lack of skill in a profession that he had entered late in his life.[3] Causing the death of a young girl through mistaken diagnosis and yet being kindly treated by her parents, who had accepted their loss as inevitable, brought him particular pain.[4] This may have been the deciding factor. His own illness may well have been the consequence of overwork and the mental burden of responsibility.

Akinari's writings that touch on his personal life reveal that he suffered from feelings of inferiority and self-pity, and such feelings seem to have been especially strong around this time.[5] Also, he had not entered medicine from interest but as a means of supporting his dependents. Moreover, it would appear that his feelings of antipathy toward unconscientious physicians intensified as the years went by. In *Kuse monogatari*, for example, which he wrote not long after retiring, he stated that physicians like those of former times were no longer to be found in the world, and he went on to castigate medical practitioners of his own day for pretending to have knowledge that they lacked, with an eye to acquiring patrons, thinking more of profit than of alleviating pain and engaging in side businesses—conduct which he considered disgraceful for a true physician.[6] In all probability it was a combination of these things that sent Akinari into retirement. Feeling his work to be a drain on both his failing health and his peace of mind, nagged by doubts about his competence, embarrassed by colleagues who gave his profession a bad name, and not having any real love for the work anyway, he seems to have decided to give it up and do what he had really wanted to do all along, be the consequences what they may.

Thus Akinari, accompanied by his mother, his wife, and his wife's mother, who had also come to live with them,[7] moved to Nagara-mura, a village on the outskirts of Osaka not far from his old haunts at the Kashima Inari Shrine.[8] Here Akinari built a small thatched hut which he called the Uzurai, or the Quail's Abode, likening himself to the bird which has no fixed dwelling but takes shelter wherever it may.[9] It was not without feelings of guilt that he brought his family to their new home. Bowing his head to the floor, he apologized to his mother for this unfilial act, but his mother accepted this change in her fortunes and took it in stride.[10] A kind and understanding woman, she may well have foreseen such a turn of events.

In his own words, Akinari had "crept back to the countryside" and "become an idler, passing the time writing poetry and prose."[11] This was surely an exaggeration, but most of his verifiable activities during his stay at Nagara concerned the world of letters—studying, teaching, editing, and writing. His excursions for sightseeing or meeting literary colleagues increased from this point, at least so far as the record shows, implying that he was free to absent himself from home without fear of the consequences. Just how he dealt with the once so acutely felt responsibility of supporting his dependents is not known. He must have realized a small income from teaching, and he probably had a substantial, though dwindling, sum on hand from savings and from the sale of his Osaka property. Nevertheless, the family's living standard had undoubtedly taken a dramatic fall. One night a thief broke into their house and made off with most of their possessions, but next morning, looking at the hole the intruder had made in the wall, Akinari merely reflected poetically:

Ware yori mo	Because there was one
Mazushiki hito no	Poorer than I
Yo ni mo areba	In this world,
Ubara karatachi	He stooped to creep through a gap
Hima kuguru nari	In the flowers and thorns.

He refashioned the hole into a window, called it his "burglar's window," and jokingly remarked to visitors that it was good for ventilation.[12] Being robbed does not appear to have been a disaster for the family, probably because they had so little to be stolen.

While living in Osaka he had acquired two promising disciples, Oka Kunio (also known as Otori) and Kuwana Masanori. They had assisted with the editing of *Kokin waka shū uchigiki*,[13] and it was Kunio's report of the eruption of Mt. Asama in 1783 on which Akinari had based his *Asama no kemuri*.[14] Akinari referred to Kunio as "a kindred spirit" and to Masanori as "a trustworthy friend," and when Kunio's wife died, he composed an elegy for her.[15] He appears to have treated his students more as friends than as disciples, just as Umaki had treated him. Kunio and Masanori are usually mentioned together in Akinari's writings, suggested that they were fellow students of comparable abilities and that they were both highly regarded by their teacher. Nevertheless, both men remain obscure, for along with their other common traits, they died prematurely, before their talents had really borne fruit. Kunio died suddenly from illness in the spring of 1788, and Masanori's death apparently occurred only a short time afterward.[16] Their loss was a personal tragedy for Akinari. Besides his genuine affection for the pair, he had seen them as disciples worthy to carry on his teachings, and he reacted to their deaths like a father to the demise of his sons. After being predeceased by these two, he said, he stopped looking for friends,[17] and it is true that in his old age he was averse to accepting disciples.

He enjoyed a longer-lasting relationship with another of his students,

Hashimoto Tsuneakira (also known by the surname of Tachibana; 1760–1806). An attendant at the Umenomiya Shrine in Umezu-mura on the western outskirts of Kyoto, Tsuneakira was to achieve some fame as a *waka* poet and as an authority on ancient court practices. The date and circumstances of their first meeting are not known, but Tsuneakira's name appears frequently in Akinari's writings after the move to Nagara. He seems to have been an intimate friend, though it is clear that he also asked Akinari's advice on matters of scholarship. On one occasion, for example, Tsuneakira acquired a copy of Kada Azumamaro's comments on a particularly thorny verse from the chronicle of Emperor Saimei in the *Nihongi*. Tsuneakira asked Akinari's opinion of the manuscript, and Akinari obliged by outlining his doubts concerning Kada's interpretation. This occurred sometime between 1787 and 1792, but clearly during the time Akinari was living at Nagara.[18]

Akinari had also become friends with the painter and haiku poet, Matsumura Gekkei (also known as Goshun; 1752–1811), a disciple of Buson, Although it was certainly not their first encounter their earliest meeting of record took place in the eighth year of the Temmei Era (1788), first month, twenty-ninth day, when Akinari went to Kyoto and stayed at Gekkei's home. Tsuneakira, who was also a friend of Gekkei's came to visit, and the three of them stayed up talking until quite late, but what happened next made the visit even more memorable. Towards dawn a fire broke out in the city. Fanned by a stiff breeze, it developed into a disastrous conflagration and burned all through the next day. By noon Gekkei's house had been destroyed, and Akinari had joined the crowds of refugees in the streets. It was an appalling spectacle, he later wrote.

> The smoke scorched the clouds, and the light of the sun and moon could not be seen. The sounds of things collapsing resounded like myriad thunders. People ran about in confusion, weeping and shouting. The scene was sad beyond compare. The several houses where I had planned to stay were now gone completely. I was terribly miserable, and could scarcely tell whether it was a dream or reality.

At last he found shelter in Takai Kitō's home, but after a short rest, he decided to return to Nagara. Late in the afternoon he set out, witnessing many scenes of pain and suffering on the way. When at last he arrived at Fushimi, he was informed that there would be no boat for Osaka that night, so he had no choice but to sleep in the open with other refugees. A thunderstorm developed, accompanied by strong winds, and the flames continued to burn, turning the dark sky red. After a miserable night, he was finally able to get on a boat and return home.[19] His decision to leave Kyoto had been prudent, for Kitō's house also was lost in the blaze.

Just a few weeks later, Akinari made a trip to Yoshino. Nishikawa Tada-
nao, a scholar with whom he was acquainted, had long wanted to see the area,
and being sixty years old was anxious to make the journey while he was still
physically able. Thinking that it would provide opportunity to keep his
promise to visit his cousin in Nagara-mura in Yamato and to call on some
other relatives as well, Akinari accepted Nishikawa's invitation to accompany
him. In his account of the excursion[20] Akinari was vague as to just when they
started out, but they passed through Kashiwara and stopped at the village of
Kuniwake to visit his kinsman named Nishio, who received them very cor-
dially. Pressing on, they came to the village of Tatsuta, where they spent a
night, and worshipped at the Dharma temple of Kataoka. Then they reached
Tawaramoto, where they found lodgings and heard to their dismay that the
cherry blossoms at Yoshino had already fallen. Next day, by now the fourteenth of the third month, they went to Miwayama and visited the shrine
there, where Akinari recalled a previous pilgrimage with his father many years
before. From there they went on to Ama no Kaguyama.

By then Nishikawa was becoming fatigued, so they cut their sight-seeing
short and made their way to an unspecified village where they were put up by a
man named Ueda, the man whom Akinari described as being like a brother.[21]
That evening they visited the nearby Tachibana Temple, and next day went to
see another relative of Akinari's, a man named Ikeda, in the village of Hirao,
but they found him ill, and although he made an effort to be hospitable,
Akinari regretted having disturbed him. Afterwards, they carried on to the
Yoshino area to find that the report heard at Tawaramoto had been correct.
Most of the blossoms were gone, and many trees had been felled by strong
winds. After spending the night, they toured the area, visiting famous spots,
while Akinari took notes on the places they passed through, asking local
people about their history and traditions, and recalling facts that he already
knew. Repeatedly he mentioned that he had passed this way long ago, and
apparently he was virtually retracing the path he and his father had followed
on that previous excursion. Next morning, after spending the night at Kamii-
chi, they descended the river by boat. Although they had enjoyed good
weather most of the time, this day was rainy. After losing their way and
finding it again, they came to the village of Nagara, where Akinari's cousin,
the man he had promised to visit, was headman. Unfortunately, Akinari
ended his account with their arrival at his kinsman's house, providing no
further details. His literary recollection of this excursion, which he wrote later
that year, is doubly interesting, for it both displays Akinari's extensive knowledge of the history and legends of the Yoshino area and also provides material
for speculation about his true parentage.

After the complete *Kokin waka shū uchigiki* was finally published in 1789,
Akinari continued to edit and publish works by Kamo Mabuchi and persons

associated with him. He prepared a fresh copy of Kato Umaki's treatise on the *Tosa Diary* and wrote a preface for it that was long enough to include some of his own detailed knowledge.[22] Publication was never carried out, possibly because of insufficient funds, but he was more successful with anthologies of verse by Mabuchi and Umaki. He had planned to publish a collection of Umaki's poems for the thirteenth anniversary of his death, but he had unfortunately missed the date. Thus, when Nomura Nobumoto, for whom he had prepared *Kokin waka shū uchigiki*, happened to approach him again, this time seeking his aid in compiling a book of poems by Mabuchi, Akinari seized the chance to issue a collection of Umaki's verses along with it. A publication request was submitted early in 1791, and two anthologies, *Agatai kashū* by Mabuchi and *Shizunoya kashū* by Umaki, were published as a single volume three months later.[23] The *Shizunoya* title may have been an allusion to the name of Yuya Shizuko (1733–52), a female disciple of Mabuchi's with whom Umaki was widely rumoured to have been romantically involved. In 1790 Akinari had written a preface for a new edition of *Ayanuno*, a collection of her poems, presumably at the request of someone who thought that in view of Umaki's reported love for Shizuko, it was fitting that his leading disciple write the preface.[24]

Meanwhile, in 1787, he had finally relented and allowed *Yasaishō* to be published. His haiku continued to appear occasionally in printed collections, and thanks to his new abundance of leisure time, his friendship with Takai Kitō took on new life. Kitō was then at the height of his career, most of the members of Buson's group having gathered around him after the master's death in 1784. It is during this period that Akinari's name appears with greatest frequency in Kitō's journals. They got together fairly often during 1789, composing poetry together or with other members of Kitō's circle or sometimes just talking and exchanging opinions on each other's work,[25] and when they were unable to meet personally, they exchanged letters. Such activities added variety to Akinari's life at Nagara, although they were to end abruptly with Kitō's sudden death in late 1789.

Akinari went to Kyoto in mid-1789 to participate in services marking the thirteenth anniversary of Umaki's passing.[26] He had barely returned to Nagara when his wife's mother died.[27] It had been only a year before that he had seen his two most prized disciples suffer untimely deaths, and now a similar tragedy struck in his immediate family.

In the autumn of the year, after the appropriate ceremonies had been completed, Akinari took his wife to Kyoto to entomb her mother's ashes. It was Tama's first visit to the Capital since moving with her foster parents to Osaka years before, and seeing her former home again helped to alleviate the sadness of the occasion. On the eleventh day of the ninth month, in appropriately rainy weather, the ashes were entrusted to a temple in the city.[28] His duty to the dead completed, Akinari went the following day to visit Kitō, and together with another member of Kitō's group, they went to the Nanzenji Temple and composed a number of poems in honour of their meeting, stopping off for refreshments on their way back.[29] Despite his apparently good health, Kitō had only a few weeks to live, and this was probably the last time Akinari saw him.

The next day, Akinari and his wife, together with a girl who seems to have been one of Tama's relations, set out for Saga, west of the city, to enjoy the autumn colours and to watch the moon. It was the thirteenth day of the ninth month, the night of *nochi no tsuki*,[30] and Saga was traditionally an ideal place for moon viewing. On the way they stopped at Umezu to call on Hashimoto Tsuneakira, but he was not at home, away attending to his priestly duties at the shrine. His mother invited them to stop there for the night, but they chose to press on to their destination. Akinari had visited Saga just one year earlier, lodging at the hut of a certain nun, and it was to her hermitage that they now went for shelter. There they spent the evening, watching the moon, and composing *waka* about the scene, until the cold wind forced them reluctantly to retire. The next day, after walking about enjoying the scenery, they returned late in the afternoon to the nun's cottage to find Tsuneakira waiting for them. Akinari seems to have found him an especially congenial companion. They conversed until evening, and when Tsuneakira started for home, Akinari and Tama accompanied him as far as the river. As a parting verse, Tsuneakira offered:

Yama no na no	Though called the mountain
Arashi ni mine no	Of tempests, from its peak
Kumo harete	The clouds have departed.
Kawase sayakeki	Tranquil the river rapids,
Tsuki wo miru kana	The moon plain to see.

To which Akinari responded:

Ōikawa	Does the moonlight,
Hayase ni kudaku	Shattered by the rapid flow
Tsuki kage no	Of Ōi River,
Sue wa kazura no	Dwell at last in waves
Nami ni sumuran	Of trailing river grasses?

In the morning Tsuneakira returned, spent the day guiding them around the famous places in the area, and towards evening escorted them to his home, where he lodged them for the night. Once settled, Tama observed, the men became deeply involved in an intellectual discussion about the distant past—

things she herself had never heard of, she said—while the women spent the time in "womanly talk." One senses that she felt left out. Although it rained heavily during the night, by morning the sky showed promise of clearing, so, anxious to be home, they declined Tsuneakira's invitation to prolong their stay and set out for Fushimi, which they reached in time to catch a boat for Osaka that evening.[31]

Upon reaching Osaka, Akinari may have sent Tama on to Nagara by herself while he stayed in the city to visit his mother, who had moved from the Quail's Abode to live with some of her relatives about two months earlier.[32] In any case, just a week later, when Tsuneakira came to Osaka to attend to some business, Akinari was on hand to meet him and escort him to the Quail's Abode to spend the night. Akinari and Tama had promised to take Tsunea-kira on a tour around Mt. Minō to repay his kindness in showing them around Saga. Their plan was to start out early in the morning, but as usual Akinari and Tsuneakira became engrossed in conversation that continued long after they had gone to bed. When morning came, both of them were too tired to get up, and in spite of Tama's urging, it was after midday when they finally left the house. Taking shelter in a mountain temple that night, they rose before dawn to watch the sunrise. From there they hiked to the waterfall of Minō, where they made tea and warmed *sake* over an open fire of pine cones and dry leaves. They spent the remainder of the day simply enjoying the scenery, until the time came for them to part at the foot of the mountain and return to their homes. Subsequently, Tsuneakira and Akinari collaborated in writing a literary account of the outing.[33]

However, these pleasant excursions were merely intervals of respite from the tragedy and misfortune that were now beginning to overtake Akinari. He still had nearly twenty years to live, but his final two decades were filled with difficulties as, one by one, his friends and family members died and left him behind. He grew more and more alienated from the world, his poverty increasing and his health slowly but relentlessly deteriorating. It was just a month after the excursion to Mt. Minō, for example, that Takai Kitō's sudden death occurred. Akinari felt the loss keenly. In *Kanetsukuba*, a commemorative volume published by Kitō's associates early the following year, he contributed this verse:

Otōto Shimmei wo kanashimu	Lamenting my younger brother, Shimmei:
Fuyu karete	Withered in winter,
Yukashige mo naki	Nothing to draw me thither,
Miyako kana[34]	Still, the Capital.

Although Akinari referred to Kitō as his brother, he did not care for some of the members of the group. He contributed the above verse out of respect for

Kitō, but nevertheless he quarrelled with Miya Shigyō, who led the circle for a time, about the compilation of *Kanetsukuba*, apparently resentful at not being called upon to play a greater role himself. Later, when Shigyō was preparing the manuscript of Kitō's *Yoshino kikō* for publication, Akinari submitted a short preface, which Shigyō rejected on the grounds that its length would add to the printing costs. He asked Akinari to shorten it, but Akinari angrily declined to do so and asked Matsumura Gekkei to inform Shigyō of his desire to cease relations with the group.[35] Significantly, Gekkei himself largely withdrew from *haikai* circles after Kitō's death and concentrated on his painting.

Kitō's ashes were scarcely cold when Akinari's mother passed away toward the end of the same year.[36] Although she had come to him as a stepmother, she had given him all the care and love that a natural parent could, and it was to her that he had given his filial devotion. From the time he was six years old, until just a few months before her death, she had lived in the same house as he, being a source of companionship and a sympathetic consultant in times of uncertainty, even after he had reached maturity. Akinari never once even hinted that looking after her in her old age was a burden. He only expressed regret that he could not care for her better.

The family now consisted of Akinari and Tama alone. Prompted by the succession of tragic events, Tama took religious vows and thereafter was known by the monastic name of Koren, which was taken from the name of a jewelled sacrificial vase mentioned in the Confucian *Analects*. It was an appropriate selection, for the name "Tama" itself meant "jewel," but despite its lofty origin, when Akinari asked his wife how her new name should be written, she merely laughed and told him to use any characters he liked. She had chosen the name, she said, because of his habit of gaining her attention by calling "*Korekore!*"[37]—an expression not unlike the English "Hey there!"

Misfortune next appeared in the form of poor health. Koren suffered from an illness early in 1790, and although she had recovered by the middle of the year,[38] she was ailing again towards its close.[39] From the spring of the same year, Akinari experienced severe pains in his hand and arm, which continued until the summer. Shortly after the suffering abated, he began to have trouble with his vision, and by the end of the summer his left eye had failed completely. He was understandably depressed, for the loss of one eye and the danger of losing the other threatened to rob him of the ability to read and write— without which his main purpose in life would be gone. He felt that he had experienced nothing but misfortune ever since the fire that had destroyed his oil and paper business, and he believed that he was being punished for the unproductive manner in which he had lived.[40] When he retired to the country-side, he had tried to see himself as following the example of men like Kamo no Chōmei and Yoshida Kenkō, famous literary recluses of the middle ages, but he could shake off neither the merchants' work ethic on which he had been raised, nor feelings of guilt for not following it. He also saw his illness and blindness as punishment for bringing his own and his wife's mothers out into the countryside to die. No one had accused him, but he blamed himself nevertheless.[41] His ailments may have been at least partly psychosomatic. Certainly he was on the verge of despair, irrationally convinced that heaven had selected him for special chastising or that some evil deity had attached itself to him. He appears to have lost temporarily the rational objectivity that had served him so well in his dispute with Norinaga.

But glimpses into his home life show that throughout these tribulations his wife remained loving and faithful and a great comfort to him. One winter's evening, as Akinari was closing the flimsy bamboo door against the cold, Koren remarked that, pleasant as their Osaka home had been, she had always been extremely busy there and faced with troubles of which her husband had been unaware. Life in this humble cottage had been so peaceful by comparison, she said, that one could scarcely say it was a worse place to live. Somewhat overcome, Akinari called her a guardian deity who had spent the years taking care of a madman like himself. Partly, but probably not entirely in jest, he bowed his head to the floor in obeisance. Smiling, Koren voiced her regret that people who misunderstood her husband could not witness this scene. She would continue to serve him, she said, no matter what transpired, and with no thought of sorrow or bitterness.[42]

It was under such circumstances that Akinari wrote *Kuse monogatari*, his best-known effort from this period. Completed in the spring of 1791,[43] it is commonly considered a work of fiction, and indeed it does contain some fictional episodes, but it is really more of a miscellany in form. It consists of a preface followed by twenty-five sketches that criticize or poke fun at the habits and personalities of scholars, physicians, haiku and *waka* poets, tea masters, priests, courtesans and their patrons, musicians, kabuki actors, and other character types. Akinari seems to have written with much the same intention he had when writing *Kakizome kigenkai*, but *Kuse monogatari*, with its broader scope and more finely tuned style, totally eclipsed that earlier work.

As its title suggests, *Kuse monogatari* is to some extent a stylistic parody of *Ise monogatari*. Akinari's interest in *The Tales of Ise* went back at least as far as his years at Kashima-mura, where he had prepared his own annotated manuscript of the work. About the same time that he was writing *Kuse monogatari*, he was preparing for publication Kamo Mabuchi's *Ise monogatari koi*, to which he was to append some of his own explanations of difficult phrases from *Ise monogatari*.[44] These were items that Akinari selected from the work he had done at Kashima—items that he apparently was still pleased with twenty years after they were written. *Kuse monogatari* may be seen in part as an outgrowth of this activity. The idea of writing a parody of *Ise* did not originate with Akinari, however. Numerous such burlesques had appeared during the Tokugawa period, probably the most famous being the early-seventeenth-century *Nise monogatari*.[45] *Kuse monogatari* reveals Akinari's thorough familiarity with and full understanding of *Ise*, and its satire and adroit blending of elegant and common language illustrates his keen wit and skillful classical style. Parodies of lines and passages from *Ise monogatari*, and to a lesser extent from other classics, dot the pages,[46] making much of the irony unintelligible to anyone not well versed in old Japanese literature. To date, few scholars have been so bold as to attempt more than a cursory study of it.

The *Kuse monogatari* title probably means "Tales of Idiosyncrasy," although an alternative reading of the characters with which the title was written, *Kampeki dan*, makes "Tales of Spleen" another possible choice. And there is some further ambiguity, for the title could be interpreted as *Kusemono katari*, or "Stories of Eccentric Persons," as well. The ambiguity was probably intentional, for all of these renditions of the title are reflected to some extent in the text. The twenty-five sketches are a hodgepodge with no apparent organization. Some are brief stories, others, merely descriptive anecdotes, but all of them attack some human shortcoming that had aroused the ire of the author. Although most of them begin with the phrase "In former times," after the manner of *The Tales of Ise*, Akinari was not really talking about the past, for the characters and events are all from his own time. He is at times lightly jesting; at others, sharply critical, but the tone is consistently one of condemnation, written from the point of view of a disapproving and sarcastic onlooker. Akinari did not take a self-righteous position, however; rather he employed a self-mocking vein as well. Indeed, if the title is seen as *Kusemono katari*, then another possible interpretation of its meaning may be "Narratives by an Eccentric Man." After making stabs at various and assorted other character types, Akinari concluded by turning his barbs on himself, as the following passage illustrates.

In former times, in the village of Fukakusa, there was a man who, weary of the world perhaps, sought out a dwelling and lived in seclusion. While he still felt as though he had been there but a short time, four or five years passed. Whenever fond memories of the Capital came upon him, he would fix his gaze on the sky in that direction. With free time in abundance, he made a pillow beneath his window his sole companion, and as he slept he heard in his dream, amidst the chirping of birds at play among the branches in his garden, a robin that spoke rapidly but precisely after the manner of men.

"I come to play at this hermitage every spring," the robin said, "yet never do I find the master doing any kind of work. What a lazy man! Is there anything to be gained living like this? How detestable he is!"

A magpie resting on a branch below heard these words and replied, "Formerly this man lived in the Capital. He is mean-spirited by nature, afraid of incurring debts should he try to earn his livelihood. Men of broader outlook will tell lies or do wrong without a thought if it does no harm to others, but as for this man, whenever he sees or hears of such things, he grows sorrowful and angry. Moreover, when he reads his books, only the past pleases him; he abhors the world of today. If he practices the arts, he looks up to the men of old, skilled and clumsy alike, as noble and refined, but as for the present, he scorns everything he sees and takes no delight in it. That is why he passes the time to no purpose. We ought to pity him."

The robin laughed aloud. "So he indulges himself," it said. ".What a wretched spirit!"

"But," said the magpie, "the master never wears fine clothing nor does he eat good food. He makes do with paper bedding and paper curtains and appears to be frugal in all matters. I see no indulgence."

"The indulgence I speak of is not of that sort," the robin replied."The master is too sensitive and getting worse. He cannot control himself. He does not exalt himself but he indulges his heart by regarding all others as impure. A world or people that he would approve of have never existed since ancient times. Do not the writings of both China and Japan state repeatedly that people in this world are dishonest, and lament that the majority are corrupt? People may accept the teachings in those books but there appear to be none who follow them. The master too is of that sort. It has nothing to do with a man's wisdom or ignorance whether he practices the teachings or not. A wise man may follow them, but if the world treats him ill, they seem to have no value. . . . To remain pure though one be buffeted by the world is good, we may say, but one can hardly mingle with society unless he presents a sullied appearance. People like the master cannot do so. When he hears of impurity, he has to despise it, but when he sees that such is the human condition, he cannot loudly condemn it. . . . If he would move with the times, he would not become angry and resentful at everything he sees and hears. When he laments over things that are contrary to the Way, he indulges his self-centred heart. He eats poor food and wears thin clothing, but if we gave him fine apparel, he would probably wear it, and if we sent him good food, he would probably eat it. It is not that he shuns luxury; he lives thus because he is poor."

So saying, the robin laughed aloud, and all the other birds joined in. The magpie too gave a merry laugh, and the mountains and moors laughed as well. Thereupon I awoke from my springtime slumber and penned these idle tales of life, which you may call *Kampeki dan*, or *Kuse monogatari*, or whatever you please.[47]

Surely this was very much the way Akinari saw himself at the time. Ideally, he believed, a man should be actively involved in the real world, working hard and cultivating himself. Even his fiction reflects this view—his characters who stray from that path invariably suffer. He did not regard literature as something appropriate for a man to devote his life to. Time and again he used the word *asobi*, or "recreation," in reference to writing prose and poetry and studying the classics, and when he finally gave in to the temptation to spend the rest of his life at such pursuits, he saw his decision as proof of his weakness, and it cost him considerable self-respect. But he had felt out of place in society from the beginning, and his alienation grew as his interest in the classics and in Japanese antiquity intensified his dislike of the present and his affinity for an idealized past. From Katō Umaki he had acquired the view that ancient society had been natural for ancient times and that contemporary society was natural for his own day. Even if it was impure, one should live in it anyway. But while he accepted this conclusion logically, he could not do so in practice. He could only withdraw. Yet he was too honest with himself to see his withdrawal as other than an act of self-indulgence. He recognized that he had done nothing for society by leaving it, that his action had inconvenienced his family and that no one but himself had benefited. The self-portrait that he appended to his castigations of others was his own admission that he really was no better than the world he criticized.

Although their confrontation was over, neither Akinari nor Norinaga had capitulated. Each man had, in effect, declared himself the winner and tried to fortify himself against future assaults. To shore up his own position, Norinaga had compiled the two works that together became known as *Kakaika*, while late in 1792 Akinari finished writing *Yasumigoto*, which summed up his own views on the subjects over which they had quarreled. He discussed history and administration in ancient Japan and considered the country in relation to other nations. He restated his view that the past cannot be recreated in the present, that Japan was not necessarily the supreme nation of the world, and that natural disasters are caused by nature, not by malevolent deities. Notably, he upheld the *Nihongi* as a historical document superior to the *Kojiki*, which he dismissed as a spurious work riddled with interpolations by various editors, and without mentioning him by name, but leaving no ambiguity, he attacked Norinaga's misguided reverence for the latter book. Akinari's criticisms of the *Kojiki* subsequently led to him being called a traitor by Katō Chikage (1735–1808),[48] a former student of Kamo Mabuchi who had become one of the day's leading *waka* poets and *kokugaku* scholars. Perhaps it was because of this remark that Akinari later called Chikage an illiterate poetaster who owed his reputation to his money.[49]

While living at the Quail's Abode, Akinari and his wife had become friendly with the family that resided next door, and they were naturally interested when the son of the house was married. In 1790 a child was born to the young couple, but the mother took sick and died the following year. Never having had any children of their own, Akinari and Koren now turned their unfulfilled parental feelings on the motherless boy next door. They took great delight in watching him grow and helping him learn to speak. Akinari would become so absorbed in playing with the child that he would forget his own bad health, and Koren, too poor to buy new cloth, would remake items of her own and her husband's clothing into things for the boy to wear. But in the autumn of 1792 the child became ill. Akinari tried frantically to find an effective medicine, and the father offered prayers without ceasing, but their combined efforts proved futile. The boy's condition worsened steadily into the following year until the day of the festival of Jizō, a guardian deity of children, when, as though this Bodhisattva had carried him away, he died. Beside himself with grief, Akinari assumed all the expenses for the funeral and cremation and personally made the journey to Osaka for the final interment of the ashes, feeling, no doubt, as though he were doing it for his own son.

There seemed little reason now to go on living. The loss of the child was only the latest in a series of events that had made Nagara a place of bitter recollections, Koren noted in her memoir,[50] and she and her husband decided to abandon their home and set out on a final journey that would end when they fell down and died. Thus they left the Quail's Abode and made their way to Kyoto, arriving in time for the Gion Festival that summer. Still sorrowful, and both of them in poor health, they had little inclination to participate in the festivities, the most gala public celebration of the year, but they ventured out into the crowded streets nevertheless, an old couple on unsteady feet. But they could only think of how the child would have enjoyed the colourful floats and pageantry, and of the pleasure they would have found in taking him to see it all. Young children in the crowd reminded them of the one they had lost, and wares in the shops made them think of the presents they could no longer give him. They went away more unhappy than they had come.

Later, when they were about to continue on their journey, friends in the Capital offered comforting words and pleaded with them to stay longer. "Your grief will lessen as time passes," they said, "and there is much to see in the Capital." Akinari and Koren gave in to their persuasion and found temporary lodgings, but though they planned to stay only for the time being, the move was to be permanent. Kyoto would be the place where both of them would spend the rest of their lives.

7

Kyoto

The move to Kyoto may not have been as fortuitous as Koren implied. The story she told was a childless woman's way of assuaging her grief, which required the sense of tragedy and loss to be portrayed without restraint and perhaps assigned a more decisive role in determining their future than it really merited. The more stoic Akinari never mentioned the child in his own writings, accounting for their removal to the Capital as a concession to his wife, who was lonely for her native home, but this was probably not the whole truth either. Since his young manhood he had had ties that had brought him frequently to the city, and by this time his interests had largely shifted from Osaka to Kyoto. He had moved to Nagara with the intention of spending the rest of his life there, but death had not come, and as the years passed he found himself increasingly dissatisfied with his attempt to withdraw from society. Most of his friends and colleagues were now in the Capital, and moving there offered easier association with them, as well as a change of scene. After their mothers' deaths, Akinari and Koren had sold articles that were of no use to them and had made frequent excursions to Kyoto on the proceeds. The desire to settle there permanently might well have developed gradually in the course of such visits. One of his companions later noted that as Akinari grew older, he felt more and more out of place in the commercial atmosphere of Osaka. Kyoto would offer quieter surroundings, he thought, and its people would be of a more congenial nature. Still, Akinari did say that the action was taken on a trial basis, and he recorded his residence as Settsu, or northern Osaka, in the autumn of the year they moved,[1] which implies that he did not yet regard the Capital as his home and that the decision to remain permanently was made at some later date. Even so, although their motives almost certainly were more complex, there seems to be no reason to doubt that the death of the child in Nagara did provide the immediate stimulus for pulling up stakes.

Akinari and Koren came to Kyoto with fifty *ryō* to their name and moved into lodgings in Fukuro-machi, near the Chion-in Temple, in what is now Matsubara-chō, Higashiyama-ku, where the flat valley of the Kamo River begins its abrupt rise into steep pine-clad hills. Here, in Akinari's words, they "lived a plain and simple life, eating grain and drinking tea made from parched rice." For sustenance Akinari relied upon the pittances he received from his publishers, probably some occasional remuneration from teaching, and just possibly some revenue from practising medicine on a part-time basis.[2] Together these would have amounted to only a small and irregular income, but even though Koren described their quarters as "difficult to bring both knees inside," and although Akinari said that they arrived in the Capital to find, like Urashima Tarō, that the people they could call upon had all vanished, they appear to have been reasonably contented, and they did have a number of friends who gave them help.[3]

One such person was Hakura Nobuyoshi (also known by the surname of Kada; b. 1750), a disciple of the poet Ozawa Roan. Akinari had met him before moving to Kyoto, and they had become quite intimate by that time, it would appear, for Nobuyoshi took him to meet Roan just shortly after his arrival in the Capital, and it is unlikely that Nobuyoshi would have honoured a short-term casual acquaintance with a formal introduction to his teacher. Akinari may have originally met Nobuyoshi through Hashimoto Tsuneakira, who was a mutual friend, but their relationship developed into a genuine bond, whatever its origin may have been, and Nobuyoshi proved to be an unfailing source of aid from the time of Akinari's arrival in Kyoto until his death.

Roan also became a true and lasting friend. When Akinari first visited his home, Roan received him kindly and appeared as though he had been impatiently awaiting his arrival. No doubt Roan had already read, and been impressed by, some of Akinari's work and was looking forward to meeting him in person. Akinari too, in his younger days, had heard much about Roan from Kojima Shigeie, the man whom he credited with introducing him to classical studies. Mutual esteem for Shigeie and their fond reminiscences of him helped Akinari and Roan to feel a common bond from the moment of their first encounter. Tsuneakira also was present at this meeting. He and

Roan played the koto together, while Akinari, having noted the two old pine trees in Roan's garden, offered the verse:

Yamazato no	The voices of two pines
Futaki no matsu no	In a mountain village
Koe aite	Were joined in harmony
Aki no shirabe wa	And to my ears were the sound
Kiku bekari keri	Of an autumn melody.

Roan responded with:

Yama kage no	The autumn voices
Futaki no matsu no	Of the two pine trees
Aki no koe	In the mountains' shade
Hito ni kikaruru	Awaited the time
Toki mo machikeri	They might be heard by men.

Akinari noted that he had Nobuyoshi act as scribe on his own behalf, implying that his eyesight was giving him some trouble.[4]

Akinari may have found his dwelling at the Chion-in with the assistance of Murase Kōtei, who was one of Matsumura Gekkei's associates. Kōtei's residence was very close to Akinari's lodging, and considering their mutual friendship with Gekkei, this proximity was likely the result of more than pure chance. For some time Akinari had had a growing interest in the ceremonial preparation of tea, and since Kōtei was a tea master of some standing, Akinari found his companionship very rewarding. During the time they were neighbours, Kōtei did much to guide and develop Akinari's own interest in the art of tea.[5]

Yotsugi Makazu, a wealthy merchant in the Capital, was another of Akinari's friends who enjoyed the tea ceremony. Again, the origin of their friendship is unclear, but Akinari had become acquainted with him at least a few years prior to moving to Kyoto, perhaps introduced by Gekkei or Tsuneakira. In a letter to Gekkei in 1791, Akinari mentioned receiving a painting from Yotsugi,[6] and shortly after getting settled in the Capital, he made an excursion with Yotsugi to Uji in order to visit Tsuneakira, who was staying there at the time. They took shelter in Tsuneakira's lodgings on this trip, where they made tea with pure water from the river and went through the usual round of poetry composition, after which they set out by boat to see the nearby Byōdō-in Temple, a rare architectural relic of the eleventh century. En route they were surprised to encounter numerous small boats on the river, their occupants picking bundles of firewood from the water. In answer to their query, they learned that a wagon loaded with firewood had overturned a few miles upstream, spilling its contents into the river and that the local inhabitants were simply profiting from the mishap. Akinari seems to have found this incident most interesting, for he described it in detail in his account of the trip, while saying virtually nothing about the Byōdō-in itself.[7] Perhaps he had seen enough of temples, while novelty continued to impress him.

Another good friend was the poet and *kokugaku* scholar Ban Kōkei (1733–1806), a close associate of Roan and known along with him as one of the "Four Heavenly Kings" of the Capital's *waka* circles.[8] Nevertheless, it would appear that Akinari had met him independently of Roan before going to Kyoto, as Kōkei mentioned in his own writings sending correspondence to Akinari at Nagara. It was reported by a third party that when Akinari first went to live in the Capital he relied on Kōkei for assistance, but that shortly a rift developed between them and he turned to Roan.[9] But even if this were true, their estrangement could not have been serious. Akinari wrote a preface for an item by Kōkei in the winter of 1793,[10] and they were clearly on good terms a few years later. This does not mean that they saw eye to eye all of the time, however. Kōkei once sharply criticized a verse that Akinari had written, for example, and on another occasion, when Kōkei suggested that the two of them try composing poetry after the fashion of the then-defunct *shokunin uta awase*—poetry competitions in which the participants composed verses on the skills of the various artisans—Akinari sarcastically replied that in the present day, poetry having become so commercialized, the name should be changed to *shōnin uta awase*, or "merchants' poetry competitions." He recorded this incident in his memoirs, adding with obvious satisfaction that his retort silenced Kōkei most effectively.[11] But such episodes are not necessarily evidence of ill feeling between them. More likely they merely indicate that neither Akinari nor Kōkei was inclined to compromise his firm beliefs for the sake of harmonious relations. When they disagreed, they made their feelings known, but they were able to tolerate opposing viewpoints. Indeed, it is not inconceivable that Akinari might have become friendly even with Norinaga, had Norinaga not been so adamant and patronizing.

Akinari's students in Kyoto also gave him assistance at times. Not much is really known about them, but they did include a Ueda Saneyuki, who was apparently quite well-to-do, to judge from Akinari's record of visiting his villa in the northern hills of the Capital. Akinari described him as "not a writer of poetry"—perhaps he was not particularly talented, but their friendship was such that Saneyuki prepared the final copies of Akinari's manuscripts on at least two occasions.[12] Another student was Tani Naomi (also called Etsu Gyoshin), who, among other things, wrote a collection of notes on Akinari's lectures.[13]

Akinari and Koren lived an unsettled existence in the Capital. They left their hut at the Chion-in in the spring of 1794, less than a year after settling there, and at the invitation of unspecified persons, moved into quarters within the precincts of the Nanzenji Temple, not far away. The new dwelling was small, but larger than the one they had been occupying, and Akinari liked the increase in living space and the stream of clear water that flowed nearby. The house consisted of a single eight-mat room, about half of which was taken up by household furnishings. There was also a verandah outside, shaded by means of a reed screen hung from the eaves. The windows provided a pleasing view of the mountain scenery, and the cries of birds could be heard mingled with the sound of running water. Akinari called this hut Uzurai, after his former dwelling in Nagara.[14] It was a quiet and relaxing environment, but before long, for unstated reasons, they moved into the tenement building where Gekkei was living, at Tōdō-in Shijō, about a mile and a half west of the Chion-in. But their stay here was also brief. Soon they moved, again for unspecified reasons, to the vicinity of Marutamachi and Koromo no tana, about a mile to the north. This abode likewise proved temporary. "We did not stay there either," Akinari wrote, "but moved back to our former *fukuro* ["bag"] in Fukuro-machi, in front of the gate of the Chion-in."[15] Their nomadic life drew laughs from some of the people they knew, he noted, but he was now too old to be much concerned about public opinion. When an acquaintance asked him where he was planning to move next, Akinari replied with an impromptu verse:

Kaze no ue ni	Like the clouds that dance
Tachi mau kumo no	On the wind, with no destination,
Yukue naku	I shall decide on
Asu no ari ka wa	Tomorrow's dwelling place
Yoku zo sadamen	When tomorrow comes.

Akinari noted that the man reacted to this verse by making a gesture of scorn and calling him detestable, but he gave no indication of being upset himself.[16]

One little-known fact about Akinari is that he was a vegetarian and a teetotaller. He claimed to have disliked *sake* and preferred tea since his younger days, and on the wall of his home he hung a list of "forbidden things," which included wine, fish, tobacco, and oily foods—as well as literary men, tea masters, rich people, anything having a strong smell, and the selling of medicines.[17] Abstaining from intoxicants was consistent with Akinari's strict nature, but the fact that he had shunned them even while engaging in other forms of dissipation in his youth suggests that his aversion may have been physical as well as temperamental. And he appears to have been tolerant of those who did not share his aversion, including his wife, who, he noted, enjoyed a drink on occasion.[18]

Akinari's preference for tea over wine nurtured his interest in its preparation. He had probably become at least roughly acquainted with the tea ceremony when he was relatively young, for one of the few pieces of information he gave about his sister was that she had studied under a master of the art.[19] His subsequent deeper interest may have been aroused by such men as Tsuga Teishō and Kimura Kenkadō. He became conspicuously active in the way of tea while living at Nagara-mura and after moving to Kyoto—a period when he and Kenkadō were getting together quite often, to judge from the entries in Kenkadō's diary—but even his *Ashikabi no kotoba*, which he had written for Kenkadō in 1774, mentioned tea in its opening lines.[20] If Akinari was really a descendant of Kobori Enshū, and aware of the fact, then a desire to emulate his progenitor may also have contributed to his interest. Moreover, in Kyoto he enjoyed the companionship of Murase Kōtei and Yotsugi Makazu, both of whom were tea enthusiasts, and he frequently praised the pure water that flowed past his Nanzenji dwelling as ideal for making tea.[21]

It was in the *senchadō*, or the way of ordinary green tea, that Akinari achieved distinction. This was a ritual method, Chinese in origin, of preparing common green tea, simpler than the formal ceremony using the powdered *matcha*. The *senchadō* had been introduced from the continent early in the Tokugawa period and was still in its evolutionary stages by Akinari's time. Indeed, he and Murase Kōtei are today known as two of the men who brought its rules to their final form.[22] It was Akinari's own "Book of Tea," *Seifū sagen*, that earned him much of this credit. The work was published late in 1794, though it is uncertain just when it was written. In the preface which he wrote for it, Murase implied that Akinari composed *Seifū* during his leisure hours in Kyoto, and in a letter written when he was seventy-two (that is, in 1805), Akinari mentioned having produced such a work ten years earlier. From the text itself, however, Nagara-mura would appear to have been the place of writing.[23] Of course, this does not rule out the possibility that Akinari revised it in Kyoto prior to publication.

Seifū sagen covers such topics as the nature of tea, the varieties of the beverage, its history in China and Japan, areas of production, methods of cultivating tea plants, the manufacture of tea, and ways of preparing it for drinking. Details of the tea ceremony and general information for the gentleman of taste are also included. Akinari drew his information from a wide range of Chinese and Japanese works, but he did not plagiarize. He cited the sources for all of his conclusions, supplemented what he had gleaned from books with his personal experiences, and expressed his own views freely. *Seifū* displays both the wide extent of Akinari's knowledge and research and his appreciation of tea as a true art form. To him, the way of tea was a spiritual art. He had long considered himself a seeker after purity in an impure world, and in tea he found not just a drink, but a temporary relief from the pains of life; something that did not corrupt the heart, as did wine, but purified it. His attitude is reflected in the verse:

> *Nigorishi to* Though I cannot flee
> *Yo wa nogarenedo* From this world of corruption,
> *Tanimizu ni* I can prepare tea
> *Cha wo nite kokoro* With water from a mountain stream
> *Sumasu bakari zo*[24] And put my heart to rest.

In the soothing effect of the drink and in the tranquil beauty of its ritual preparation, he could find peace of mind. It was as an extension of this feeling that he began to delve into tea lore and ultimately create his own earthenware vessels for making tea. In this latter pursuit he achieved a high degree of skill and a far-reaching reputation. People came to learn pottery-making from him, and a teapot that he and Murase designed became so popular, it was reported, that there was no dealer in tea wares, from the three main urban centres to the farthest outlying regions, who did not sell it.[25] Some of the tea vessels that Akinari made with his own hands are still in existence, highly prized by collectors, and as his ceramics are, so is his book. *Seifū sagen* was only one among many similar works, but it established Akinari as a first-ranking authority on tea. It seems to have been widely read when it first appeared, and it still is highly acclaimed.[26]

Akinari continued as an active scholar in other fields as well. After coming to Kyoto, or perhaps even before, he began to write *Reigotsū*, a comprehensive work in six sections, one each on the names of Shinto deities, the names of Japan's provinces, noted products of the various regions, poetry, terminology, and systems of *kana* orthography. The *kana* section was completed by the winter of 1795 and published in early 1797.[27] Unfortunately, this was the only portion ever to be published, and the manuscripts of the other five sections have all been lost.

In the *kana* section of *Reigotsū*, Akinari took issue with most of the scholars of his day on the matter of *kana* orthography. It would appear that toward the end of the Heian period (794–1185), the Japanese language underwent appreciable phonetic changes that eliminated distinctions between the pronunciations of such *kana* symbols as お and ゑ, ゐ and ひ, ゑ and ゑ, resulting in confusion as to which symbol should be used in a given word. Writers generally followed the historical spelling, using the symbols that had always been used for each word, but some disunity was inevitable. A very real problem had developed by the thirteenth century, and proposals for standardization were being heard from such figures as Fujiwara Teika and Minamoto Chikayuki. In the latter half of the fourteenth century their ideas were finally codified by Chikayuki's grandson, Gyōa, in *Kana moji zukai*. This system, known as the Teika method, became the standard among *waka* poets and was followed by most other persons as well until the Edo period, by which time further phonetic changes had occurred in the language, and competing views on *kana* orthography began to emerge once again. The strongest advocate of reform was Keichū, who thoroughly revised the Teika system on the basis of the old historical conventions he had gleaned from ancient writings. Keichū's system won wide acceptance among *kokugaku* scholars and people in related lines of study, but there were dissenters, one of the most prominent being Tayasu Munetake (1715–71), a son of the eighth Tokugawa shogun, Yoshimune, and a student of Kamo Mabuchi. He contended that *kana* should be written according to the sound. If a phonetic change occurred in the language, the symbol used to express the particular sound in writing should also be changed, he said. In *Reigotsū*, Akinari built upon Munetake's opinions, maintaining that the rules for *kana* orthography were all man-made, not natural laws, and so one need not feel bound to adhere to any particular system.[28] He saw the preserving of more than one symbol to express the same sound as needless pedantry, which made what was simple appear complex, and he went to great lengths to show the irrationality of contemporary *kana* usage. In ancient times, he said, *kana* had been written according to the sounds that were vocally expressed, and so it was no more than common sense to do likewise in his own day. Thus he advocated no codified system, but simply the discarding of old outmoded conventions and writing words as they were pronounced at the present time. Such a view brought Akinari some censure from other scholars, notably from Murata Harumi (1746–1811),[29] but more recently he has been seen as one of the early advocates of a truly phonetic script, an idea which began to acquire true momentum in Japan only after the Meiji Restoration.[30]

His other writings from this period include *Man'yōshū kaisetsu*. His first general discourse on the *Man'yōshū*, it was completed in 1794,[31] though the bulk of it could have been written earlier. A short piece, it briefly treats such topics as the meaning of the *Man'yōshū* title, the identity of the compiler, the number and variety of the poems included, and so on. For the most part, Akinari was content to echo the conclusions of other scholars, expressing few opinions that were clearly his own, but despite the lack of originality, the work remains noteworthy as another forerunner of his more exhaustive *Man'yōshū* scholarship.

In collaboration with Hakura Nobuyoshi, he collected stray items of poetry by Kada Azumamaro and compiled them into an anthology, to which he gave the title *Shun'yōshū*. It was completed by the autumn of 1795, according to the postscript to the collection,[32] though not published until 1798. Also in the field of poetry, Akinari appointed himself to carry on the work begun by Mabuchi in his 1757 work, *Kanjikō*, a study of "pillow words" (*makura kotoba*, conventionalized epithets used in poetry as modifiers), in the *Man'yōshū*. Mabuchi had arranged selected words in phonetic order and explained the origin and meaning of each one in minute detail. In 1796, Akinari completed *Kanjikō zokuchō*,[33] which, like its predecessor, consisted of selected "pillow words," listed in phonetic order, defined, and commented upon. It was a solid work of philology that modern scholars still mention as an extension of the important work that Mabuchi had begun.[34]

Akinari's earliest known *waka* poems appeared in his *uikyo-zōshi*, and he continued to compose them for the rest of his life,[35] but it was only after he moved to Kyoto and was introduced to poetry circles there that he achieved any real standing as a *waka* poet. After Katō Umaki's death Akinari had carried on by himself, but without the backing of a teacher it was difficult to gain recognition or acceptance in poetry circles. In Kyoto, Ozawa Roan offered invaluable assistance in this regard. Not only did he go out of his way to assist Akinari materially, keeping a close watch over his welfare and sending him fuel every winter,[36] but he also took special pains to put him in contact with men of common interests. He often invited Akinari to his home, and through taking part in poetry sessions there, Akinari began to get acquainted with prominent *waka* poets in the Capital. Thus he formed connections with Tadagoto school, of which Roan was a leader, and with poets from the imperial court as well. The record shows that in 1799 he participated three times with the court poets in their New Year poetry sessions.[37] He did not become a member of any group, however, but remained an outsider. He himself was most inclined toward the Kogaku style of poetry, advocated by Kamo Mabuchi, which aimed at recapturing the purity and simplicity of ancient times, subordinating craftsmanship to the direct portrayal of human feelings and looking for its models to the *Man'yōshū*, or even beyond it to the poetry of the *Kojiki* and *Nihongi*. This style was generally opposed by the poets in Kyoto, who tended to look to the *Kokinshū* as their ideal, but Akinari remained flexible in the matter of poetry. He clung to his independence, but he was willing to explore poetic styles other than his personal favourite, and so he did manage to win the companionship, if not the unqualified acceptance, of poets in the Capital.

It was probably while he was still living at Nagara that he had acquired Ikenaga Hatara as a student. A member of an Osaka merchant family, Hatara had shown literary talent from his childhood, and he ultimately abandoned commercial pursuits entirely, much as Akinari had done before him.[38] He is known to have visited Akinari early in 1794, and the fact that he stayed for several days[39] implies a strong degree of intimacy. Although there were probably other visits as well, the next one of record took place late in 1795, nearly two years later, when Hatara brought the manuscript of his commentary of the *Man'yōshū* to show to Akinari. He asked his teacher to read and criticize it, but Akinari was not feeling well and declined, pleading the difficulty of doing the job with only one eye. Nor was he in the mood to listen while Hatara read his manuscript aloud. Hatara was moved to tears by this refusal, so eagerly had he been anticipating Akinari's help, and in the end left the manuscript with Akinari anyway, promising to come back for it in the spring. He was never to return, however. He became sick near the end of that spring and died in the sixth month, not yet thirty years old. Akinari was shocked and repentent. Hatara was his third promising disciple to die prematurely, and Akinari now described their relationship as having been like that of father and son. Not long afterwards, the publisher who had agreed to print Hatara's *Man'yōshū* commentary called on Akinari, in search of the manuscript. Akinari now at last took the trouble to read Hatara's work and found much that he could not approve. He refused to let the manuscript go to press in its current form, but wrote a revision, which he turned over to the publisher in the winter of that year.[40] The final version, which was not published until 1809, may actually be more Akinari's work that his disciple's.

Even more bitter for Akinari may have been the loss of Tsuneakira, for it came through desertion. Notwithstanding his high regard for Akinari, Tsuneakira appears to have been something of an opportunist, not one to be deterred by feelings of loyalty if he felt that his interests lay elsewhere. Shortly before Akinari moved to Kyoto, in 1793, Motoori Norinaga also had gone there to live. Tsuneakira had helped Norinaga to meet certain persons of influence and continued to associate with him thereafter. Under those circumstances, it would have been hard for Akinari to remain kindly disposed toward Tsuneakira, and relations between them appear to have cooled shortly after Akinari's arrival in the Capital. There is no specific proof of estrangement, but verifiable contacts between them ceased not long afterward. As late as 1793, or possibly even later, Akinari wrote that he regarded Tsuneakira as a brother,[41] but the last record of good relations between them was the preface that Tsuneakira wrote for *Shun'yōshū* in 1795. Thereafter, Akinari made no mention of him, not even when Tsuneakira died in 1806, nor is Akinari mentioned in any of Tsuneakira's writings. It is interesting to note than in 1800 Ozawa Roan formally rejected Tsuneakira as a disciple on grounds of "bad behaviour."[42] Perhaps he too had had occasion to feel slighted by Tsuneakira's opportunism.

In the autumn of 1797 Akinari and Koren made an excursion to Kusakamura in the province of Kawachi to visit the nun Yuishin, the widow of Hirase Sukemichi with whom Akinari had gone to Arashiyama in the spring of 1787. Her husband was now dead, and as her parents too were no longer living, she had taken the tonsure and retired to a hermitage in Kusaka where, Akinari said, she spent the time reading and practising calligraphy. Presumably she and her husband had been friendly with Akinari and Koren in Osaka, for

Akinari said that he had known her for twenty years or more by this time.[43] Perhaps he had even given her some assistance in her literary interests. In any case, both he and his wife must have considered her a valuable friend to make a special trip of considerable distance to call on her. As part of this trip they took the opportunity to pass by the Kashima Inari Shrine and renew their acquaintance with the Fuji family as well.[44]

This must have been the last time that Akinari and his wife ever made an excursion together, for Koren died quite suddenly that winter, on 31 January 1798 (Kansei Era, ninth year, twelfth month, fifteenth day).[45] Akinari was prostrated with grief. "Casting myself down, I writhed about, stamped my feet, and wept," he wrote, "but, as there was nothing to be done, I sent her to the moors and let her go up in smoke. Inside her coffin I wrote this complaint:

Tsurakarishi	To take your revenge
Kono toshi tsuki no	For the pain and misery
Mukui shite	Of these years and months,
Ika ni seyo to ka	Have you cast me aside,
Ware wo suteken"[46]	Telling me to do as I may?

Undemonstrative though he may have been with his affection, Akinari had loved Koren and needed her. She had stayed beside him through thirty-seven years of married life, few of which could have been pleasant for her. Now she was gone, leaving him in poor health, with failing eyesight and his financial resources exhausted. This was the low point of his life. There is a note of resentment in his expression of grief, as though he felt that she had died deliberately, as an act of betrayal.

Roan in particular offered considerable assistance and sent numerous verses of condolence, and most of Akinari's other friends also came to express their sympathy, but he refused to be comforted, and in time they left him to himself.[47] As he was sorting through Koren's belongings, to his surprise he came upon a pair of manuscripts that she had written, the existence of which he had until then been unaware. These were *Tsuyu wake goromo*, Koren's account of their journey to Kyoto in 1789 to entomb her mother's ashes, and *Natsuno no tsuyu*, in which she recounted the death of the child in Nagara and their subsequent move to the Capital. Akinari's first impulse was to throw them away, lest they call back painful memories, but after reading them over he thought them worthy of preservation for the literary talent they displayed. The manuscripts were in very rough form, with many words and phrases crossed out and corrected. It was obvious that Koren had planned to rewrite them, so during the early part of 1798 Akinari addressed himself to the task of preparing clean copies. After completing the work, he entrusted the manuscripts, together with the messages of condolence that his friends had sent, to the Jippō-in Temple.[48] This was probably on the forty-ninth day after Koren's death, when her ashes were interred.

Shortly thereafter, at the end of cherry blossom season, Akinari went by himself to Kawachi to visit Yuishin and apparently stayed for some time. He had remained despondent and had even contemplated taking his own life, but retracing the path that he and Koren had followed on their last journey together and sharing reminiscences with Yuishin about their late spouses brought him some comfort. But misfortune persisted. Eight years before, as though brought on by grief over the death of his mother, he had lost the use of his left eye. Now, in the same way, close on the heels of his wife's death, the trouble spread to his remaining eye, and within five months of her passing he was completely blind.[49]

8

The Final Years

Although one might expect Akinari to have become a helpless old man after losing both his wife and his eyesight, he was not really alone. A girl whom he and Koren had adopted as their daughter at some previous time stayed on in the house and gave him the assistance he needed. Aside from her existence, however, almost nothing is known about this woman. Her name is believed to have been Mineko, and it has been supposed that she was the girl who accompanied Akinari and Koren on their excursion to Saga in the autumn of 1789,[1] but even these points are mere assumptions. Akinari did not get along well with her—this fact is implied, if not explicitly stated, in nearly every reference to her that appears in his writings—which suggests that the adoption had been Koren's idea and that Akinari had simply acquiesced in the matter. The daughter is known to have taken religious vows, presumably after Koren's death, and to have suffered from poor health, which apparently rendered her unable to give Akinari and the domestic tasks her undivided attention. It was probably for this reason that a second woman, an elderly nun from Osaka named Matsuyama Teikō, joined their household. It has been suggested that she had been a maidservant in Akinari's home when he was practising medicine,[2] but this too is pure conjecture, and she remains, indeed, just as obscure a person as the adopted daughter. Nevertheless, between them, these two women took care of Akinari and provided him with a measure of companionship.

Yuishin remained a third woman in his life. Even though they continued to live far apart, she and Akinari maintained close ties and enjoyed one another's company. It was at her invitation that in 1798, towards the end of the fifth month, Akinari and his daughter set out for her home in Kawachi, intending both to visit with her and to consult an optical physician in Osaka. Ozawa Roan came to see them off, and they stopped at Ban Kōkei's place on the way and exchanged parting verses.[3] They must have passed through Osaka en route to Yuishin's home, for Kimura Kenkadō recorded a visit from Akinari and his daughter on the twenty-eighth day of the fifth month.[4] Most likely Akinari made his first visit to the eye physician then as well, for it is apparent from his account of the trip that he could see well enough to enjoy watching the moon at Kusaka-mura on the evening of the twelfth day of the sixth month. Just what sort of treatment he received is not known—indeed the precise nature of his malady is uncertain—but he did credit his physician with restoring a degree of vision to his left eye,[5] which had been sightless for the past eight years. Strangely, it was his right eye, which had failed only a month or so earlier, that proved beyond remedy. Still, even in his left eye, the cure must have been less than complete, for he continued to dictate much of his work to a scribe and stated repeatedly that his eyes were dim and of little use. Moreover, on the fourteenth day of the month, just two days after the above-mentioned moon viewing, when he found Yuishin suffering from severe abdominal pains, he was in no condition to look after her, but rather went with his daughter, who was also ailing, to a nearby temple to be taken care of himself. He stayed there for a full month, associating with people in the district and keeping busy conducting poetry competitions, even though Yuishin made a quick recovery and called on him at the temple nearly every day.

In spite of continuing depression over the loss of Koren and notwithstanding the condition of his eyes, Akinari did a fair amount of writing during his stay at Kusaka. He made frequent mention of Yuishin urging him to write and acting as his amanuensis;[6] perhaps she was making a deliberate effort to turn his mind away from his sorrows and rekindle his interest in life. Her concern for his well being is beyond doubt and raises the question of whether her association with him went further than friendship and assistance. Yuishin was forty-two years old at this time,[7] perhaps attractively young to a man of sixty-five, and with neither husband nor parents she was probably much in need of companionship herself, so romantic developments are by no means unimaginable. Apparently she accompanied Akinari to Osaka late in the ninth month of that year and stayed with him at the same inn for about a week, as is apparent from Kimura Kenkadō's diary entries. He had been away from home when Akinari had come to call on the twenty-fifth and twenty-eighth days of that month, so he went to Akinari's inn on the twenty-ninth, where he saw Akinari and also met Yuishin for the first time.[8] Although it was Kenkadō's custom to record the names of all members of a party, he made no mention of Akinari's daughter, which suggests that she was not present. But whatever fuel for speculation this may provide, if there was anything beyond friendship in his relationship with Yuishin, it was a matter on which Akinari maintained a discreet silence.

Although it is not certain just when Akinari returned to the Capital, the stay in Osaka was likely a stopover on the way back. Shortly thereafter, he moved with Teikō and his daughter to a detached dwelling at the home of Hakura Nobuyoshi in Marutamachi near the Kamo River, expecting to die there.[9] In fact he had almost eleven more years to live, but the feeling that his days were numbered, perhaps strengthened by the encouragement that Yuishin had offered, seems to have roused him to an unprecedented level of literary activity. Despite his failing health and vision, the last decade of his life was the most productive of all in terms of sheer volume of material, which included a number of short pieces of prose and poetry and some very lengthy works of scholarship and fiction as well.

He also gave lessons on the classics to a young Kyoto aristocrat by the name of Ōgimachi Sanjō Kiminori.[10] The Ōgimachi Sanjō family had been involved in the so-called "Hōreki Incident" of 1758, when the Tokugawa Bakufu had taken punitive action against members of the Imperial Court who had spoken directly to the emperor against the despotic rule of the shogunate. The head of the family had been dismissed from office, placed under house arrest, and subsequently ordered to take the tonsure. It was not until 1769 that his son, Kiminori's father, was allowed to hold a government position. Akinari's friendship with members of the family need not be taken as evidence that he himself opposed the Tokugawa hegemony, for the first record of his affiliation with them is the congratulatory verse that he sent on the occasion of Kiminori's ceremonial initiation into manhood in 1786.[11] Akinari appears to have seen Kiminori as a promising student who would carry on his teachings. He once told of sending three boxes of his books to Kiminori, together with the verse:

Ima wa tada	There now is nothing
Oinami yosuru	But a crumbling shore, washed
Kuzuregishi	By the waves of age,
Fumi todomeyo to	And yourself, asking me
Tanomu kimi kana	To leave these writings to you.

He received ten *ryō* in gold in return.[12] He was finding it necessary to sell his personal library in order to make ends meet, but in this case the material seems to have been a gift, and Kiminori's money more a donation than a payment. There is no doubt that they were very close. But one might almost be justified in concluding that there was a curse attached to becoming Akinari's favoured disciple, for, like Oka Kunio, Kuwana Masanori, and Ikenaga Hatara before him, Kiminori was to die in the autumn of 1800, at the age of twenty-eight.

Early in the summer of 1800 Akinari commenced writing a projected commentary on the entire *Man'yōshū*,[13] but he stopped well short of completion. He was writing it primarily for Kiminori and so had little inclination to continue after his student's death, but his immediate reason for suspending the task was further deterioration of his vision and general health. By autumn it had become necessary to go to Osaka for more treatment. Thinking it probable that he would never return, he took pains to put his personal affairs in order before leaving, requesting the Jippō-in Temple to hold appropriate rites at the proper times for his adoptive parents, his real mother, his wife, his mother-in-law, and for himself, if he should die on the journey. His depression at the time is obvious from the letter he wrote to the abbot. He had no knowledge of his true father, and little of his real mother, he said, and he had been unfilial to his foster parents, losing his entire inheritance in a fire and spending the rest of his life aimlessly, until now he was separated from his old home and family, blind, and living off the charity of others. In his life he had accomplished nothing of value but had merely earned the world's censure for his useless writings. He was ashamed of himself and wished to die, but he kept on living. Thus he set out for Osaka, with instructions hung around his neck that his ashes, or at least word of his death, be sent to the Jippō-in.[14]

It is not clear whether his daughter accompanied him. Matsuyama Teikō had died the previous winter, and with just two of them in the house, relations between Akinari and his daughter, never very harmonious, had become even more strained. Indeed, not long after Teikō died, Akinari had dreamed that she appeared to him with a message from Koren, whom she had met in the nether world, urging him to try to get along better with their daughter[15]—a clear indication that the problem was very much on his mind.

The real purpose of his journey to Osaka was probably as much to pay final visits to certain friends as to improve his vision. As he was truly expecting to die, he was anxious to be off without delay. Kiminori had been taken ill a week or two before, but Akinari left Kyoto anyway, about the middle of the eighth month, going first to Yuishin's hut in Kusaka-mura.[16] He was there when word reached him, on the sixth day of the ninth month, that Kiminori had died five days before. Having Yuishin write the message, he sent his condolences to the family, expressing his profound shock and grief, but his own weak condition ruled out a hasty return to the Capital. Instead, he had someone carry him to a temple in Osaka where he offered prayers for Kiminori.[17] Not long afterwards, he went to Kashima-mura and stayed until sometime the following year.[18]

It may have been while he was at Kashima-mura that he had his first meeting with Ōta Nampo, which took place at the Jōganji Temple in Osaka. Nampo had been impressed by "a strange piece of writing" by Akinari—presumably *Ugetsu monogatari*—that he had read, so he made a point of meeting the author when his duties as a shogunate official took him to Osaka. The encounter went well. Each man was favourably impressed with the other, and though opportunities for subsequent meetings were few, it was nevertheless the beginning of a real friendship.[19] Although Akinari later said bluntly that Nampo, despite his exalted reputation, was an inept writer of poetry, he had high praise for his *kambun*. Nampo had no such reservations about Akinari, however. When it came to writing, he said, Akinari possessed eight *to* of the nation's *koku* of talent (a *to* being the tenth part of a *koku*). The remark was made in jest, of course, but it indicates Nampo's regard for Akinari's ability.[20]

Akinari appears to have been away from Kyoto and slow to be informed when Ozawa Roan died in mid-1801, for there is no record of his attending the funeral and very little reference to Roan's death in his writings, although he did express his sense of loss poignantly in the verse:

> *Tamagoto no*　　　　　The jewelled koto's
> *O wa tachishikaba*　　Strings being broken,
> *Kimi ga io no*　　　　At your hermitage
> *Futaki no matsu yo*　There are only the two pines
> *Tada aki no koe*[21]　And the voices of autumn.

But very likely he was still at Kashima and unable to do much more. There must have been some such reason, for he had had a long and genuine friendship with Roan and owed him a debt of gratitude as well. Akinari had, of course, been writing *waka* for many years before coming to Kyoto, but his poems had not attracted much notice until after his arrival in the Capital, when Roan had begun giving him periodic guidance and instruction. Thereafter, his work was often included in collections of *waka* by Roan's recognized disciples, showing that he was accepted as one of them. Roan believed that true *waka* poetry embodied the innate spirit of Japan and therefore should not slavishly follow convention at the expense of spontaneity. According to his view, a poet should not consciously strive for any goal other than to express his thoughts simply and naturally in his own words. This was not unlike what Katō Umaki had preached, and Akinari had no trouble accepting it. Thus, unlike most of his contemporaries, Akinari took no poet or poetic collection as his handbook, but sought to learn from all while giving allegiance to none. Rules were to be a guide, he believed, but not unbreakable laws. He had grown up thinking *waka* composition to be a courtly pursuit, but over the years his attitude changed so much that he was able to argue with strong conviction that a person's worth as a poet had nothing to do with his social status. It was the heart that was of critical importance. A man of good character could produce good poetry even though he might be of low birth or mean occupation.[22] Thus, he concentrated on simplicity and freedom of expression, confident of his own ability. He studied the classics for what guidance they could offer, but refused to be tied down. His *waka*, as a result, are rich in variety, some being reminiscent of the *Man'yōshū* or the *Kokinshū*, or of other collections, while many others defy classification.

Since he subscribed to no set of conventions, it is not surprising that he left no coherent discourse on poetic theory. His thoughts on the subject appear as random remarks scattered through his writings, which the reader must piece together for himself. Even so, Akinari did state plainly that he considered the source of Japanese poetry to be the *Man'yōshū*, and he advised all would-be poets to study it.[23] He shared Kamo Mabuchi's view that perfection in poetry was not something to be discovered, but to be rediscovered and emulated. To do this, one should study the *Man'yōshū* and try to capture its essence in one's own poems. He considered *waka* a medium for expressing the thoughts and feelings of the heart, but he felt that excessive emphasis on poetic artistry had led people to forget the outstanding feature of the *Man'yōshū*, which was the expression of human emotions. But while he condemned the Kyoto poets for failing to comprehend the *Man'yōshū*'s spirit, he himself did not necessarily try to imitate its style. He saw the *Man'yōshū* much the same way as he saw the distant past. Neither was a thing to be restored in the present, but simply to be understood and learned from. He sought to write poetry that incorporated the spirit of the *Man'yōshū*, which is why his style appears relatively straightforward and unadorned compared to most of the other poets of the day. He was opposed to lavish verbal embellishments, for he believed that the ancient poetry had been written in the vernacular and merely expressed what the people felt in their hearts. To do more than this, he believed, was to cultivate artificiality. Thus, in order to be good, a verse had to be natural, not forced, and the poet himself must have a heart free from deceit. It was not necessary to memorize large numbers of old *waka* before trying one's own hand at writing them. If the poet's heart was right, he would automatically produce poetry without effort.

It was partly his belief that there were few upright hearts around that made him consider it useless to teach the techniques of poetry composition. In his view, literary ability was something one either had or did not have. For those born with talent, a teacher was not really necessary; for those without the gift, no amount of teaching could supply it. Roan once strongly urged him to take poetry students as a means of supplementing his meagre income, but Akinari refused, saying that to do so would make fools of those who were not talented by birth. A person might be capable in some pursuits, but he could never master those for which he was not gifted. He added, in his account of this incident, that Roan offered no rebuttal.[24] His opinion that poetic talent was inborn, not acquired, was precisely what Umaki had told him years before.[25] Thus, he believed, it was useless to rely on a teacher. One could scarcely acquire half of one's teacher's ability, and that teacher would have acquired only half of his own teacher's proficiency.[26] Together with his conviction that any effort to teach a person how to write poetry was bound to fail came his reluctance to follow the example of many of the local teachers who, he felt, were plying their trade strictly for profit. Such was a prostitution of one's own talent, he believed. Deeply pained by the commercialism in nearly all of the arts, as well as in scholarship, he was loath to follow the crowd, even if poverty were the alternative. In this respect he was much the same as an artist as he had been as a physician.

Akinari must have been considered a good poet in his day. Roan would hardly have urged him to teach if he had thought otherwise, and the fact that forgeries of Akinari's calligraphy were being sold while he was still alive[27] may be seen as a further indication. Nor would the recognized masters in the Capital have deigned to permit an unknown amateur to participate with them formally. In *Kōjinshū ruidai*, a collection of more than 2700 *waka* by poets of the Tokugawa period, published in 1812, Akinari ranks fifth in terms of the number of verses included among the thirty-seven poets represented. He is surpassed by men like Kamo Mabuchi and Kada Azumamaro, but trailed by Keichū, Motoori Norinaga, Ban Kōkei, Katō Umaki, Ozawa Roan, and others, and some outstanding poets are not even represented. If nothing more, this provides some idea of Akinari's popularity with the compiler.[28] But after Roan died, Akinari seems to have dropped out of *waka* circles and continued on his own, following his old preference for private study. It was hard to achieve lasting recognition as a poet unless one became a renowned teacher, but Akinari shunned this role, and none of the few men who could be called his students became sufficiently well-known to advertise his name. Nor did he belong to any particular school or make any real contribution to *waka* theory. Moreover, his poetry, like his fiction and his scholarship, has been overshadowed by *Ugetsu monogatari*. It is for reasons such as these that he had not been remembered as a *waka* poet.[29]

He had been expecting to die ever since he moved to Nagara-mura in 1787, but in 1801 he was still alive. He was now sixty-eight years old and saw his attainment of that age as a fulfilment of the prophecy given to his father many years before by the deity of the Kashima Inari Shrine. To express his gratitude he composed a series of sixty-eight *waka* and presented them to the priests.[30] But having now exhausted his allotted life span, he no doubt felt that he was living on borrowed time.

Kimura Kenkadō's death early in 1802 continued the trend of Akinari's friends leaving him behind. Still, though their ranks were thinning, his old friends remained loyal, and he had made some new ones as well. These included Morikawa Chikusō, a calligrapher from Osaka; and Shōdō (d. 1811), a priest from the province of Bingo, who had been a student of Ozawa Roan and of Murase Kōtei, and apparently of Akinari as well to some degree. It was at their instigation that a collection of Akinari's poetry and short prose works was readied for publication. Akinari had never attempted to edit his own numerous verses into a single collection, thinking that such a task was best left for a poet's admirers to carry out after he was dead, much as he had done for Mabuchi and Umaki. It was not his ideal to publish his poetry in order to gain recognition. In 1802, as part of his preparations for death, Akinari had prepared his own grave under a plum tree at the Saifukuji, a subsidiary temple of the Nanzenji, and ordered a coffin to be made for him.[31] At the same time, he had entrusted to the head priest a basket containing a number of unpublished manuscripts. Knowing of these writings' existence, Shōdō, by his own account, took the initiative in obtaining them from the abbot and commenced editing them. When Akinari became aware of what was going on, Shōdō said, he was most displeased and only reluctantly allowed the work to proceed.[32] Nevertheless, he must have co-operated to some degree, for a few items that were not among those in the basket were included when the work was published. Because of the source of most of its material, the collection was given the title of *Tsuzurabumi*, or "A Basket of Writings."

In the summer of 1802 Takizawa Bakin visited the Capital and apparently tried, but without success, to meet Akinari. Later he expressed high praise for Akinari's talent but described him as a man who hated the world and did not associate with others.[33] Similar opinions were expressed by other persons, but these are clearly exaggerations. Akinari went to Osaka with his daughter in mid-1803, and stayed in quarters near the Ōe Bridge, not far from his old home in Dōjima, and while he was there, his Osaka friends held a party to congratulate him on reaching the age of seventy.[34] Ōta Nampo sent his good wishes from Edo for the occasion. About two weeks later, Akinari participated in a memorial service for Roan.[35] He went to Osaka again, slightly more than a year later and became sick during the visit,[36] but he was well enough to enjoy a visit from Nampo, who was on his way to a new assignment in Nagasaki. Nampo had called on him in Kyoto in the spring of 1802, but this was their first meeting in more than two years. At this encounter Nampo was asked to supply a postscript for *Tsuzurabumi*, which was then being readied for the press. Shōdō may have been present and made the request himself, though Akinari's words are too ambiguous to be certain. Shōdō had already asked Murase Kōtei to write this postscript, but Kōtei kept postponing the task, so Shōdō finally transferred his request to Nampo. Nampo agreed and sent the promised postscript from Nagasaki after he had arrived there.[37] Murase's failure to write the postscript may indicate that relations between him and Akinari were strained at the time. When they met in 1807 it was said to be for the first time in eleven years,[38] which, if true, would mean that in spite of the proximity of Murase's dwelling, Akinari had had no association with him during his second period of residence at the Chion-in, and indeed there is no record of any contact between them during the eleven-year period.

Shōdō's preface to *Tsuzurabumi* was dated Bunka Era, first year (1804), third month; Nampo's postscript in mid-winter of the same year.[39] The first three volumes were published in 1805; a new edition consisting of all six volumes, but with a few changes in the first three, came out in the autumn of 1806. For undetermined reasons, another edition, again with certain revisions, was issued the following spring.[40] *Tsuzurabumi* had been conceived as a collection of Akinari's poems, to be supplemented with a few prose writings, but it emerged in its final form as an anthology of his poetry, miscellaneous jottings, travel diaries, and fiction. The first two volumes were devoted entirely to poetry, containing a total of 656 *waka* and the longer *chōka*, many of them composed for specific occasions and with accompanying explanatory prose passages. The third volume is taken up by Akinari's poetic account of his trip to Kinosaki in 1779, *Akiyama no ki*, while the last three together include twenty miscellaneous items, four travel accounts, three short stories, and a congratulatory piece. Additional poems appear in most of these. To complete the assortment, the two accounts by Koren were appended. Thanks to this collection's publication, many of Akinari's shorter works that might otherwise have disappeared have been preserved. At the time, however, it sold poorly, and the publisher suffered a severe loss.[41]

While *Tsuzurabumi* was being edited, Akinari had been writing *Kinsa*, an interpretative collection of outstanding verses from the *Man'yōshū*, which, with its brief supplement, *Kinsa jōgen*, is by far his longest work. *Kinsa* itself bears no date, but Akinari claimed to have written it in the same year as *Jōgen*, which he completed in the first month of 1804.[42] He implied that he wrote it during a short period of concentrated effort, but even if he were in the best of health, he could hardly have completed the whole project in less than a month. A more plausible view is that he began the work during the autumn of 1803, since he mentions looking at the autumn scenery while writing near the beginning of *Kinsa*.[43] Presumably, he finished *Kinsa* shortly after the beginning of the New Year and then proceeded with *Kinsa jōgen*. Even so, it shows a remarkable surge of energy on Akinari's part. He arranged *Kinsa* under a variety of topical headings and selected for each one appropriate verses from throughout the *Man'yōshū*, transcribing them into contemporary script, including the name of the poet, and adding his own critical comments. *Kinsa jōgen* complemented this selective work with a general consideration of the

Man'yōshū as a whole. Together, the two works prove beyond any doubt that Akinari was thoroughly acquainted with the whole *Man'yōshū* collection, and mark the culmination of his classical scholarship.

It was probably about this time that he finished writing *Machibumi*. "Stopped writing" might be more accurate, for he had been adding bits and pieces to the manuscript over the years since starting it at Nagara-mura in 1787. A miscellany, in some respects a literary diary, it is a catalogue, in poetry and prose, of events that transpired while he was living in Nagara and Kyoto. The contents are of an intensely personal nature, and for this reason it was never published. Akinari's expressions of discouragement and self-pity on its pages often show him in an unflattering light. Shōdō said in his preface to *Tsuzurabumi* that the editors had considered including *Machibumi*, but that Akinari had been ashamed of it and had adamantly witheld his permission.

During the autumn of 1805, Akinari moved out of Hakura Nobuyoshi's establishment and took up temporary residence at the Saifukuji, which three years earlier he had decided upon as his burial place. He stayed there for about two hundred days, until the spring of the following year,[44] when more permanent quarters at the Nanzenji were ready for him. He had gone to Nobuyoshi's mansion expecting to die shortly, but, "Since I was not able to die," he wrote, "I again built a hut on the site of my Nanzenji hermitage of former times, and moved there in the spring of my seventy-third year."[45]

It would appear that his daughter was no longer with him at the time of this move. She is on record as serving as his scribe toward the end of 1803, and as accompanying him and Nobuyoshi on a visit to the Shūgakuin Detached Palace about a year later,[46] but when Akinari next mentioned her, it was to say that she had run away. This apparently had happened by the fourth month of 1805.[47] Akinari is known to have been visiting Osaka at that time,[48] and it may well be that she took advantage of his absence to abscond. About this same time Akinari wrote a short story about an old man who lived with his daughter. In this tale the girl loses a shell of priceless value while her father is away. The old man is so grieved at the loss that he takes to his bed, but, after being comforted by his friends, he comes to accept the misfortune and forgives his daughter. This has been seen as an allegorical representation of the events underlying Akinari's own daughter's disappearance, the story being interpreted to mean that the girl was seduced while Akinari was away from home and ran off with her lover. Akinari was at first very upset, but at length he gave in to his friends' remonstrations and extended his forgiveness.[49] This is no more than speculation, but it does give a plausible explanation for the daughter's flight. Still, even though Akinari may have pardoned her misconduct, she was never again mentioned in his writings. One may search his works in vain for a complimentary reference to her, yet she had stayed with him for at least seven years after his wife's death and so must have had strong feelings of obligation, if not of love, toward him. When Akinari went in the winter of 1801 to visit the Kitano Kamo Shrine, as recounted in Chapter 4, he lost his way and arrived home late, convinced that a fox had bewitched him. In his accounts of the experience he noted that when he finally reached his home it was to find his daughter standing by the roadside in the heavy rain, watching for him.[50] This does indicate that she was concerned for his welfare, as does the fact that she often accompanied him on his travels in spite of her own poor health. But this regard had its limits, and now she was gone, leaving him to his own devices.

Akinari appears to have become relatively at ease after moving back to the Nanzenji. Dissatisfied with the world, but recognizing the impossibility of creating a better one, he had decided to accept stoically whatever fate would bring, patiently waiting for death to overtake him. Indeed, he wanted to die. His body was worn out, and all of his family members were dead, as were most of his old friends. Hosoai Hansei had died in 1803, and Ban Kōkei's death in 1806 depleted their number even further. For all practical purposes, his life was over; it was a divine punishment, he believed, that he should continue to live, and he concluded that he must be paying for some misdeed committed either in the present, or in a previous, incarnation.[51] "I can do nothing more," he wrote, "so I drink green tea and look forward to death."[52] He had achieved a degree of inner peace.

Even so, he had not mellowed completely. The Ōsawa and Isogai families, who continued to assist him, remembered him as having a gentle disposition, but there were occasional flashes of his old temper. A member of the Ōsawa family who was born nearly fifty years after Akinari died recalled being disciplined as a child with the warning that Yosai-san would come and scold him if he misbehaved. Nor had Akinari lost his sense of humour. Each night an elderly woman from the Isogai house would prepare a bath for him, and he would usually invite her to make use of the water herself after he had finished. The old woman would often accept his invitation, but the edge of the tub was unusually high, and Akinari had many a laugh watching her efforts to climb in. Again, one hot summer day, when Akinari was dozing inside his hut, his nap was disturbed by a stranger who introduced himself as the poet Shikatsube Magao (1753–1829). A student of Ōta Nampo, he had probably come at Nampo's suggestion. When Akinari asked the purpose of his visit, the caller replied, in extremely pompous language, that he had taken the opportunity to come by while making a journey to various places celebrated in poetry. Piqued by his haughty demeanour, Akinari responded with an impromptu verse, mercilessly mocking his visitor's name with puns that defy translation.

> *Shikatsube na*   Oh, you who journey, clad
> *Asa gamishimo no*   In formal linen attire,
> *Uta makura*   Through places known in song,
> *Sonna magao wa*   Put off that solemn countenance,
> *Maa yoshinasai*   Shikatsube Magao.

The traveller did no such thing, however, but promptly ran away.[53] Obviously Akinari's mind remained keenly alert. Nor was the condition of his body so bad that he was unable to make a journey in the autumn of 1806 over the mountains to Ōtsu, where he stayed at the villa of an acquaintance and enjoyed watching the moon on Lake Biwa at night.[54] Also, he apparently assisted the priests at the Saifukuji with their record keeping and perhaps with other miscellaneous tasks on occasion. The temple's principal function was to conduct funerals, and there are some entries in its death register that appear to be in Akinari's handwriting.[55]

He maintained good relations with the small circle of loyal friends that remained. Around 1804 he and Gekkei collaborated in producing a series of fourteen sketches by Gekkei and twenty-five haiku by Akinari on a variety of annually observed events.[56] To celebrate his seventy-second birthday, his Kyoto friends joined with him in composing *waka* on seventy-two topics that he had selected, and when he went to Osaka not long afterward, he showed the results to his friends there, and they promptly tried their own hands at a similar effort, though this time in *kambun*.[57] Towards the end of 1805 Ōta Nampo called on him at the Saifukuji, and reported a cordial reception.[58] Nampo was one of the leading writers of comic *waka* in Edo, and may have been the inspiration behind a collection of such verse that Akinari wrote the same winter.[59]

But in spite of these friends and the companionship they provided, he felt lonely and out of place. He once said that he had found two friends in the Capital, but none whom he really considered a kindred spirit, and on another occasion he stated that he had no intimate friends in any of the three main urban centres and only three acquaintances—Ōta Nampo in Edo, Ozawa Roan and Murase Kōtei in Kyoto, and none in Osaka.[60] One may think it strange that he would accord such an honour to these three, for he had looked up to Roan as a senior, his acquaintance with Nampo was relatively new and their meetings were infrequent, and he had gone for eleven years without seeing Kōtei. But he explained that those whom he called "acquaintances" (the word he used was *chiki*) were not people who trifled with literature, but who were able to understand and exchange ideas about it. Such was his estimation of Roan, Kōtei, and Nampo, but he specifically denied that they were friends. Apparently he felt that for him there was no person who really filled the role. Still, despite crushing poverty, he remembered those who were or had been close to him. Early in 1808, in preparation for memorial services for his wife and father, he wrote a short story, and begged Yotsugi Makazu to buy it for a sum sufficient to provide flowers and incense.[61] A year and a half earlier he had offered commemorative verses before Umaki's grave on the thirtieth anniversary of his death.[62] On a happier note, when Nampo celebrated his sixtieth birthday in Edo in 1808, Akinari sent him 106 verses with the wish that he might live to be 106 years old.[63]

In 1806, as part of his attempt to put his affairs in order prior to death, he commenced writing *Chaka suigen* (Drunken Words of a Tea Addict). The title would suggest that it was planned as a further commentary on tea, and Akinari and Murase Kōtei spoke of it as such at their 1807 meeting, but Akinari apparently changed his mind while writing. He included a number of personal opinions and experiences, and the result, which was probably completed toward the end of 1807, was a miscellany.[64] The personal references would appear to be part of his attempt to show himself as he wanted to be remembered. It was this same desire that led him, in the autumn of 1807, to throw five bundles of his manuscripts down a well. He felt very much relieved after doing so, he said,[65] and he penned the lines,

Nagaki yume	Long-felt delusions
Mi-hatenu hodo ni	Shall never more disturb me,
Waga tama no	For my soul has gone
Furu i ni ochite	Cast into an ancient well—
Kokoro samushi mo[66]	And how cold my heart now grows.

In *Chaka suigen* he noted that these manuscripts had included *Kinsa*,[67] but if this was true, someone must have been waiting nearby to fish the papers out of the well as soon as Akinari's back was turned, for the work survives. It has been observed that the extant manuscripts of *Kinsa* and *Nubatama no maki* do look as though they had once been in the water.[68]

Sometime in 1807 he prepared *Aki no kumo* (Autumn Clouds), a collection of his own poems, together with his comments about them. Earlier, he said in the preamble, he had compiled 360 of his verses, but since they had not been appreciated by those to whom he had shown them, he had decided instead to prepare this collection, with his own comments, explanations, and self-criticism. The larger collection has been lost, but *Aki no kumo* appears to be a selection of poems that were included in it, and with which Akinari was especially pleased.[69] As such, it may be seen as a guide to what he considered good poetry to be; this too may have been a deliberate step toward getting his affairs in order.

Another such step was the publication in 1808 of *Fumihōgu* (Discarded Letters), a collection of his letters and miscellaneous fragmentary writings.[70] It was said to have been published because Ōsawa Shunsaku had secretly made copies of the materials and entrusted them to Matsumoto Ryūsei, a former disciple of Roan's, for editing. This is doubtful, however, for the explanatory notes contain information that could hardly have been obtained without Akinari's co-operation, and, moreover, a manuscript copy of *Fumihōgu* in Akinari's handwriting is extant today. The contents range from letters that Akinari sent to Katō Umaki to some items written as late as 1807. Together they constitute a valuable source of biographical information.

Even more valuable for what it tells us about him is *Tandai shōshin roku* (A Record of Courage and Cowardice). This collection of stray notes was probably a miscellany in the true sense of the word, added to from time to time over the years, though it is evident from the text that it was put into its final form in 1808. Written in a mixture of colloquial and literary language, it provides a good cross section of his opinions on such matters as history, scholarship, poetry, and contemporary society, along with considerable information about himself and his associates—including biting criticism of some who were supposed to be his friends. Another collection of notes about his life, untitled, but now known as *Jiden* (Autobiography), was also written in 1808, perhaps originally intended to be a part of *Tandai*.[71] He wrote a further collection of jottings, different versions of certain sections of *Tandai*, early in 1809.[72]

His activity in the *haikai* world continued right up to the year of his death, with his compilation in 1809 of a collection of 104 verses that he had personally selected from among his numerous compositions.[73] Since *haikai* had been the first kind of literary activity that he mentioned participating in, it might be said that this was the literary form that he practised more consistently than any other. Yet it amounted to only an insigificant fraction of his total output. Despite his long involvement in the pursuit, few of his verses survive, and of these even fewer belong to his independent works. He never achieved fame as a *haikai* poet, but he did not aspire to such fame; indeed he shunned it, for he did not consider *haikai* an art form whose practitioners were worthy of adulation. To him, *haikai* poetry was never anything more than a pleasant way of passing the time. It had originated as a recreational pursuit, he believed, and such it ought to remain; its true character would be lost if one tried to elevate it to the level of serious art. And on the exaltation of what he considered frivolty, he was far from neutral, having harsh words for Bashō, and even more for men who aped his lifestyle, travelling about the country calling themselves "masters" and trying out of greed to peddle their art, under the pretence of making a *haikai* pilgrimage.[74]

During the last years of his life—perhaps as much as the last decade— Akinari was working sporadically on his second major work of fiction, *Harusame monogatari* (Tales of the Spring Rain). He probably never finished it to his own satisfaction. It was read as a manuscript by a small number of admirers, but it was not published until 1907, and then only in fragmentary form. Not until after World War II did the complete text become available in print.[75] Akinari may never have intended the work for publication, for its contents are not aimed at the general reader. A work of deep meaning, it is pervaded by a philosophical element and covers a wide range of subjects, including historical events, literature and literary conventions, religion, ethics, and social problems, with Akinari's personal views on them. Its lack of form is an outstanding feature. The ten tales have no uniformity of length, the longest one being about twenty times the length of the shortest. Some of the stories are scarcely worthy of the name, being little more than collections of random thoughts or disjointed narrations of events, while even those which do qualify as tales suffer from imperfect organization and roughness of narrative. The uneven quality may be no more than evidence that Akinari was still revising *Harusame* when he died, but in any case the reader will appreciate the collection more if he examines its component parts, rather than the work as a whole.

The two stories that begin the collection may be considered together, since the second is a continuation of the first. "Chi katabira" (The Bloodstained Robe), is set during the reign of the emperor Heizei (774–824; r. 806–9), who is the central character and whose gentle and upright nature is the focal point of the story. Heizei is the embodiment of *naoki kokoro*, that legendary quality of the ancients that encompassed the virtues of purity and sincerity and total lack of deceit, leading them to do as a matter of course that which was right and proper. The tranquility of the realm is idyllically portrayed, but it soon becomes apparent that this is a façade. Heizei is a vanishing species, for the native Japanese virtues are being assailed by corrupting influences from China. In contrast to the simple and guileless Heizei stands his brother, the Crown Prince Kamino. Well-versed in Buddhist and Confucian teachings and in continental manners and culture, he is talented and sagacious and, above all, ambitious. Although supernatural manifestations portend disaster, Heizei proceeds with his plans to abdicate and so retires to the former capital of Nara, where scheming courtiers, led by Fujiwara no Nakanari and his sister Kusuriko, conspire to persuade him to rescind his abdication, rally support to his side, and declare Nara to be the imperial capital once again. Prince Kamino, now reigning as the emperor Saga (r. 809–23), hears of the plot and has Nakanari put to death. Kusuriko is placed in confinement, but she stabs herself to death, unrepentant. The depth of her corruption and resentment are made clear when the blood that has stained her clothing refuses to dry. Arrows cannot cause her robe to move, and swords shatter against it. Recognizing his own negligence in having been unaware of the conspiracy, Heizei takes monastic vows.

"Amatsu otome" (The Celestial Maidens), continues the action of "Chi katabira." The efforts of Saga and his successors, the emperors Junna (r. 823–33) and Nimmyō (r. 833–50), to reproduce in Japan the splendour of China, are portrayed together with the further rise of the continental influences, the increasing luxury and frivolty of the court, further plots against the throne, Buddhist influence on domestic politics, and the concomitant decline of the Japanese spirit. But the material is not clearly represented. The sentence structure lacks polish, and the events are isolated from one another, not following smoothly in logical sequence. In sum, the tale emerges as little more than a collection of brief episodes and does not succeed as a story.

The didactic element overshadows the story in "Chi katabira," and overwhelms it in "Amatsu otome." In these two tales Akinari used literature as a podium from which to propound his view of history as a process of decay, rather than of progress. Like many other scholars of his time, he saw the early Heian period as an era of upheaval in Japanese thought which had led to corruption of the native spirit. Confucian and Buddhist teachings, with their promise of limitless rewards had, he believed, stimulated human desires, causing men to forget the simple virtues of the past and provoking power struggles even among members of the imperial family, who ought to have been above such things. Thus in "Chi katabira" it is continental learning that has corrupted Prince Kamino and made him eager for authority. Heizei is portrayed as a man who is good, but not in step with the times. His nature is better suited to the past, when ruler and subject alike possessed upright hearts and the Japanese emperor could rule like the Taoist sage-king, through non-action. In his own day, Heizei's extreme simplicity appears not so much a virtue as an unfortunate naivete, but Akinari's tone is not condemnatory. Rather he is lamenting for a bygone era. Retaining his own virtue while others are losing theirs, Heizei transcends the corruption around him with a kind of greatness. But though he transcends, he lacks the power to overcome, and therein lies the tragedy.

Akinari saw the decay that had begun in the Heian period as extending to his own time. His later writings, especially *Tandai shōshin roku*, are filled with passages lamenting that things are no longer as they were in his youth. Everything had changed, and for the worse. Scholars had become lax, no longer rigorous in their pursuit of truth. Artists were no longer striving for excellence, but thinking only of money. In former times, courtesans had been good-hearted, wearing simple costumes with few adornments, and they had been besieged by wealthy patrons; now they had become scheming women with petty thieves for customers. Even the sumō champions of his old age were inferior to those of his youth, he felt, succeeding only through lack of competition. "In Shikoku," he once said, "it is badgers that take possession of people; in Kyushu, water imps. In Kyoto and Osaka it is courtesans, teachers, and tea masters who possess you and cause you grief. You cannot be at ease anywhere in this world."[76]

The third tale, "Kaizoku" (The Pirate), takes as its setting the poet Ki no Tsurayuki's voyage back to the Capital in 935 after completing his term as governor of the province of Tosa. In his *Tosa Diary*, Tsurayuki spoke repeatedly of the danger of pirates, though none were actually encountered, but in Akinari's version a pirate does overtake the ship and comes aboard. His objective, however, is not to plunder, but to criticize Tsurayuki and expound his own views on poetry, scholarship and society. At this point, what has been an interesting narrative gives way to an undisguised polemic that touches on such topics as the correct interpretation of the *Man'yōshū* title, whether the varieties of poetry can be classified or whether they are as numberless as the human emotions they express, the doubtful propriety of including poetry about illicit love in the imperial anthologies, and other matters. No doubt most readers will find "Kaizoku" the least satisfying of *Harusame monogatari*'s ten items. It begins quite well as a tale, but it fails to fulfil its promise. The story stops in midstream to end in a welter of disconnected scholarly arguments, most of them hair-splitting and pedantic and not clearly presented. The story and the polemic stand apart from each other; there is no fusion of the two, and neither is really successful.

After these first three attempts, however, Akinari managed to settle into the role of storyteller and yet retain that of moral apologist. The next two tales, while quietly didactic, remain stories from beginning to end. "Nise no en" (The Destiny that Spanned Two Lifetimes), is a satirical tale with a religious theme. A young farmer, sitting up late one night reading, becomes aware of the sound of a bell. Mystified, he searches for its source, finally determining that it comes from beneath a stone in a corner of his garden. Next morning, when his servants excavate the site, they unearth a coffin in which lies a man, old and shrivelled, his hair grown down past his knees, but alive. They realize that he is a priest in a state of *zenjō*, a trancelike condition of suspended animation said to be achieved by certain devout followers of religious disciplines. At length they succeed in reviving him, but the words of inspiration they expect to hear are not forthcoming. The priest cannot even remember his own name, let alone his former life or the paradise he sought. As his condition improves, he exhibits an ordinary man's desire for food, including forbidden things such as fish. When he has fully recovered, he makes his living at the lowest sort of menial labour. He takes a wife and proves to have a normal sexual appetite. He displays anger. His wife nags and henpecks him. Such is the man who had aspired to spiritual greatness. He seems, if anything, even lower than the average man, as though his religious austerities have had a negative effect. With this example of the fruits of piety before their eyes, the villagers lose their faith and turn away from religious activity, disregarding their priests' efforts to explain the situation.

Observers laughingly suggest that the priest has remained in the world in order to fulfil the saying, *Fūfu wa nise*, which refers to the teaching that a married couple's relationship extends from this life into the next. The implication is tht the man's new wife is a reincarnation of his former mate, and this is the reason for the title, "Nise no en." Phonetically, however, the same words may be interpreted to mean "fake destiny," and the pun was probably intentional, since the Buddhist teachings on the relationship of cause and effect are made to appear false. Still, Akinari had not simply become anti-Buddhist, for it becomes clear in subsequent tales that this was not the case. It was not religion as such, but the hypocritical practice of religion for ostentatious display or personal gain that he was opposed to. He recognized that there were many among both clergy and laity who were motivated by selfish concerns, and he abhorred that kind of false piety, but true religious devotion, which led to personal peace of mind and rectitude of heart, remained his ideal.

"Me hitotsu no kami" (The One-Eyed God), may remind readers of *Ugetsu monogatari,* for it has the strongest supernatural element of all the *Harusame* tales, but it is a light-hearted and amusing supernatural, the world of "Muō no rigyo" or of "Himpukuron." Aspiring to become an accomplished *waka* poet, a youth from Sagami, in the uncultured eastern part of the country, sets out for Kyoto to take instruction from the masters there. On the last night of his journey, he lies down to sleep in front of a small shrine in the midst of a forest. He is awakened by the arrival of a Shinto priest, an itinerant Buddhist mendicant, and two women who are actually foxes in disguise. A weird-looking deity with only one eye emerges from the shrine to join them. Terrified, the lad pretends to be still asleep. A cask of wine is carried in by a monkey and a hare, and the group begins to drink. At length they call on the youth to join them. The situation is reminiscent of that on Mt. Kōya in "Buppōsō," though these supernatural beings are a good-humoured, harmless lot, and the sinister and terrifying atmosphere of that tale is totally missing. As the boy consumes wine with the group, the one-eyed god counsels him against going to study under the so-called masters of poetry in the Capital. Such men are all imposters with no real ability, he says, and in any case, it is better to develop one's talents by oneself. He concedes that a teacher may be necessary to get started, but he maintains that true poetry comes only from the heart and cannot be learned. The story concludes with the youth agreeing to accept this advice and being whisked back to his home in Sagami by supernatural power. In this tale, the polemic element does not intrude into the story. It fits in smoothly and is kept short enough to prevent it from overshadowing the action. The mood is light and entertaining throughout. Akinari was particularly successful in this attempt to tell a story and at the same time restate his oft-repeated views on poetic talent. It should not be overlooked that he himself was a one-eyed person when he wrote the tale.

In four of the last five stories, overt didacticism virtually disappears, and the emphasis shifts from scholarship to human interest, with stress on what Akinari considered virtues to be cultivated and vices to be avoided. "Shikubi no egao" (The Smiling Death's-Head), a tragic tale of romantic love, is based upon the same incident that Takebe Ayatari had used as his source for *Nishiyama monogatari*. There are varying reports of the actual event, but the basic facts are that in 1767, in a village on the northern outskirts of Kyoto, a youth named Watanabe Unai, the son of the village headman, fell in love with Watanabe Yae, who lived in the neighbouring house with her mother and two brothers. The families, though related by blood, were on bad terms, and the affair was carried on secretly until it became a matter for village gossip. The girl's mother had her elder son, Genta, try to arrange a marriage, but Unai's father refused the overtures and sent his son away to the home of a relative. At last, in a final attempt to allow the young people to marry, the mother sent her daughter to her lover's home once again, escorted by Genta. When the father ordered them away, Genta abruptly drew his sword and decapitated his sister on the spot.[77] In 1806 Akinari, who had long been interested in the incident, had chanced to meet the now elderly Watanabe Genta in person and had heard his version of the affair. Following this encounter, he had written *Masurao monogatari* (A Tale of a Man of Valour), in which he related the facts as Genta had presented them, and condemned Ayatari (for whom, it will be remembered, he had little regard) for the way he had distorted the truth in *Nishiyama*.[78]

Nevertheless, having set the record straight, as he supposed, with *Masurao monogatari*, Akinari went on to adapt the events to suit his own purpose in "Shikubi no egao." Gosōji, as the father is called in this tale, is a very prosperous *sake* brewer, but the epitome of miserliness, while his son, Gozō, is quite a different person, accomplished in the arts, refined in his behaviour, and considerate of others. Nearby lives Mune, the daughter of a once-wealthy family now forced to rely upon the meagre wages of the son, Motosuke, to maintain a state of genteel poverty. Gozō and Mune pledge themselves to each other, but Gosōji violently opposes a marriage with a girl from such a family and forbids his son to visit her home. His wife is more sympathetic but begs Gozō to obey, even so. Mune becomes genuinely ill with grief and longing, and her mother summons Gozō in desperation. Gozō affirms his vow to Mune, whose condition thereupon shows a marked improvement, but then he must return home to face his father's wrath and his mother's pleas. He begs their forgiveness and thereafter spends each day diligently working in the brewery, obeying his father's every command and neglecting his pledge to Mune, who once again starts to pine away. When she seems to be at the point of death, word is sent to Gozō. Going to her home, he tells her mother to send her to his house the next day as his bride, and together they celebrate the betrothal before he has to return home. But next morning, when Motosuke and his sister, dressed for her wedding, appear at his door, Gosōji is taken completely by surprise and orders them away. Gozō, it would appear, has not spoken to his father. Now he attempts to leave his home and family, taking Mune with him, but Motosuke forestalls such action by drawing his sword and striking off his sister's head. Throughout the story, to this point, Motosuke has presented an air of indifference, as though he did not care what happened to his sister, but at last this seeming insensitivity is revealed as stolid self-control. He has felt deeply and acted in accordance with those feelings, killing his sister with no outward display of emotion in order to spare her the disgrace of going through life as the wife of a disinherited son and to save his own family name from Gosōji's insult. Although his crime is a capital offence, the judge recognizes the purity of his motives and lets him off with banishment. Motosuke continues as the filial son he has been, working to support his mother, who accompanies him into exile. Gosōji's wealth and property are confiscated, and he and Gozō are likewise banished from the province. Unrepentant and greedy to the end, Gosōji disinherits his son and goes into exile vowing to become rich once more. Gozō himself becomes a monk.

Akinari left no doubt as to where his sympathies lay in this conflict between romantic love and filial duty, but Gozō's behaviour is subject to differing interpretation. On the surface, he appears to be vacillating, led first by love to pledge himself to Mune, then by duty to obey his parents, and lacking the determination to adhere strictly to either course. The tragedy may be seen to result from his indecision, and thus his entering the priesthood becomes an act of penance. But this is probably not what Akinari had in mind. More likely, considering his praise of Gozō's character, he wanted to portray him as striving to win his parents' approval for his love through his exemplary conduct as a son, but this is nowhere clearly stated, and the resulting ambiguity is the story's fundamental weakness. There is no such uncertainty as to Akinari's view of the other characters, however. Mune, who dies a martyr to her love, and Motosuke, who saves her from shame, both display the courage and uprightness of heart that Akinari so much admired. Unable to wed the man of her choice, Mune seals her love for him with her death, and the smile that remains on her lifeless face symbolizes the victory of this pure love over the squalid world she has left. But, Akinari would appear to be saying, such purity has little place in the present day. One must leave the contemporary world if one is to be unsullied by it. The gap between the ideal and the reality cannot be bridged in any other way.

"Suteishimaru" also has its roots in fact, though much more loosely than "Shikubi no egao." It was suggested by the actions of the priest Zenkai, who devoted thirty years of his life in the mid-eighteenth century to digging the Ao no Dōmon tunnel in what is now Shimoge-gun, Ōita-ken, in order to bypass a precipitous mountain route over which many travellers had lost their lives.[79]

Akinari's story, however, begins in the far northeastern part of Honshu, where Suteishimaru, the protagonist, is in the service of a wealthy landowner. He is a natural man, exceedingly strong, unrefined, naive and simple, uneducated, and relatively untouched by philosophies or religion. The master, an inveterate tippler, often invites Suteishimaru to join him in his cups. During one such spree Suteishimaru, befuddled by drink, begins to struggle with his master, and thinking that he has killed him, he takes flight. When the master actually does die during the night, Suteishimaru is branded a murderer. The master's son, Kodenji, is ordered by the local magistrate and the provincial governor to go and bring back the supposed killer's head or have the property to which he is heir confiscated. Kodenji is neither physically strong nor skilled in the use of weapons, but he spends the next two years assiduously training under a master of the martial arts, and then sets off on his mission of revenge.

Meanwhile, Suteishimaru makes his way to Edo where, after making his living as a *sumō* wrestler for a time, he enters the service of a daimyo and goes to the domain in Kyushu. At length his habit of drinking to excess produces abscesses in his legs which render him a cripple. Now he begins to reflect on his past life and is struck with remorse at having killed his former master. To atone for his supposed crime he vows to spend the remainder of his life digging a tunnel through the nearby mountain, making the hazardous route safe for travellers. Thus when Kodenji, after three years of searching, at last tracks him down, it is to find him engaged in this labour. Touched by his virtue, Kodenji loses all desire for revenge and stays to help dig the tunnel. Together they work on, completing the task just before Suteishimaru dies. Akinari was not the only person to write a fictionalized account of Zenkai's labour,[80] but while others concentrated on the avenger's change of heart, he placed the emphasis on Suteishimaru's spiritual growth, which changes him from a natural man to a saint. He saw the simple, unsophisticated Suteishimaru as the clay from which a Buddha may be fashioned; it is the same theme that he developed more fully in "Hankai," the final story in the collection.

Miyagi, the heroine of "Miyagi ga tsuka" (The Grave of Miyagi), evokes memories of the Miyagi of "Asaji ga yado" and of Fujino of *Seken tekake katagi*—the gentle, pure, self-sacrificing, and above all, faithful woman whose virtue transcends the worldly corruption around her. Miyagi is the daughter of an imperial councillor who dies, leaving her, her mother, and a servant of the family in desperate poverty. Through the machinations of the servant, the mother is deceived into selling her daughter to a brothel. Though hating the life she now leads, Miyagi dutifully accepts her fate for her mother's sake. Soon she becomes a celebrated beauty, beloved of Jūtabei, a wealthy and refined young man who determines to ransom her and make her his own. But Miyagi is also coveted by Fujidayū, a man of considerable authority. Fujidayū arranges for Jūtabei to be murdered and then courts Miyagi himself. She, unaware of his responsibility for her lover's death, finally yields to him, and only later, to her dismay, learns the truth. Just at that time, it happens, the priest Hōnen, known as the founder of the Pure Land sect of Buddhism, is about to depart from the Capital on his way into exile in Shikoku. Hearing that his boat is to pass her way, Miyagi has herself taken out into the middle of the river to meet him. As the priest's boat draws near she calls out to him, asking what a person like herself must do to obtain salvation. Then and there Hōnen teaches the efficacy of the *nembutsu*, whereupon Miyagi, chanting this invocation to the Buddha Amida, casts herself into the river and drowns.

Akinari's tale of Miyagi was based on a purportedly factual incident. The grave of the real Miyagi was located at Kanzaki, just across the river from Akinari's dwelling at Kashima-mura, where he had first heard her story more than thirty years before. The tale closes with an account of his visit to her grave and with the long poem he had composed in her memory. His lingering affection for the area is apparent in this postscript, but more important is his view of Miyagi herself, as a strong, intelligent, faithful, and pure woman whose spirit remains unsullied by what her body is compelled to do. She was only the latest manifestation of this kind of woman in his writings, indicating that he retained her as his ideal woman nearly all his life.

The polemic element revives briefly in "Uta no homare" (The Glory of Poetry). This item is no more than a short discourse; Akinari did not even attempt to tell a story. Rather he presented four *waka* from the *Man'yōshū*, each of which describes cranes crying out as they fly over the sea. The wording in all four poems is similar, which fact, says Akinari, is not the result of plagiarism, for the upright men of old would never have stooped to pirate the work of another. In former times, he maintains, since people were not burdened with restraining conventions, they simply expressed in poetry what they perceived with their senses. The result was a brand of verse independent of theory and rules, which came directly from the heart of man. Since two upright hearts would see the same thing in the same way, it was only to be expected that they would describe it in similar terms. Thus, he argues, the four poems were composed independently of one another, and their common expressions are a reflection of the spirit of ancient times.

Finally, there is "Hankai." It is the story of a rough, untutored, wild and impulsive young man who fears neither gods nor men and makes no distinction between good and evil, relying on his own near-superhuman strength to surmount all difficulties—much like Suteishimaru. His character becomes apparent right at the beginning of the tale when, challenged to pay a nocturnal visit to the shrine of a reputedly ferocious deity, he goes with no hesitation and with some bravado. He is punished for his sacrilege and returns home chastened and subdued, but the lesson does not last. Greed leads him to steal from his family. He murders his father and brother in the process and must flee.

Akinari uses this flight to take his hero on a journey to enlightenment—an odyssey whereby he comes to recognize the limits of physical strength, to distinguish right from wrong, and at last to change from a scoundrel to a saint.

As Hankai begins his journey he is much the same as he has always been, living by his own means, removing obstacles by brute force. In Hakata and Nagasaki he makes his way by gambling; in Shikoku he joins a band of robbers. Gradually, however, it becomes apparent that his character is not all bad. He saves a family from being deceived by a dishonest merchant. During the winter he cultivates his own musical talent. After robbing the treasury of a wealthy man, he handsomely rewards his friend who had once saved his life. And in Edo he risks his own life out of genuine concern for the welfare of his two comrades. The action moves rapidly from one place to the next, and Akinari manipulates his character, not always logically, in order to give him the experience prerequisite to his conversion. The tale is episodic, but the grand tour of Japan on which the reader is taken is engrossing in itself.

There are two key episodes in Hankai's transformation. The first takes place in a dilapidated temple where, for the first time in his life, he is soundly beaten in a fight—and by a most unlikely opponent—and comes to realize that he is not invincible. The second occurs on the Moor of Nasuno where, impressed by the virtue of a priest he has robbed, he experiences an abrupt but lasting change of heart. No details of his subsequent life are given, but the final glimpse of him is as the abbot of a Zen temple in northeastern Honshu, at the point of death and entry into enlightenment.

Akinari's final comment on the action: "All who rule their passions have the Buddha nature; all who set them free are monsters,"[81] sums up the theme of "Hankai." It is well to note that Hankai, like Suteishimaru, reforms not through the preaching of others, but through himself. His salvation is not something acquired, but simply the result of his own innate goodness coming to the fore; it comes not so much through religious or philosophical teachings as through cultivation of qualities that he already possesses. This is not to say that Akinari rejected such teachings. He recognized their value, and they do prove helpful to Hankai in his quest for salvation. Akinari himself was affiliated with religious institutions throughout his life. As before, it was the misuse of religion, not religion as such, that he was against. He had no sympathy for those who self-consciously strove for salvation as personal gain or who sought for magical formulas which would produce salvation without effort on their own part. In sum, he believed that in ancient times people had been good by nature. By his own day, human nature had become corrupt. It was not possible to go back to the past, but one could, nevertheless, incorporate the spirit of former times into oneself. The virtues of old Japan had not vanished; they had merely become tarnished. A man could still discover this ideal nature within himself and nourish it to fruition. But there were no shortcuts; to rely on them was to shirk responsibility. It was only through simple living, shunning worldly matters, upright conduct, and strict self-mastery that one could obtain peace within his own mind and in the world. Such was Akinari's conviction, and if one looks for a common theme running through the diversities of *Harusame monogatari*, this must be it. Indeed, it runs through much of his other writing as well.

It is not always the work into which a writer puts his greatest effort that wins the most favour with the critics. *Harusame* is a good example. Though recognized as an important work, it has suffered from the natural tendency to compare it with *Ugetsu*. The style of *Harusame* is relatively straightforward with little artistic embellishment, and its structure and organization are lacking in polish. Reading it does not provide the aesthetic experience of *Ugetsu*. In part, this may be just a reflection of the fact that Akinari was in poor health and nearly blind when he wrote it, and that he died before he considered it finished, but his basic intentions when he wrote the two works were not the same. *Ugetsu* was conceived and executed as a work of pure literature; *Harusame*, more as a summary of what Akinari considered truth to be. When writing the latter, he saw his role to be more one of informing his readers than of pleasing them. This was relative, of course. Some of the *Harusame* tales are first-rate examples of the storyteller's craft, and Akinari's opinions are propounded to some degree in all of the *Ugetsu* pieces. But even in the openly didactic *Ugetsu* tales, Akinari paid such attention to the artistic element that they remain primarily literature, and only secondarily intellectual discourses. The essential difference between *Ugetsu* and *Harusame* is that in the former work the scholarly and literary qualities are fused and digested, while in the latter they tend to be separate. *Harusame* is clearly unequal to *Ugetsu* as a work of literature, but such a comparison is neither fair nor, in the end, possible, for they are not really specimens of the same kind of writing.

In 1808, the same year that *Harusame monogatari* and *Tandai shōshin roku* were completed, Akinari declared that he had cast his writing brush away.[82] In 1809 he did revise some of his entries in *Tandai* and compile his favorite haiku compositions, and he apparently wrote a new draft of *Harusame* as well, but his statement was probably an accurate reflection of his state of mind, nevertheless. *Tandai* and *Harusame* together amounted to a summation of what he wanted to leave behind. Thus, "All who rule their passions have the Buddha nature; all who set them free are monsters," may be seen not only as his final comment on "Hankai," but as his final comment on life. He now felt that his work was finished. There was little more to say, he was almost totally blind, and his general health was failing rapidly.

He was well enough to make the journey to Osaka toward the end of 1808 to observe the fiftieth anniversary of his father's death,[83] but he had little time remaining. Sometime in 1809, probably sensing that the end was truly near, he left his Nanzenji dwelling to live once again at the home of Hakura Nobuyo-shi. It was there that, 8 August 1809 (Bunka Era, sixth year, sixth month, twenty-seventh day), the death he had so long awaited, and had at times longed for, claimed him at last. His grave may still be seen today, standing by itself in honoured isolation in the garden of the Saifukuji Temple, marked by the simple stone monument that his surviving friends erected on the thirteenth anniversary of his death.[84]

Akinari's reputation as an author was already secure long before he died. Both Ōta Nampo and Takizawa Bakin had given him high praise, and the continuing popularity of *Ugetsu monogatari* and *Shodō kikimimi sekenzaru*, and the posthumous publication of some of his other works attest to the regard in which he was held. His popularity suffered for a time in the general preoccupation with things Western and the corresponding indifference to traditional Japanese culture that followed in the wake of the Meiji Restoration, but by the last decade of the nineteenth century the pendulum was starting to swing back. Akinari again became a subject for appreciation and, for the first time, academic research. Beginning in the 1880's and 90's, a solid base of scholarship was gradually built up over the next few decades and after a brief hiatus during World War II, study of Akinari truly began to flourish. Some of the stimulus, both in Japan and elsewhere, may be credited to Mizoguchi Kenji's film, *Ugetsu monogatari*, based primarily on the tales, "Asaji ga yado" and "Jasei no in," which won the grand prize at the Venice Film Festival in 1953 and remains an international classic. The discovery of the complete text of *Harusame monogatari* (purchased during the war in a secondhand bookshop for a mere twenty sen[85]) and its publication in 1950 made possible more extensive scholarship on that work and led to a more complete appreciation of Akinari's talents. It may in part be the emphasis on scholarship and *waka* verse in *Harusame* that has sent some researchers delving into Akinari's role as a *kokugakusha* and poet. Much remains to be done, especially in these latter areas, but the trend shows every sign of continuing and is gradually rounding out the general view of the man who once was known almost exclusively as a writer of supernatural fiction.

In the West, Akinari has attracted attention ever since Lafcadio Hearn retold the *Ugetsu* tales, "Kikuka no chigiri" and "Muō no rigyo" in his *A Japanese Miscellany* in 1905. English translations of individual *Ugetsu* stories have been appearing since 1927, and two complete versions came out during the 1970's. *Ugetsu* has also recently appeared in French, German, Hungarian, Polish, Spanish, and Czech translations, and a complete English rendition of *Harusame* has come off the press as well.

Study of Akinari's works is rewarding both for its own sake and for the debt owed him by other Japanese writers. Tanizaki Jun'ichirō, Ishikawa Jun,

Mishima Yukio, Satō Haruo, Kawabata Yasunari, Kōda Rohan, Izumi Kyōka, Akutagawa Ryūnosuke, Dazai Osamu, Ibuse Masuji, and Enchi Fumiko have all acknowledged his influence on their own writings. Today Akinari's place in the literature of Japan is secure and interest in him is, if anything, growing. A recent report from Japan indicated that university students are turning from modern to classical Japanese literature, and suggested that studies of Akinari may rank closely after *The Tale of Genji* in popularity as topics for graduation theses.[86] It is as though there is something in an age of rational scepticism and scientific technology that sends people back to the haunting imagery, absorbing fantasy, and pursuit of traditional beauty to be found in his works. Likewise, in a world of confusion with the breakdown of long cherished social and moral attitudes, the study of Akinari's life reveals a man who did not seek to ingratiate himself with the world, but strove, sometimes unsuccessfully, but without ceasing, to live according to his own principles and beliefs.

Abbreviations

The following abbreviations are used in footnote references and in the bibliography.

HJAS—Harvard Journal of Asiatic Studies
JAS—Journal of Asian Studies
JK—Joshidai kokubun
KBKKK—Kokubungaku kaishaku to kyōzai no kenkyū
KK—Kokugo kokubun
KKB—Kokugo to kokubungaku
KKK—Kokubungaku kaishaku to kanshō
KZ—Kokugakuin zasshi
MN—Monumenta Nipponica
NB—Nihon bungaku
NKBT—Nihon Koten Bungaku Taikei

Notes

NOTES TO CHAPTER ONE

1. See *Jizō hakogaki*, in *Akinari ibun*, ed. Fujii Otoo (Tokyo: Shūbunkan, 1919), pp. 498, 499; and Akinari's letter to the abbot of the Jippō-in, ibid., pp. 631-33.

2. The Saifukuji's record of his death is quoted in Takada Mamoru, *Ueda Akinari nempu kōsetsu* (Tokyo: Meizendō Shoten, 1964), p. 347. In Akinari's day, a person's age was equivalent to the number of calendar years in which he had lived. He was considered to be a year old at birth and a year older at the beginning of each succeeding year. To avoid confusion, all ages of persons in this study will be expressed in traditional Japanese terms.

3. From a manuscript in the Nihon University Library, quoted in Asano Sampei, "Ueda Akinari no shussei to kazoku," *JK* 36 (Feb. 1965): 1-10; also quoted in Mori Senzo, "Muchō Okina zakki," *Kamigata* 45 (Sept. 1934): 54-62, but here "25th day" is mistakenly printed as "20th."

4. Fujita Gyō, *Kashima Inari Sha ken'ei wakajo*, in *Ueda Akinari zenshū*, ed. Iwahashi Koyata (Tokyo: Kokusho Kankō-kai, 1918; rpt. 1969), 1:149. It is not certain who Fujita Gyō was, but since he deferentially refers to Akinari as *Sensei*, or "teacher", he was presumably one of Akinari's pupils.

5. Letter to the Jippō-in, *Ibun*, p. 631. Akinari gives his natural mother's death date incorrectly as Meiwa, ninth year, *kanoe ne* (cyclical sign of metal and the rat), fifth month, twenty-ninth day. But *kanoe ne* was actually the cyclical designation for the ninth year of the An'ei Era (1780), and the proclamation of a new era during the ninth year of Meiwa (1772) caused that year to be officially redesignated An'ei 1. For these reasons it had been assumed until recently that the mother died in 1780, Akinari having inadvertently written "Meiwa" instead of "An'ei", but this assum-ption has now been shown to be incorrect. See note 8, below.

6. See *Iwahashi no ki, Ibun*, pp. 263-86. The reference to the cousin in Nagara is on p. 286.

7. First pointed out by Takada Mamoru in "Akinari no himitsu," in *Akinari nempu*, pp. 350-60, this fact provided the hint for further research by Nagashima Hiroaki which established the identity of Akinari's natural mother. See Nagashima Hiroaki, "Akinari no jitsubo to sono shūhen," *Bungaku* 50 (May 1982): 86-104.

8. Supporting evidence comes from the records of the Ryūshōji Temple in Nagara. Both sources give Myōzen's death date as Meiwa, fifth year, *tsuchinoe ne* (cyclical sign of earth and the rat), fifth month, twenty-ninth day. Although the year and its cyclical designation differ from those given in Akinari's letter to the Jippō-in, the month and the day coincide. See Nagashima, "Akinari no jitsubo," p. 89.

9. Quoted in Rai Momosaburō, "Akinari den kikigaki," *NB* 8 (June 1959): 6-10. Unless specifically acknowledged, all translations in this study are my own.

10. *Shōroku* is sometimes called *Kakan shōroku, kakan* being the Sino-Japanese reading for Kasumigaseki.

11. Speculation about the identity of Akinari's natural father has been taken, from Takada, "Akinari no himitsu," with some additions and modifications from Nagashima's more recent research.

12. See Akinari, *Jiden, Ibun*, pp. 255-62; Takada, *Akinari nempu*, p. 5. Takada speculates that the family name of Mosuke's foster father was Tanaka, and that Mosuke re-assumed the Ueda surname after his wife and her father died. This may explain the report that Akinari's original surname was Tanaka.

13. Takada, "Akinari no himitsu," *Akinari nempu*, p. 354.

14. It is interesting to note that one of Akinari's relatives in Yamato was named Ueda, and that Akinari described him as "like my brother" (*harakara mekishi*, which indicates a blood relationship). See *Iwahashi no ki, Ibun*, p. 274. The common surname would suggest that Akinari was related to the man through his foster father, although geographical proximity would lead one to assume that all of Akinari's Yamato kinsmen were relatives from his mother's side. It is strange that Mosuke would have close relatives in Yamato, as his family roots were in Tamba, and his only brother, who had gone back to Tamba from Osaka, was still living there as late as 1779. See Akinari, *Akiyama no ki, Zenshū*, 43–61, N.B. p. 61. Of course, coincidence could have given Akinari a maternal relative named Ueda. The surname was by no means uncommon, and none of the four relations Akinari mentioned had the same family name. The phrase, "like my brother," does raise questions, however. One Japanese scholar has even suggested that the man was an illegitimate son of Ueda Mosuke by Akinari's natural mother. See Ōba Shunsuke, *Akinari no tenkanshō to dēmon* (Tokyo: Ashi Shobō, 1969), pp. 31, 32. While this is an extreme view, we do not have sufficient evidence to prove it incorrect.

15. See Fujita, *Ken'ei waka jo, Zenshū*, 149; Akinari, *Kashima Inari Sha ken'ei waka, Zenshū*: 150–55, N.B. p. 155. There are a few discrepancies between the two accounts, perhaps inevitably, as Fujita wrote ninety-three years after the occurrence of events that he did not witness, and Akinari, being quite young and extremely ill, probably had no clear recollection of what actually happened. The Kashima Inari Shrine, now known as the Kaguwashi Jinja, in Higashi Yodogawa-ku, Osaka, is about three miles as the crow flies from where Akinari lived, and in 1738 the journey would have entailed crossing the river by ferry boat. It is not certain why Mosuke went to such an inconvenient place to offer prayers; possibly he already had a friendly relationship with the priests of the shrine. Moreover, although Inari shrines were dedicated to agricultural deities, in the Kansai area these same deities had come to be household gods of the merchant class. See Noda Hisao, *Kinsei bungaku no haikei* (Tokyo: Kōshobō, 1964; rpt. 1971), p. 95. Besides this, the priests of the shrine were reputed to be endowed with special powers for exorcising fox spirits. See *Kaguwashi Jinja to Ueda Akinari no shiori* (pamphlet; Osaka: Kaguwashi Jinja Keishin Kenkōkai, 1965); Akinari, *Tandai shōshin roku*, in *Ueda Akinari shū*, ed. Nakamura Yukihiko, *NKBT* 56 (Tokyo: Iwanami Shoten, 1959; rpt. 1968): 251–361, N.B. no. 34, p. 276. Mosuke may have hoped as a last resort that these powers would extend to curing diseases.

16. *Tandai*, no. 89, *NKBT* 56: 305, 306.

17. Letter to the Jippō-in, *Ibun*, p. 631. *Seikōki, Zenshū*, 1: 112–115, N.B. p. 114.

18. Assumed, because she died in 1789 at the age of seventy-six. See Akinari's letter to the Jippō-in, *Ibun*, p. 631; *Tandai*, no. 69, *NKBT* 56: 294. It is not known exactly when Mosuke remarried, but it seems to have been not long after his first wife's death.

19. *Jizō hakogaki, Ibun*, p. 498.

20. For Akinari's own description of the commercial scene in his home area, see his *Seken tekake katagi*, in Moriyama Shigeo, *Ueda Akinari shoki ukiyo-zōshi hyōshaku* (Tokyo: Kokusho Kankōkai, 1977), pp. 177–313, N.B. pp. 261, 262.

21. Akinari, *Daimyō Kokushi gazō no ki, Ibun*, pp. 497, 498.

22. *Jiden, Ibun*, p. 255.

23. *Tandai*, no. 110, *NKBT* 56: 317, 318.

24. See Shigetomo Ki, "Senshi Kijin no gigō to sono raiyū" (1935), in *Akinari no kenkyū*, by Shigetomo Ki (Tokyo: Bunri Shoin, 1971), pp. 161–68.

25. See *Jiden, Ibun*, p. 255; Fujita, *Ken'ei waka jo, Zenshū*, 1:149.

26. *Tandai*, no. 26, *NKBT* 56: 267, 268. Akinari's scorn for the Nakai brothers is also apparent in this passage.

27. See *Jiden, Ibun*, p. 255. On education in general at this time, see R.P. Dore, *Education in Tokugawa Japan* (Berkeley and Los Angeles: University of California Press, 1965).

28. *Tandai*, nos. 55, 57, *NKBT* 56: 187, 188.

29. Among the characters in Akinari's first work of fiction is a courtesan who tries to amuse her patrons by composing poetry in both Japanese and Chinese. See *Shodō*

kikimimi sekenzaru, in Moriyama, *Ueda Akinari shoki ukiyo-zōshi hyōshaku,* pp. 23–176, N.B. pp. 139–48.

30. *Jiden, Ibun,* pp. 259, 260.

31. See Ibid., pp. 258, 259. Akinari dated the fire 1723, but there is no record of a fire of such proportions in Osaka in that year. It was probably an error for 1724, when such a fire did occur, perhaps made by Mosuke when recounting the story to Akinari. See Asano, "Ueda Akinari no shussei to kazoku," pp. 6, 7.

32. This rumour appears to have been widely believed during Akinari's lifetime. It is mentioned, for example, in Homma Yūsei's miscellany, *Mimitokawa,* quoted in Fuji Otoo, "Ueda Akinari den," in *Ibun,* pp. 1–52, N.B. p. 4.

33. On these excursions, see *Iwahashi no ki, Ibun,* p. 267; *Kozo no shiori, Zenshū,* 1: 165–172, N.B. pp. 167, 171; *Akiyama no ki, Zenshū,* 1: 49, 50; *Fuji Sansetsu, Ibun,* pp. 491, 492; Shigetomo Ki, "Akinari zatsuwa" (1932), in *Akinari no kenkyū,* pp. 291–93; Takada, *Akinari nempu,* p. 179.

34. Quoted in Nagashima Hiroaki, "Akinari shiryō shūi," *Kaishaku* 25 (November 1979): 24–29.

35. These verses are quoted in Nakamura Yukihiko, *Kinsei sakka kenkyū* (Tokyo: San'ichi Shobō, 1961), pp. 205, 211–15.

36. In his preface for *Zoku Akegarasu,* compiled in 1776 for the seventeenth anniversary of Kikei's death, Akinari said it had been twenty years before that he had met Kikei. The preface is quoted in Fujii, "Ueda Akinari den," *Ibun,* pp. 6, 7.

37. The sequence is reproduced in Nakamura, *Kinsei sakka kenkyū,* pp. 207–9.

38. Quoted in Iwahashi Koyata, "Haijin Muchō," *KZ* 18 (July 1912): 55–62.

39. See *Tandai,* no. 23, *NKBT* 56: 266, 267.

40. See Akinari's preface to the 1789 commemorative collection of Seigyo's verses, *Nishinomiya gusa,* quoted in Takada,

Akinari nempu, pp. 167, 168.

41. See Akinari, *Aki no kumo, Zenshū,* 1: 157–64, N.B. p. 157.

42. On Tama's background see Akinari, *Tsuzurabumi, Zenshū,* 1: 1–142, N.B. p. 141. The year of marriage is calculated from her age at death (fifty-eight) in 1797. There has been speculation, based on a remark by Akinari in *Yomotsubumi, Zenshū,* 1: 132–35; N.B. p. 134, that Tama had come into the Ueda house, perhaps as a serving maid, when she was about fourteen. The passage is ambiguous, however. For discussion of its meaning, see Fujii, "Ueda Akinari den," *Ibun,* p. 35; Takada, *Akinari nempu,* pp. 28–30; and Takada," "Ueda Akinari nempu kōsetsu' hoi," in *Kinsei chūki bungaku no shomondai,* ed. Kinsei Bungakushi Kenkyū no Kai (Tokyo: Meizendō Shoten, 1966), pp. 69–113, N.B. pp. 75, 76. The latter source, in which Takada concludes that there is no evidence that Akinari and Tama had any contact before their marriage, is especially convincing.

43. See *Jiden, Ibun,* p. 260; for the date of Mosuke's death, see Akinari's letter to the Jippō-in, *Ibun,* p. 631. In *Jizō hakogaki, Ibun,* p. 498, Akinari said that he was thirty-seven years old when his father died. This must have been a slip of the pen for twenty-seven, for additional evidence supports 1761 as the date. (By Japanese reckoning, Akinari would have been twenty-eight in 1761, but *Jizō hakogaki* was written in 1804, so an error of one year is not surprising.) In 1801 Akinari said that he had been separated from his father for over forty years, and in 1808 he wrote of his plans to hold services observing his father's fiftieth death anniversary. He would scarcely have been thinking of such rites if Mosuke had not died until 1770. See *Seikōki, Zenshū,* 1: 114; *Seburui no okina den, Ibun,* pp. 395–400, N.B. p. 399.

NOTES TO CHAPTER TWO

1. *Jiden, Ibun*, p. 255, 260.
2. *Tandai* nos. 61, 62, *NKBT* 56: 289, 290. Akinari also recalled this experience in *Reigotsū, Zenshū*, 2: 409-38, N.B. p. 422. Concerning Korean embassies to Japan at this time, see George B. McCune, "The Exchange of Envoys between Korea and Japan During the Tokugawa Period" (1946), in *Japan: Enduring Scholarship*, ed. John A. Harrison (Tucson: University of Arizona Press, 1972), pp. 83-100; pp. 85-89 give some information about this particular embassy. See also Matsuda Osamu, "Sei tōbōsha Ueda Akinari," *Subaru* 13 (June 1973): 25-37.
3. See *Yamazuto, Ibun*, pp. 345-63, N.B. p. 349.
4. See Noda, *Kinsei bungaku no haikei*, p. 117; Dore, *Education in Tokugawa Japan*, p. 20.
5. See Richard Lane, "The Beginnings of the Modern Japanese Novel (*Kanazōshi*, 1600-1682)," *HJAS* 20 (Dec. 1957), 644-701; Donald Keene, *World Within Walls: Japanese Literature of the Pre-Modern Era, 1600-1867* (New York: Holt, Rhinehart and Winston, 1976), pp. 149-166.
6. For a general treatment of *ukiyo-zōshi*, see Ivan Morris, ed. and trans., *The Life of an Amorous Woman and Other Writings by Ihara Saikaku* (Norfolk, Connecticut: New Directions, 1963); Howard Hibbett, *The Floating World in Japanese Fiction* (New York: Oxford University Press, 1959); Hasegawa Tsuyoshi, *Ukiyo-zōshi no kenkyū* (Tokyo: Ōfūsha, 1969). Keene, *World Within Walls*, pp. 167-229.
7. See Noda, *Kinsei bungaku no haikei*, p. 138.
8. Ōsaka Tosho Shuppangyō Kumiai, ed., *Kyōhō igo Osaka shuppan shoseki moku-roku* (Osaka: Ōsaka Tosho Shuppangyō Kumiai, 1936), p. 65. The actual publication data from the 1766 edition is quoted in Takada, *Akinari nempu*, p. 42.
9. On the monkey's significance in oriental art and literature, see U.A. Casal, "Far Eastern Monkey Lore," *MN* 12 (1956): 13-49.
10. The most ambitious and authoritative study to date of Akinari's literary sources, both Chinese and Japanese, for *Seken-zaru* is Takada Mamoru, *Ueda Akinari kenkyū josetsu* (Tokyo: Nara Shobō,

1968), pp. 15-74. For information about the live character models, see Nakamura Yukihiko, "Akinari ni egakareta hitobito," Part I, *KK* 32 (Jan. 1963): 1-11.
11. This point is discussed more fully in Asano Sampei, "Shodō kikimimi seken-zaru ron," *JK* 15 (Oct. 1959): 46-56.
12. Moriyama, *Ueda Akinari shoki ukiyo-zōshi hyōshaku*, p. 150.
13. Both publication requests and publication data from the first edition are quoted in Takada, *Akinari nempu* pp. 46, 47, 50, 51.
14. Most of the ideas expressed in this paragraph are treated more fully in Asano Sampei, "Seken tekake katagi wo megutte— Shokoku kaisen dayori, Uta makura some-buroshiki ni oyobu," *KKB* 36 (May 1959): 38-48.
15. *Ihon Tandai shōshin roku, NKBT* 56: 370-77, N.B. pp. 372, 373.
16. Fujita Gyō, *Ken'ei waka jo, Zenshū*, 1: 149.
17. This and subsequent references to Uma-ki's whereabouts at given times are taken from Takada Mamoru, "Umaki nyūmon nendai kō", in *Akinari nempu*, pp. 361-76.
18. *Ihon Tandai, NKBT* 56: 373.
19. Ibid.
20. Despite ample debate, Japanese scholars have yet to agree on the date of Akinari's first meeting with Umaki. In "Umaki nyū-mon nendai kō," Takada argues in favour of 1768. Maruyama Sueo supports the 1770 view in "Akinari no Umaki nyūmon no toshi sono ta," *Wagimo* 13 (Mar. 1936): 42-45; while in "Akinari den no mondaiten," *KKK* 265 (June 1958): 7-11, Nakamura Yukihiko proposes that the first meeting took place in 1767. All three reach their conclusions by accepting some pieces of evidence, rejecting others, and making certain arbitrary assumptions. No matter which view one subscribes to, some of the evidence must be assumed erroneous.
21. *Tandai shōshin roku kakioki no koto, NKBT* 56: 363-70, N.B. p. 366.
22. Probably a deliberate fabrication, since it appears in both *Ihon Tandai* and *Kakioki no koto*. See *NKBT* 56: 365, 372.
23. See *Ihon Tandai, NKBT* 56: 373. *Masu-rao monogatari, Ibun*, pp. 406-18. Akinari's criticism of *Nishiyama* appears on p. 408 of the latter source.

24. An attempt to draw inferences about their relationship through analyzing the written record has been made by Nakamura Yukihiko in "Umaki to Akinari" (1958), in *Akinari*, ed. Nihon Bungaku Kenkyū Shiryō Kankōkai (Tokyo: Yūseidō, 1972), pp. 150–57.

25. Letter from Tamiya to Nampo in *Ichi wa ichi gen*, in *Shin hyakka zeirin Shoku Sanjin zenshū*, ed., Yoshikawa Kōbunkan (Tokyo: Yoshikawa Kōbunkan, 1907, 1908), 4: 806.

NOTES TO CHAPTER THREE

1. *Setsuyō kikan*, in *Naniwa sōsho*, ed. Funakoshi Seiichirō (Osaka 1927), 4: 157. The date of the fire is given as Meiwa Era, fifth year (1768), third month, twenty-third day. National Diet Library.
2. See ibid., p. 181; *Tandai*, no. 69 *NKBT* 56: 293; *Jiden, Ibun*, p. 260; *Jizō hakogaki, Ibun*, pp. 498, 499.
3. See *Jiden, Ibun*, pp. 255, 260; *Jizō hakogaki, Ibun*, p. 499.
4. Fuji Teibu, *Kokin jo kikigaki*, quoted in Takada, *Akinari nempu*, p. 72. Teibu was also called Ietoki. This may be the earliest recorded use of the name "Akinari", but Takada himself ignores this instance and states that the name first appeared in *Kusagusa no fumi*, completed in 1775 by Teibu's brother Utsuna (also called Ietaka). See *Akinari nempu*, p. 76; for a text of *Kusagusa no fumi*, see *Kinsei bungei* 5 (May 1960); 47–52. Another scholar contends that the name's earliest appearance was in the preamble to a verse composed on the occasion of Katō Umaki's departure from the Kamigata region after his first period of association with Akinari, which would probably have been about 1770. See Ōiso Yoshio, "Ueda Akinari wa futari ita," *Kokugo kokubungaku hō* 13 (April 1961): 11–16. Ōiso surmises that Akinari received his name from Umaki, or perhaps even earlier from his Shimo no Reizeike instructor, since it is most often used in connection with *waka* and *kokugaku*.
5. Suggested by Nakamura in *Kinsei sakka kenkyū*, p. 210. However, there would have been nothing to stop Akinari from simply submitting one of his earlier compositions.
6. *Jiden, Ibun*, p. 255.
7. See Asano Sampei, *Akinari zenkashū to sono kenkyū* (Tokyo: Ōfūsha, 1969), p. 58.
8. Now the Kanzaki River. At the conclusion of his *Nagara no miyako kō* (unpublished

manuscript preserved at the Kaguwashi Jinja), Akinari said that he had written it while residing near the Mikuni River. On the basis of that statement, and the verse quoted above, it has been surmised that Akinari's dwelling was beside the dike on the river, not far from the shrine. See Noma Kōshin, "Kashima insei jidai no Akinari," *Kamigata* 58 (Aug. 1936): 2–10.
9. See *Jiden, Ibun*, p. 225; *Tandai*, no. 69, NKBT 56: 293.
10. Fuji Utsuna, *Kusagusa no fumi*, quoted in Takada, *Akinari nempu*, p. 76.
11. *Ise monogatari kō* as pointed out in Takada, *Akinari nempu*, p. 76.
12. *Ōsaka shuppan shoseki mokuroku*, p. 94; for a text of *Yasaishō*, see *Zenshū*, 2: 449–77.
13. Publication data in *Zenshū*, 2: 477.
14. See Takeoka Masao, "Fujitani Nariakira to Ueda Akinari to no kankei," *Kokugo* 2 (Sept. 1953): 222–28.
15. See Buson's letter to Masana dated ninth month, sixth day (presumably of 1776), in *Buson shū*, ed. Ōtani Takuzō, Okada Rihei, and Shimasue Kiyoshi, *Koten Haibungaku Taikei* (Tokyo: Shūeisha, 1972), 12: 433.
16. *Ugetsu monogatari, NKBT* 56: 33–141, N.B. p. 77.
17. See Ōba, *Akinari no tenkanshō*, p. 44.
18. From his students' preface to *Yasaishō, Zenshū*, 2: 450; unpublished translation by Leon M. Zolbrod.
19. Ibid.
20. Asano, *Akinari zenkashū*, p. 227. In the second line there is a pun on "Naniwa" (Osaka) and *nanika ni tsukete* (whatever one does).
21. See Akinari, *Ashikabi no kotoba, Zenshū*, 1: 185–90.
22. *Ashikabi* was written in the second month of 1774. See Ibid., p. 190.
23. See Akinari's letter to Umaki in *Fumihōgu, Zenshū*, 1: 191–228, N.B. pp. 193, 194. For Kimura's record of contacts with

Akinari, see Mizuta Norihisa, ed. *Kenkadō nikki* (Osaka: Kenkadō Nikki Kankōkai, 1972), pp. 6, 9, 16, 39, 41, 45, 51, 58, 69, 75, 77, 78, 89, 96, 97, 122, 129, 130, 133, 145, 151, 160, 163, 165, 167, 171, 187, 355, 357, 386, 396, 416, 424, 425, 441, 450. The entries on these pages record a total of forty-four meetings between Akinari and Kenkadō.

24. See Takada, *Akinari nempu*, pp. 88, 89. Technically, Iehide's death occurred early in 1776, according to the Western calendar.

25. *Jiden, Ibun*, p. 255.

26. See Asano, *Akinari zenkashū*, p. 204.

27. The possibility that the move took place late in 1775 cannot be ruled out. In *Tandai*, no. 5, *NKBT* 56: 254, Akinari said that he was forty-three when he began to practice as a physician, but in Ibid., no. 69, p. 293, he said that he was forty-two. 1776 is most likely the corrrect date, however, because Akinari probably would not have left Kashima while Iehide was seriously ill and because spring would have been a more convenient time than the dead of winter to find a new home.

NOTES TO CHAPTER FOUR

1. The first edition is dated "An'ei 5th year, early summer"—that is, mid-1776. See Takada, *Akinari nempu*, p. 92.

2. See Moriyama Shigeo, *Hōken shōmin bungaku no kenkyū* (Tokyo: San'ichi Shobō, 1960; rpt. 1971), pp. 253–62.

3. For an exhaustive catalogue of the sources, both Chinese and Japanese, related to each *Ugetsu* tale, see Uzuki Hiroshi, *Ugetsu monogatari hyōshaku* (Tokyo: Kadogawa Shoten, 1969), pp. 707–12.

4. See Nakamura, *Kinsei sakka kenkyū*, p. 161.

5. *Yasumigoto, Zenshū*, 1: 465–89; for Teishō's preface see p. 465. Teishō's signature appears on the manuscript copy in the Tenri Library. See Nakamura, *Kinsei sakka kenkyū*, p. 163.

6. Bakin, *Kinsei mono no hon Edo sakusha burui*, ed. Kimura Miyogo (Nara: privately published, 1971), p. 128.

7. *Hanabusa sōshi, Nishiyama monogatari, Ugetsu monogatari, Harusame monogatari*, ed. Nakamura Yukihiko, Takada Mamoru, and Nakamura Hiroyasu, *Nihon Koten Bungaku Zenshū*, 48 (Tokyo: Shōgakukan 1973); 73, 74.

8. For these experiences and opinions, see *Tandai*, nos. 13 and 29, *NKBT* 56: 258, 270–72; see also Akinari, *Kitano Kamo ni mōzuru ki, Ibun*, pp. 372–80.

9. *Shonin ichidai michi no naka zukai*. This was compiled by the same firm that published *Ugetsu* in Kyoto. Photographic reproductions of the notice can be seen in Takada, *Akinari nempu*, p. 65, and Uzuki, *Ugetsu hyōshaku*, p. 703.

10. Suggested in Uzuki, *Ugetsu hyōshaku*, p. 699.

11. For a detailed explanation of the title, see Leon M. Zolbrod, trans., *Ugetsu Monogatari: Tales of Moonlight and Rain* (Vancouver, University of British Columbia Press, 1974), pp. 19–21. See Zolbrod's complete introduction to the collection (pp. 19–94) for a critical discussion of the background of *Ugetsu*.

12. *NKBT* 56: 47, 48; Zolbrod, trans., *Ugetsu*, p. 109.

13. *NKBT* 56: 53, 54; Zolbrod, trans., *Ugetsu*, p. 114.

14. For a discussion of this recurring character type in Akinari's works, see Komiyayama Eiko, "Miyagi ron: ningen tsuikyū no kokoromi toshite" (1959), in *Akinari*, ed. Nihon Bungaku Kenkyū Shiryō Kankōkai, pp. 127–33.

15. See *Man'yōshū*, nos. 431, 432, *NKBT* 4: 206, 207; nos. 1807, 1808, *NKBT* 5: 416, 417; nos. 3386, 3387, *NKBT* 6: 416, 417.

16. *NKBT* 56: 77; Zolbrod, trans., *Ugetsu*, p. 139.

17. *Kansei kaigen, Ibun*, pp. 425–29.

18. *Eurystomus orientalis*. A small bird, green rust in colour. It was called *sambōchō*, or "bird of the three treasures," because it was supposed to emit a cry sounding like *buppōsō*, that is, the Buddha, the sutras, and the monastic orders, the "three treasures" of Buddhism. Actually this is the cry of another bird, the *konohazuku* (*Otus scops japonicus*), but the error was not discovered until 1935. See *Dai Nihon hyakka jiten* (*Encyclopedia Japonica*) (Tokyo: Shōgakukan, 1967–1972), 7: 535; 15: 629.

19. See *Tandai*, nos. 27 and 28, *NKBT* 56: 269, 270.

20. These stories are related in *Akiyama no ki, Zenshū,* 1: 54–57. For the *Nihongi* version of the story of Hada no Ōtsuchi and the wolves, see *NKBT* 68: 62, 63; W.G. Aston, trans., *Nihongi: Chronicles of Japan from the Earliest Times to A.D. 697,* (London: George Allen & Unwin, 1956), 2: 36, 37.

Akinari also relates this story and comments on it in *Tandai,* no. 31, *NKBT* 56: 272, 273.

21. See *Tandai,* no. 13, *NKBT* 56: 258; see also nos. 30, 31, pp. 272–74.

22. *NKBT* 56; 126, Zolbrod, trans., *Ugetsu,* p. 189.

NOTES TO CHAPTER FIVE

1. See *Tandai,* nos. 5 and 69, *NKBT* 56: 253, 293.
2. *Tandai,* nos. 14 and 69, *NKBT* 56: 258, 259, 293. Compare Samon's treatment of Akana in "'Kikuka no chigiri," p. 49.
3. See *Jiden, Ibun,* p. 255, *Tandai,* nos. 50 and 69, *NKBT* 56: 283, 293. A map showing the locations of Akinari's birthplace (Sonezaki), the Shimaya, his rented home in Amagasaki, and the new residence is included in Takada, *Akinari nempu,* p. 111.
4. From an entry in Kitō's manuscripts, dated An'ei Era, fifth year (1776), second month, eighteenth day. Quoted in Takada, *Akinari nempu,* p. 90.
5. Implied in a letter from Buson, apparently to Kitō, dated An'ei fifth year, second month, twenty-first day. See *Buson-shū,* ed. Ōtani, et al, p. 360. Buson also mentioned a visit to Kyoto by Akinari, perhaps the same one, in a letter to Tōshi dated An'ei fifth year, second month, eighteenth day. See Ibid., p. 431. In *Akinari nempu,* p. 96, Takada, for unstated reasons, dates this letter a year later.
6. Quoted in Takada, *Akinari nempu,* p. 94.
7. In addition to those mentioned in note above, see Buson's letters in *Buson shū,* ed. Ōtani, et al, to Kitō, dated An'ei fifth year, ninth month, twenty-eighth day (p. 365); to Masana, dated An'ei fifth year, ninth month, sixth day (p. 433); to Masana (?), dated An'ei fifth year, ninth month, twenty-second day (pp. 433, 434); to Tōshi, dated An'ei fifth year, twelfth month, thirteenth day (pp. 435, 436); to Masana and Shunsaku, dated An'ei sixth year, fifth month, twenty-fourth day (pp. 436, 437).
8. This was *Baiō hokku mukashi guchi.* See Takada, *Akinari nempu,* p. 97. Takada points out that this was the first collection of Sōin's haiku to be published.
9. *Amayo monogatari tami kotoba;* for Akinari's preface, see *Ibun,* pp. 507, 508. Publication data is given in Takada, *Akinari nempu,* pp. 98, 99.
10. Akinari gave Umaki's death date as "sixth month, tenth day." See *Fumihōgu, Zenshū,* 1: 194. This corresponds to the date in the register at the Sambōji, where Umaki was interred. See Takada, *Akinari nempu,* p. 99.
11. *Fumihōgu, Zenshū,* 1: 195.
12. See Takada, *Akinari nempu,* pp. 99, 100.
13. See *Akiyama no ki, Zenshū,* 1: 43; *Kozo no shiori, Zenshū* 1: 165–72, N.B. p. 165. The baths at Kinosaki are considered especially effective for neuralgia, gastrointestinal complaints, and gynecological disorders. See *Dai Nihon hyakka jiten,* 5: 483.
14. Some twenty years earlier, as mentioned in *Akiyama no ki, Zenshū,* 1: 43, 49.
15. Ibid., p. 44. Previously Akinari had referred to the traditional fates of Murasaki and Lo in his preface to *Ugetsu.* See *NKBT* 56: 35.
16. *Zenshū,* 1: 165. See also p. 172, where Akinari says that he wrote *Kozo* during the winter of the year after the one in which he wrote *Akiyama.*
17. *Nubatama no maki, Ibun,* pp. 95–124. For the preface, see pp. 95, 96.
18. For instance, he once composed a sequence of fifty-four *waka,* each one related to one of the fifty-four chapters of *The Tale of Genji.* See *Zenshū,* 1: 39–42.
19. Sōchin was not a figment of Akinari's imagination, but a real person, a *waka* poet who was also noted for making copies of *The Tale of Genji.* See Miyama Yasushi, "Nubatama no maki ni tsuite," *Kōgakkan Daigaku kiyō* 8 (March 1970), 95–112.
20. Compare the physical description of this man with that of the priest who discourses on *Genji* in *Akiyama,* and Akinari's description of the moonlight on the beach with his account of the same kind of scene

at Ōkuradani. See *Ibun*, p. 98; *Zenshū*, 1:
44, 46.

21. See *Ōsaka shuppan shoseki mokuroku*, p.
118. Akinari once stated that the expression *no naru matama* was equivalent to
nubatama. See *Koyō jōgen, Zenshū*, 2:
235–44, N.B. p. 236.

22. *Kaseiden, Zenshū*, 2: 245–65. Although
the exact date of its completion is unknown, Takada feels that it is indebted to
a work that was published in 1774 and so
could not have been finished earlier than
that year. See *Akinari nempu*, p. 102.
Even so, in 1799 Akinari mentioned having written *Kaseiden* some thirty years
before. See *Mitake sōji, Zenshū*, 1: 71, 73.
A postscript to *Kaseiden*, called *Kaseiden
tsuikō*, is dated 1785. See *Zenshū*, 2:
266–70. In sum, *Kaseiden* must have been
completed between 1774 and 1785, though
it may well have been started even earlier.
For a list of the sources quoted from in
Kaseiden, see Takada, *Kenkyū josetsu*,
p. 408.

23. In a letter to Akinari, Umaki spoke of
lending him *Man'yōshū* manuscripts. See
Fumihōgu, Zenshū, 1: 193.

24. *Manihōshū*, a collection of *kyokā* verses
published in 1775, was reported to be the
work of Akinari and probably antedated
Kaseiden. But the evidence for Akinari's
authorship is quite tenuous, and it seems
unlikely that his first *Man'yōshū*-inspired
work would be a satirical treatment. See
Takada, *Akinari nempu*, pp. 86–88.

25. *Hakoya no yama, Ibun*, pp. 382–84; *Mina-
segawa, Zenshū* 1: 89. It is not stated in so
many words that these two accounts describe aspects of the same excursion, but
their common dates make it very likely.

26. *Yamazuto, Ibun*, pp. 345–63.

27. For the publication requests, see *Ōsaka
shuppan shoseki mokuroku*, pp. 125, 131,
132. Nomura Nobumoto's preface, which
is dated Temmei Era, fifty year (1785),
tenth month, and which establishes the
time by which editing of all twenty volumes
must have been completed, is quoted in
Takada, *Akinari nempu*, p. 131. For publication data, see ibid., p. 160.

28. See *Ōsaka shuppan shoseki mokuroku*, p.
132, Takada, *Akinari nempu*, p. 140.

29. For texts, see Morita Kirō, "Ueda Akinari, *Kakizome kigenkai*: honkoku to
kaidai," *Bungaku kenkyū* 34 (Dec. 1971),
80–90; Miyama Yasushi, ed., *Harusame

monogatari. Kakizome kigenkai (Tokyo:
Shinchōsha, 1980), pp. 155–96. Akinari
disclosed his authorship of the work in a
letter to Nakahara Ōe, dated third month,
twenty-third day, apparently of 1791. Por-
tions of this letter are quoted in Takada,
Akinari nempu, pp. 138, 177. See also
Asano Sampei, "Kakizome kigenkai ni
tsuite," *KKK* 35 (Feb. 1958): 41–49; *Harusame monogatari*, ed. Maruyama Sueo
(Tokyo: Koten Bunko, 1951), pp. 26–36.

30. The meaning of the title, and other aspects
of *Kakizome* are examined in Asano,
"Kakizome kigenkai ni tsuite." See also
Asano's "Mitsu no fūshiteki sakuhin—
Kakizome kigenkai, Kuse monogatari,
Manihōshū," *KKK* 23 (June 1958): 42–46.

31. See his letter to Nakahara in Takada,
Akinari nempu, p. 138.

32. Ibid.

33. See *Tandai*, no. 101, *NKBT* 56: 312.

34. On Kikuya Hyōbe and his relations with
Akinari, see Ōkubo Tadashi, "Akinari to
Norinaga—ronsō no kei-i to tairitsu no
imi," *KBKKK* 12 (Aug. 1967): 121–26;
Takada, *Akinari nempu*, p. 123; Akinari,
Yamazuto, Ibun, p. 354; *Fumihōgu, Zen-
shū*, 1: 195.

35. *Asama no kemuri, Ibun*, pp. 190–201,
N.B. p. 194.

36. See Takada, *Akinari nempu*, p. 120;
Ōkubo, "Akinari to Norinaga," p. 122.

37. *Kan Ito Koku-ō kin'in kō, Zenshū*, 1:
491–95.

38. *Fumihōgu, Zenshū*, 1: 195.

39. The letter is found in *Kakaika, Zenshū*, 1:
423–64, N.B. p. 464. It is dated eighth
month, twentieth day, but no year is given.

40. See *Kakaika, Zenshū*, 1: 440, 441.

41. See ibid., p. 441.

42. Roland A. Lange, in *The Phonology of
Eighth-Century Japanese* (Tokyo: Sophia
University, 1973), includes no syllabic
nasal in his phonetic table. For a discussion of the appearance of this sound in the
Japanese language, see Roy Andrew
Miller, *The Japanese Language* (Chicago
and London: University of Chicago Press,
1967), pp. 207–20.

43. For more technical and detailed analysis
of the phonetic side of the quarrel, see
Fukunaga Shizuya, "Akinari to Norinaga
no ronsō," *JK* 31 (Dec. 1963): 7–19; Takada Mamoru, "Kakaika ronsō no keisei
katei shikō," in *Akinari nempu*, pp.
385–401.

44. Although no original manuscript is known to exist, the work was probably entitled *Kenkyōjin hyō*; it forms the basis of Akinari's criticism in *Kakaika*. It has been suggested that the pen name Rakugai Hankyōjin, with which Akinari signed *Kakizome kigenkai* (published the year after *Kenkyōjin hyō*) was a reference to the *Kenkyōjin* title. See Morita Kirō, *Ueda Akinari no kenkyū* (Tokyo: Kasama Sōsho, 1979), p. 221.
45. See *Kakaika, Zenshū*, 1: 425–27.
46. See ibid., pp. 425–30.
47. See *Yasumigoto, Zenshū*, 1: 480, 487–89.
48. *Ueda Akinari ronnan dō ben*. For the date, see *Kakaika, Zenshū*, 1: 464. In *Akinari nempu*, p. 139, Takada points out that this date also appears on Norinaga's original handwritten manuscript.

49. *Ueda Akinari Kenkyōjin hyō dō ben*. The printed version was taken from a copy of the original, dated Kansei Era, second year (1790), sixth month. See *Kakaika, Zenshū*, 1: 437.
50. See *Fumihōgu, Zenshū*, 1: 195, 196.
51. *Tandai*, no. 5, *NKBT* 56: 254. I have copied the translation of the verse that appears in Donald Keene, *World Within Walls*, p. 387.
52. *See Tandai*, nos. 100, 101, *NKBT* 56: 311–13.
53. More detailed treatment of the debate on Japanese traditions may be found in Nakamura Hiroyasu, "Yūkō na honshitsu, mukō na honshitsu—'Hi no kami' ronsō ni tsuite," in *Akinari*, ed. Nihon Bungaku Shiryō Kankōkai, pp. 158–74; Takada, *Kenkyū josetsu*, pp. 362–81.

NOTES TO CHAPTER SIX

1. Akinari, *Uzura no ya, Ibun*, pp. 418–25; for his account of this excursion, see pp. 419–23. The historical record states clearly that Takatsukasa Sadahei was raised to the office of *kampaku* in the Temmei Era, seventh year, (1787), third month, first day. See *Dokushi biyō*, ed. Tokyo Teikoku Daigaku Shiryō Hensan-jo (Tokyo: Naigai Shoseki Kabushiki Kaisha, 1933), p. 245. It is Akinari's report of seeing the procession of the new *kampaku* that enables us to date this trip.
2. See *Uzura no ya, Ibun*, p. 423. Akinari gave the date of their move from Osaka as fourth month, twentieth day, apparently of 1787, as he described the shift as though it was made directly after his excursion to Arashiyama. In two other sources, however, he said that he was fifty-five when he gave up medicine, which would have been in 1788. See *Jiden, Ibun*, p. 256; *Tandai*, no. 5, *NKBT* 56: 254. Still, both of these writings were completed during Akinari's final years, while *Uzura no ya*, to judge from its style, was written during the same year as the events it describes, and so is probably the more reliable source.
3. *Tandai*, no. 5, *NKBT* 56: 254; *Jiden, Ibun*, pp. 256, 261. In both of these references, Akinari restated that poor health was one of his reasons for giving up his medical practice.
4. *Jiden, Ibun*, p. 261.

5. See particularly the opening lines of *Uzura no ya, Ibun*, p. 418.
6. *Kuse monogatari, Zenshū*, 1: 329–50, N.B. p. 332.
7. See *Tandai*, no. 69, *NKBT* 56: 294. Tama's "mother" was most likely her foster mother, Mrs. Ueyama, whose husband, presumably, had died before she came to live with them. It is not certain whether she actually accompanied them to Nagara-mura or joined them there later.
8. Nagara-mura was also known as Awajishō-mura, but its precise location is not clear. Most scholars believe it was in present-day Osaka's Higashi Yodogawa-ku, but Asano Sampei, in "Akinari den ni okeru ni san no mondaiten," *KKB* 38 (June 1961), 42–52, argues for a location in Oyodo-ku, on the opposite side of the Yodo River. Takada Mamoru presents a convincing case against Asano's view in *Akinari nempu*, pp. 146, 147; see also the maps on p. 145.

   Care should be taken to avoid confusing this Nagara-mura with the Nagara in Yamato where Akinari's cousin was village headman. Awajishō-mura also should be kept distinct from Awaji-chō in Osaka where Akinari had been living. The coincidence of place names is interesting, but does not seem to have any significance.
9. See *Uzura no ya, Ibun*, pp. 423, 424; *Tsuzurabumi*, Part 2, *Zenshū*, 1: 37.

10. See *Tandai*, no. 69, *NKBT* 56: 294.
11. *Jiden, Ibun*, pp. 256, 261, 262.
12. *Tsuzurabumi*, Part 2, *Zenshū*, 1: 37.
13. See *Kokin waka shū uchigiki fugen, Ibun*, pp. 520–27, N.B. pp. 526, 527.
14. Kunio was a native of the province of Kōzuke, which suffered severe damage in the eruption. For Akinari's quotations from his report, see *Asama no kemuri, Ibun*, pp. 196–200.
15. *Machibuni, Ibun*, pp. 212–44, N.B. pp. 217, 218. For the complete poem, see *Tsuzurabumi*, Part 1, *Zenshū*, 1: 19, 20.
16. For the time of Kunio's death, see Akinari's letter to Tsuneakira, quoted in Takada, *Akinari nempu*, p. 153. On Masanori's death, close on the heels of Kunio's demise, see *Tsuzurabumi*, Part 2, *Zenshū*, 1: 37.
17. *Tsuzurabumi*, Part 2, *Zenshū*, 1: 37.
18. See *Kada Shi kundoku Saimeiki wazauta zongi, Zenshū*, 2: 1–7. Tsuneakira's copy was dated 1787 (see p. 2); the published version of Akinari's comments was taken from a manuscript dated 1792 (see p. 7).
19. Akinari recounted this adventure in *Kagutsuchi no arabi, Ibun*, pp. 363–68.
20. *Iwahashi no ki, Ibun*, pp. 532–37.
21. See chapter 1, note 14.
22. *Tosa nikki kai jo, Ibun*, pp. 532–37. This was written in 1790.
23. See *Ōsaka shuppan shoseki mokuroku*, p. 139; *Agatai kashū jo, Ibun*, pp. 540–43; *Shizunoya kashū batsu, Ibun*, pp. 543, 544.
24. Suggested by Takada in *Akinari nempu*, p. 175. For Akinari's preface to the 1790 edition of *Ayanuno*, see *Saihan Ayanuno jo, Ibun*, pp. 538, 539. The first edition had been published in 1758.
25. Concerning Akinari's meetings with Kitō in 1789, see Takada, *Akinari nempu*, pp. 159, 161–63.
26. The *nagauta* that Akinari offered on this occasion appears in *Tsuzurabumi*, Part 1, *Zenshū*, 1: 17, 18. The fact that Akinari remained loyal to Umaki long after his death is underlined by the visit he received from Umaki's adopted son while living at Nagara. See his letter to Tsuneakira in *Kada Shi kundoku Saimeiki wazauta zongi, Zenshū*, 2: 7.
27. In his letter to the Jippō-in, *Ibun*, p. 632, Akinari gave the date as sixth month, twentieth day. See also *Tandai*, no. 69, *NKBT* 56: 294.
28. Tama, *Tsuyu wake goromo, Zenshū*, 1: 135–38.
29. Kitō, *Shimmei shū*, quoted in Takada, *Akinari nempu*, p. 165.
30. See p. 109.
31. These events are all related in *Tsuyu wake goromo*.
32. See *Tandai*, no. 69, *NKBT* 56: 294, and note 8 for comment.
33. *Minō yuki, Ibun*, pp. 368–71.
34. Quoted in Takada, *Akinari nempu*, p. 172.
35. See Akinari's letters to Matsumura Gekkei, dated simply "twenty-eighth day," and sixth month, second day (presumably 1790), *Ibun*, pp. 583–89.
36. On the twenty-first day of the eleventh month. See Akinari's letter to the Jippō-in, *Ibun*, p. 631. In *Tandai*, no. 69, *NKBT* 56: 294 Akinari said that his mother died five years after he left Osaka, which would have been 1792, but this was probably just a slip of the pen. In the same passage he said that both Tama's and his own mothers died in the same year, and his letter to the Jippō-in gives 1789 as the year of death for both women.
37. *Tandai*, no. 69, *NKBT* 56: 294. It is not certain just when Tama took her vows, but Akinari's letter to Gekkei, sixth month, second day (presumably 1790) refers to her as "Koren." See *Ibun*, p. 588. For the term *koren*, and commentary on it, see *Rongo, Shinshaku Kambun Taikei* (Tokyo: Meiji Shoin, 1960) 1: 103. See also Arthur Waley, trans., *The Analects of Confucius* (New York: Vintage Books, 1938), p. 107.
38. Letter to Gekkei, *Ibun*, pp. 588, 589.
39. Letter to Gekkei, probably 1790 (see note 40, below), twelfth month, sixteenth day, *Ibun*, pp. 577, 578.
40. Ibid. In *Jizō hakogaki, Ibun*, p. 499, Akinari said that he was fifty-seven when he lost this eye. It is this statement that enables us to date the letter to Gekkei.
41. *Machibumi, Ibun*, p. 212.
42. *Uzurai, Zenshū*, 1: 115–18, N.B. pp. 115, 116. Akinari said this incident happened thirty years after their marriage—thus in or around 1790.
43. In his letter to Nakahara Ōe, Akinari said that *Kakizome kigenkai* (published 1787) had been written four years prior to *Kuse monogatari*. See Takada, *Akinari nempu*,

pp. 177, 178. Since the final words of *Kuse*
seem to have been written in the springtime, we may assume that it was completed in spring, 1791. It was not published until 1822.

44. These two works were published together
in 1793. Akinari called his own work
Yoshi ya ashi ya. There is a text in *Zenshū*,
2: 385–408; see p. 408 for publication data.
Akinari's preface to Mabuchi's *Ise monogatari koi* appears in *Ibun*, pp. 544–46.

45. See Jack Rucinski, "A Japanese Burlesque:
Nise Monogatari," *MN* 30 (Spring 1975):
1–18.

46. For examples, see Asano, "Mitsu no
fūshiteki sakuhin," pp. 43, 44; Morita,
Ueda Akinari no kenkyū, pp. 263, 267.

47. *Kuse monogatari, Zenshū*, 1: 348–50.

48. See Nakamura Yukihiko's introduction to
NKBT, 56: 6. Nakamura does not give the
source of this information.

49. *Tandai*, no. 111, *NKBT* 56: 318.

50. Koren, *Natsuno no tsuyu, Zenshū*, 1:
138–41. The account of the child's death,
and of their subsequent move to Kyoto are
drawn from this item.

NOTES TO CHAPTER 7

1. See *Kaifūsō batsu, Ibun*, pp. 552, 553.

2. In his *Kikō omoide gusa*, Tsumura Seikyō
mentioned becoming ill while on a visit to
Kyoto and receiving medicine from Ueda
Yosai, to whom he was introduced by
Murase Kōtei. This was in mid-1793, just
after Akinari had come to the Capital. See
Takada, *Akinari nempu*, p. 187. On
Murase Kōtei, see p. 105, above.

3. Concerning reasons for the move to Kyoto,
and their initial living conditions there, see
Koren's *Natsuno no tsuyu, Zenshū*, 1: 141;
Fujita's *Ken'ei waka jo, Zenshū*, 1: 149;
and Akinari's *Tandai*, no. 69, *NKBT* 56:
294, 295, and *Machibumi, Ibun*, p. 213.

4. Akinari described his first meeting with
Roan in *Machibumi, Ibun*, p. 213. See
also *Aki no kumo, Zenshū*, 1: 157; *Tsuzurabumi*, Part 2, *Zenshū*, 1: 36.

5. See *Tandai*, no. 69, *NKBT* 56: 294; also
Kōtei's preface to *Seifū sagen, Zenshū*, 2:
479, 480.

6. See *Ibun*, p. 577.

7. See *Machibumi, Ibun*, pp. 213–15. Akinari described this excursion as though it
was made in the same year that he moved
to the Capital. A verse in *Tsuzurabumi*,
Part 2, *Zenshū*, 1: 24, with a prefatory
note to the effect that it was composed the
morning after a night spent at Tsuneakira's home in Uji "about the Godless
Month", suggests that the visit was made
around the tenth month of the year.

8. *Heian no Waka Shitennō*. The other two
were Chōgetsu (1714–98) and Jien
(1748–1805).

9. See Nakamura Yukihiko's quotations from
Kōkei, *Kanden fumigusa* and Homma
Yūsei, *Mimitokawa*, in *NKBT* 56: 397.

10. The preface was for Kōkei's *Utsushibumi
warawa no satoshi*, which was published
in the sixth year of Kansei (1794). Since
Akinari's preface is dated "Winter of this
year of Kansei," it must have been written
in 1793. See Takada, *Akinari nempu*, pp.
191, 192.

11. See *Machibuni, Ibun*, pp. 230, 231; *Tandai*, no. 3, *NKBT* 56: 252.

12. These were *Jūu yogen* and *Man'yōshū
kaisetsu*. See *Zenshū*, 1: 147, 148; 2: 20.
See also *Machibumi, Ibun*, p. 216.

13. *Man'yōshū uchigiki*; unpublished, and of
uncertain date. See Maeno Sadao, "Ueda
Akinari no Man'yōgaku," *KBKKK* 4
(June 1959): 62–71.

14. See *Uzurai, Zenshū*, 1: 120, for a detailed
description of this dwelling; and Akinari's
letter to Roan in *Fumihōgu, Zenshū*, 1:
200. It may have been the Ōsawa and Isogai families, who were very helpful to
Akinari while he lived at the Nanzenji,
who invited him to come to live there.
Concerning these two families, see Iwahashi Koyata, 'Zuiryūzan ka no Ueda Akinari," *Wakatake* 13 (March 1920): 5–10;
(May 1920): 7–13.

15. Concerning these moves, see *Tandai*, no.
69, *NKBT* 56: 294, and notes 23 and 25
same page. See also Takada, *Akinari
nempu*, p. 214; Tsujimori Shūei, *Ueda
Akinari no shōgai* (Tokyo: Yūkōsha,
1942), p. 40.

16. *Tsuzurabumi*, Part 2, *Zenshū*, 1: 36, 37;
see also *Machibumi, Ibun*, p. 213.

17. See Akinari's letter to Ōdate Kōmon,
Ibun, pp. 572–77; and *Kabegaki, Ibun*, p.
570. By literary men and tea masters, Akinari must have meant those who engaged

in the pursuits for monetary gain rather than for love of their art.

18. See *Jiden, Ibun*, p. 255; *Tandai*, no. 69, *NKBT* 56: 294.
19. *Tandai*, no. 53, *NKBT* 56: 286.
20. See *Ashikabi no kotoba, Zenshū* 1: 185.
21. See, for example, *Cha no uta, Ibun*, pp. 457, 458.
22. They are so mentioned in the article on *senchadō* in *Dai Nihon hyakka jiten*, 11: 44.
23. *Seifū sagen, Zenshū*, 2: 479-502. For publication data, see p. 502; for Murase's remarks, pp. 479, 480; pp. 480, 492 imply that the writing was done at Nagara. See also Akinari's letter to Ōdate, *Ibun*, pp. 573, 577.
24. From *Cha no uta, Ibun*, p. 457.
25. Stated by Tanomura Chikuden (1776–1834), who was a painter and an associate of Murase, in *Toseki sasaroku*, quoted in Takada, *Akinari nempu*, p. 207. See also *Fumihōgu, Zenshū*, 1: 202.
26. For more comprehensive treatment of Akinari's activities in the art of tea, see Sakada Motoko, "Ueda Akinari to senchadō," *JK* 31 (Dec. 1963): 62–76; Tsujimori, *Ueda Akinari no shō*gai, pp. 321–36.
27. *Reigotsū, Zenshū*, 2:409–38. For publication data, see p. 438. The preface by Etsu Gyoshin (pp. 409, 410) was written near the end of 1795, but says that Akinari had been working on *Reigotsū* for the past two years. It is this preface that tells us the nature of the missing sections.
28. I am indebted to *Nihon bungaku daijiten*, ed. Fujimura Tsukuru, (Tokyo: Shinchōsha, 1950–52), 2: 24–26 for most of the information on the history of *kana* orthography. For Akinari's comment on this specific point, see *Zenshū*, 2: 421, 422.
29. See *Tandai*, no. 4, *NKBT* 56: 252, 253.
30. See *Nihon bungaku daijiten*, 1: 23.
31. *Man'yōshū kaisetsu, Zenshū*, 2: 9–20. for the date of completion, see p. 20.
32. Quoted in Takada, *Akinari nempu*, p. 211. Akinari's preface to *Shun'yōshū* appears in *Ibun*, pp. 555–57.

33. *Kanjikō zokuchō, Zenshū*, 2: 271-384. For the date of completion, see p. 275.
34. See *Nihon bungaku daijiten*, 2: 112.
35. A purported complete collection of his *waka*, Asano Sampei, *Akinari zenkashū to sono kenkyū* (Tokyo: Ōfūsha, 1969), contains 2337 such verses.
36. See *Fumihōgu, Zenshū*, 1: 201.
37. Twice in the last month of Kansei 11, and once in the first month of Kansei 12. See Asano, *Akinari zenkashū*, pp. 514–19.
38. Sugino Tsune, *Tenseki sakusha benran* (comp. 1812), quoted in Takada, *Akinari nempu*, p. 215.
39. For Akinari's record of this visit, see *Machibumi, Ibun*, pp. 218–21; for the date, see *Yuki wa kiku, Zenshū*, 1: 94–97, N.B. pp. 94, 95.
40. See *Man'yōshū miyasu hosei jo, Ibun*, pp. 553–55.
41. He wrote this in a copy of the *Izumo fudoki* that Tsuneakira had borrowed, mistakenly thinking it to be Tsuneakira's own book. It is not clear just when Akinari did this, but the printing date of the *Izumo fudoki* copy was Kansei, fifth year (1793), second month. See *Harusame monogatari*, ed. Maruyama, p. 41.
42. See Takada, *Akinari nempu*, pp. 260, 261.
43. See *Tsuzurabumi*, Part 2, *Zenshū*, 1: 36; *Machibumi, Ibun*, pp. 223, 224 *Yamagiri no ki, Ibun*, pp. 287–314, N.B. p. 287.
44. Material at the Kaguwashi Jinja, quoted in Takada, *Akinari nempu*, pp. 218, 219. It is not definite that this visit was part of the trip to Kusaka, but such is a reasonable assumption.
45. See *Machibumi, Ibun*, p. 222; also Akinari's letter to the Jippō-in, *Ibun*, p. 632.
46. *Machibumi, Ibun*, p. 222.
47. Ibid., pp. 222, 223; see also *Fumihōgu, Zenshū*, 1: 202, 203.
48. See *Natsuno no tsuyu shikigo, Ibun*, p. 560; Akinari's postscript to *Tsuyu wake goromo* and *Natsuno no tsuyu, Zenshū*, 1: 141; Ban Kōkei's postscript to the two manuscripts, quoted in Takada, *Akinari nempu*, p. 222; *Machibumi, Ibun*, p. 223.
49. See *Machibumi, Ibun*, pp. 223, 224.

NOTES TO CHAPTER 8

1. Suggested by Takada in *Akinari nempu*, p. 165. For the name, Mineko, see *Fumihōgu, Zenshū*, 1: 216, 217, although it is not certain that this passage actually refers to the daughter. See also *Machibumi, Ibun*, p. 224.
2. See *Yomotsubumi, Zenshū*, 1: 132, 133; Takada, *Akinari nempu*, pp. 223, 244.
3. The events of this excursion are described in Akinari's *Yamagiri no ki, Ibun*, pp. 287–314. See also *Ama kawazu, Zenshū*, 1: 109–12.
4. *Kenkadō nikki*, p. 416.
5. *Jizō hakogaki, Ibun*, p. 499.
6. See, for example, *Kōbai, Zenshū*, 1: 122–25; *Jūu yogen, Zenshū*, 1: 147, 148; *Kosenjō, Zenshū*, 1: 92–94.
7. For information on Yuishin, including her age and family, see Takada, *Kenkyū josetsu*, pp. 336–61.
8. *Kenkadō nikki*, pp. 424, 425.
9. *Tandai*, no. 69, *NKBT* 56: 295. This must have been the time that he took up residence at Nobuyoshi's home, as he said in 1808, eleventh month, that he had been there for six years. See *San'yo, Zenshū*, 1: 131, 132. In any case, he was definitely at Nobuyoshi's place by the third month of the following year. See *Mitake sōji, Zenshū*, 1: 71, 80.
10. See *Machibumi, Ibun*, p. 235.
11. From a manuscript in the Tenri Library, quoted in Takada, *Akinari nempu*, p. 134.
12. See *Tandai*, no. 98, *NKBT* 56: 310; *Machibumi, Ibun*, p. 238.
13. Entitled *Nara no soma*. The introductory portion of this work is included in *Ibun*, pp. 597–625; for the date of writing, see p. 625.
14. Letter to the abbot of the Jippō-in, *Ibun*, pp. 631–33.
15. See *Yomotsubumi, Zenshū*, 1: 132–35.
16. Takada Mamoru, in "Ueda Akinari no kyōtō," *Dentō to gendai* 3 (July 1972): 40–46, reports talking to elderly people in what used to be Kusaka-mura and hearing their tradition of "the Beggar Yosai," who sometimes visited the area. He was described as an old man dressed in dirty rags, his clothing fastened with a rope instead of a sash, grimy, and accompanied by a foul odour.
17. See *Machibumi, Ibun*, p. 236; *Fumihōgu, Zenshū*, 1: 205–7.

18. Presumed because the Kaguwashi Shrine preserves verses written by Akinari which give his age as sixty-seven and sixty-eight, indicating that he visited the shrine in both 1800 and 1801. Since he was in the area during the latter part of 1800, not healthy enough to travel extensively, and considering his close ties with the Fuji family, it is logical that these verses were written on a single prolonged visit. See Noma Kōshin, "Kashima insei jidai no Akinari," *Kamigata* 68 (Aug. 1936): 2–10.

    This excursion in 1800 was his last contact with Yuishin of which there is any record. His only known reference to her after this was in *Mizu yari hana*, written in 1802 after the heavy rains and disastrous floods of that year. He mentioned being told that Yuishin had gone to Osaka shortly before the calamity and noted that she had not returned by the time he commenced writing. See Takada, *Akinari nempu*, pp. 281, 282. It is known, however, that she lived unti 1827. See Takada, *Kenkyū josetsu*, p. 340.
19. For Nampo's account of this meeting, see his *Chōyashitsu no ki*, in *Tsuzurabumi, Zenshū*, 1: 124; for the year, see Nampo's postscript to *Tsuzurabumi*, p. 142. In his diary, *Ashi no wakaba*, Nampo spoke of a poetry session held at the Jōganji Temple on the sixteenth day of the sixth month, though he did not specifically mention Akinari as being present. The passage is quoted in Takada, *Akinari nempu*, p. 265. For Akinari's account of their meeting, see *Tandai*, no. 108, *NKBT* 56: 315, 316.
20. *Tandai*, no. 108, *NKBT* 56: 316; see note 12 on the source of Nampo's statement.
21. *Tsuzurabumi*, Part 2, *Zenshū*, 1: 36. Another verse by Akinari lamenting Roan's death appears in *Tsuzurabumi datsurō, Zenshū*, 1: 143–46. N.B. pp. 145, 146.
22. *Tandai*, no. 10, *NKBT* 56: 256, 257.
23. *Nara no soma, Ibun*, p. 597.
24. *Tandai*, no. 2, *NKBT* 56: 251.
25. See Umaki's letter to Akinari in *Fumihōgu, Zenshū*, 1: 193.
26. *Tandai*, no. 51, *NKBT* 56: 285.
27. Ibid., no. 94, p. 308.
28. See Asano, *Akinari zenkashū*, pp. 524–27.
29. See Tsujimori, *Ueda Akinari no shōgai*, pp. 129, 130.

30. *Kashima Inari Sha ken'ei waka, Zenshū,*
    1: 150–55. The collection is dated Kyōwa
    Era, first year (1801), ninth month.
    Since it is not certain when he returned to
    Kyoto, he may still have been visiting at
    the shrine when he wrote these poems.
31. See *Kōbai, Zenshū,* 1: 122–24; Ōta Nampo,
    Chōyashitsu no ki, Zenshū, 1: 124. See
    also a letter, apparently from Akinari, to
    Morikawa Chikusō, quoted in Takada,
    Akinari nempu, p. 275.
32. See Shōdō's preface to *Tsuzurabumi,
    Zenshū,* 1: 3, 4.
33. Takizawa Bakin, *Kiryo manroku,* Tsu-
    kamoto Tetsuzō, ed., *Nikki kikō shū*
    (Tokyo: Yūhōdō Bunko, 1931), pp.
    489–679, N.B. p. 597.
34. See chapter 1, p. 1, and note 3; see also
    Akinari, *Makura no nagare, Zenshū,* 1:
    129–31.
35. See Akinari, *Akikaze no hen, Ibun,* pp.
    625, 626. For a list of the participants and
    the poems each one contributed, see Tak-
    ada, *Akinari nempu,* pp. 290, 291.
36. See *Fumihōgu, Zenshū,* 1: 225. The date is
    not included in the published version, but
    it does appear on the original manuscript
    copy, according to Takada in *Akinari
    nempu,* p. 30.
37. For Akinari's account of this meeting, see
    Tandai, no. 108, *NKBT* 56: 316. For
    Nampo's see *Mizunoe inu kikō,* quoted in
    Takada, *Akinari nempu,* p. 276. Nampo
    stayed in Osaka from the tenth to the
    eighteenth of the eighth month of that
    year. See Takada, *Akinari nempu,* p. 301.
38. Tanomura Chikuden, *Toseki sasaroku,*
    quoted in Takada, *Akinari nempu,* p. 326.
39. Nampo's postscript appears in *Zenshū,* 1:
    142. Actually it was written quite early in
    the winter, as is shown by Nampo's letter
    to Akinari in Iwahashi Koyata, "Ueda no
    hitsuji," *KZ* 33 (June 1927): 29–48, N.B. p.
    31.
40. See Maruyama Sueo, "Akinari no haikai
    to waka," *KKK* 265 (June 1958): 12–19,
    N.B. p. 16; Takada, *Akinari nempu,* pp.
    314, 321, 328. It is the 1806 version that is
    included in *Ueda Akinari zenshū.*
41. See *Jiden, Ibun,* p. 256.
42. *Kinsa, Zenshū,* 2: 21–216; *Kinsa jōgen,
    Zenshū* 2: 217–34. For *Kinsa jōgen*'s date
    of completion, see p. 234; for Akinari's
    statement that he had written *Kinsa* that
    same year, p. 226.
43. *Kinsa, Zenshū,* 2: 40.

44. See *Yamamura gantan, Ibun,* pp. 451,
    452; *Fumihōgu, Zenshū,* 1: 213, 215. *Zen-
    shū,* 1 p. 213 gives 1806 as the date of
    moving to the Saifukuji, but it is clear
    from the other sources that this was a slip
    of the pen.
45. *Tandai,* no. 69, *NKBT* 56: 295.
46. See *San'yo, Zenshū,* 1: 132. *Saikei Hakoya
    no yama, Ibun,* pp. 384–88.
47. According to a passage in the manuscript
    copy of *Fumihōgu,* not included in the
    published version. See Takada, "Akinari
    nempu' hoi," pp. 110, 111.
48. See Akinari, *Tsuigi kagetsurei, Ibun,* pp.
    175–89, N.B. p. 175.
49. For the original story, see Fujii Otoo,
    "Akinari itsubun," *Kokubungaku kō* 1
    (April 1935): 1–6; for comments, Naka-
    mura Yukihiko, "Akinari den no mon-
    daiten," *KKK* 265 (June 1958): 7–11, N.B.
    pp. 10, 11, and Takada, *Akinari nempu,*
    pp. 310, 311.
50. See *Kitano kamo ni mōzuru ki, Ibun,* p.
    373; *Tandai,* no. 29, *NKBT* 56: 271.
51. See *Shichi-jū-ni kō, Ibun,* pp. 125–74,
    N.B. p. 125.
52. *Tandai,* no. 69, *NKBT* 56: 295.
53. These anecdotes are related in Iwahashi
    Koyata, "Zuiryūsan ka no Ueda Akinari,"
    Wakatake 13 (March 1920): 5–10; (May
    1920): 7–13.
54. *Donkodō no ki, Ibun,* pp. 487–91. On p.
    491 his age is given as seventy-three, and
    the time is specified in the text as mid-
    autumn.
55. See Asano, "Akinari den ni okeru ni, san
    no mondaiten," pp. 50, 51. These entries
    were made during the early months of
    1807. Considering the Saifukuji's proxim-
    ity to the Nanzenji, there is no reason to
    accept Asano's contention that Akinari
    was actually residing at the Saifukuji at
    that time.
56. *Nenjū gyōji zukan.* He had collaborated
    in a similar manner in 1802 with Kawa-
    mura Bumpō, producing *Shiki fūryū
    emaki,* a collection of twenty-two pictures
    by Bumpō and ten *waka,* sixteen haiku,
    and one Chinese poem by himself. Akina-
    ri's contributions to both collections are
    reproduced in Asano Sampei, "Ueda Aki-
    nari bannen no haikai: sono haikai san ni
    kan wo megutte," *KKB* 40 (July 1963),
    36–44.
57. *Shichi-jū-ni kō, Ibun,* pp. 125–74, *Tsuigi
    kagetsurei, Ibun,* pp. 175–89.

58. Their meeting took place on the fifth day of the eleventh month. See Nampo, *Kohara kikō*, in *Ōta Shokusanjin zenshū*, 1: 252.
59. *Kaidō kyōka awase, Ibun*, pp. 335–44. For the date of composition, see the note on the manuscript copy, quoted in Takada, *Akinari nempu*, p. 316. Since the collection was published in 1811, two years after Akinari's death, together with sketches by Kawamura Bumpō and Watanabe Nangaku, Bumpō also may have influenced Akinari to write these verses.
60. *Machibumi, Ibun*, p. 213, *Tandai*, nos. 108, 139, *NKBT* 56: 315, 343, 344.
61. *Seburui no okina den, Ibun*, pp. 395–400. Akinari's request to Yotsugi (here called Kyozentei) is appended to the tale.
62. According to manuscripts in the Tenri Library, quoted in Takada, *Akinari nempu*, p. 323.
63. See *Tandai*, no. 108, *NKBT* 56: 317.
64. There are two extant *Chaka suigen* manuscripts. One, in Akinari's own hand, contains sixty-six sections; the other, written by a scribe, only fifty-six. Forty of the sections are common to both manuscripts, but even most of those have their differences. Both versions are reproduced, with introductory comments, in Nakamura, *Kinsei sakka kenkyū*, pp. 219–49.
65. *Tandai*, no. 98, *NKBT* 56: 310.
66. *Fumihōgu, Zenshū*, 1: 227; trans. Zolbrod, *Ugetsu*, p. 28.
67. See Nakamura, *Kinsei sakka kenkyū*, p. 247.
68 Fujii, "Ueda Akinari den," *Ibun*, p. 48.
69. *Aki no kumo, Zenshū*, 1: 157–64. On p. 164 he gives his age as seventy-four at the time of writing. On the larger collection, see Asano, *Akinari zenkashū*, pp. 477–509.
70. Publication data in *Zenshū*, 1: 228. For the account of its compilation, see pp. 191, 228.
71. Presumed by Fujii Otoo, who gave the manuscript its title. See his preface to *Ibun*, p. 5. The date of its composition is inferred from Akinari's statement that he was seventy-five at the time. See *Ibun*, p. 256.
72. *Ihon Tandai shōshin roku, NKBT* 56: 370–77. See p. 377 for his statement that he was seventy-six when he wrote it.
73. *Haichō giron*. For a text, see Fujii Shiei [Otoo], "Ueda Akinari no Haichō giron," *KK* 11 (Oct. 1941) 70–79.
74. See, for instance, *Kozo no shiori, Zenshū*, 1: 170, 171; *Kuse monogatari, Zenshū*, 1: 341. See also Takada Mamoru, "Akinari no Bashō kan," in Waseda Daigaku Haikai Kenkyū Kai, ed., *Kinsei bungaku ronsō* (Tokyo: Ōfūsha, 1970), pp. 494–508.
75. For a discussion of the various *Harusame* manuscripts, and their discovery and publication, see *Tales of the Spring Rain*, trans. Barry Jackman (Tokyo: University of Tokyo Press, 1975), pp. xix–xxiii.
76. *Tandai*, no. 35, NKBT 56: 276. See also nos. 54, 55, 70, 138, pp. 287, 295, 341–43.
77. Readers who are interested in the actual incident should consult Asano Sampei, "Genta sōdō to Ayatari, Akinari," (1962) in *Akinari*, ed. Nihon Bungaku Kenkyū Shiryō Kankōkai, pp. 231–46; Noma Kōshin, "Iwayuru Genta sōdō wo megutte: Ayatari to Akinari, " *Bungaku* 37 (June 1969): 46–55; (July 1969): 39–50. See also my "A Tale of the Western Hills: Takebe Ayatari's *Nishiyama Monogatari*," in *MN* 37 (1982) 77–121.
78. *Masurao monogatari* was, in fact, the name given to this work by Fujii Otoo when compiling *Akinari ibun*. Akinari's own manuscript was untitled.
79. See *Dai Nihon hyakka jiten*, 1: 69.
80. "Onshū no kanata ni" by Kikuchi Kan is the best-known work of fiction based on this episode, but Akinari's "Suteishimaru" was unknown at the time it was written and so could not have had any influence. For comparative notes on the two tales, see Morita Kirō, *Ueda Akinari* (Tokyo: Kinokuniya Shoten, 1970), pp. 189, 190; *Spring Rain*, trans. Jackman, pp. 117–19.
81. *NKBT* 56: 247.
82. *Jiden, Ibun*, p. 256.
83. Letter to a Mr. Kin'ya, quoted in Takada, *Akinari nempu*, p. 344.
84. See Takada, *Akinari nempu*, p. 348.
85. Reported in *Nihon Dokusho Shimbun*, 30 August, 1950, p. 4. Although the copyist had purposely omitted "Suteishimaru" and "Hankai," this was the most complete version of *Harusame* to be discovered up to that time. Edited by the finder, Urushiyama Matashiro, it was published as *Urushiyama bon Harusame monogatari* by Iwanami Bunko in 1950.
86. *The Japan Foundation Newsletter* 7 (Feb. –Mar. 1980); 20.

Bibliography

A. Collections of Akinari's Works

Akinari. Ed. Shigetomo Ki. Tokyo: Nihon Hyōronsha, 1943.

Akinari ibun. Ed. Fujii Otoo. Tokyo: Shūbunkan, 1919.

Akinari jihitsubon shū. Ed. Tenri Toshokan Zenpon Sōsho Washo no Bu Henshū Iinkai. Tenri: Tenri Daigaku Shuppanbu, 1975.

Hanabusa sōshi, Nishiyama monogatari, Ugetsu monogatari, Harusame monogatari. Ed. Nakamura Yukihiko; Takada Mamoru; and Nakamura Hiroyasu. *Nihon Koten Bungaku Zenshū*, vol. 48. Tokyo: Shōgakukan, 1973.

Harusame monogatari. Ed. Asano Sampei. Tokyo: Ōfūsha, 1971.

Harusame monogatari. Ed. Maruyama Sueo. Tokyo: Koten Bunko, 1951.

Harusame monogatari. Ed. Nakamura Yukihiko. Osaka: Sekizenkan, 1947.

Harusame monogatari. Kakizome kigenkai. Ed. Miyama Yasushi. Tokyo: Shinchōsha, 1980.

Kakizome kigenkai. Ed. Maruyama Sueo. Tokyo: Koten Bunko, 1951.

Ueda Akinari shū. Ed. Nagai Kazutaka. Tokyo: Yūhōdō Bunko, 1931.

Ueda Akinari shū. Ed. Nakamura Yukihiko. *Nihon Koten Bungaku Taikei*, vol. 56. Tokyo: Iwanami Shoten, 1959; rpt. 1968.

Ueda Akinari shū. Ed. Shigetomo Ki. *Nihon Koten Zensho*. Tokyo: Asahi Shimbunsha, 1957; rpt. 1970.

Ueda Akinari zenshū. Ed. Iwahashi Koyata. 2 vols. Tokyo: Kokusho Kankōkai, 1918; rpt. 1969.

Ueda Akinari zenshū. Ed. Suzuki Toshiya. Tokyo: Fuzambō, 1938.

Ugetsu monogatari. Kuse monogatari. Ed. Asano Sampei. Tokyo: Shinchōsha, 1979.

Urushiyama bon Harusame monogatari. Ed. Urushiyama Matashirō. Tokyo: Iwanami Shoten, 1950.

B. Translations of Akinari's Works in Western Languages

Allen, Lewis. " 'The Chrysanthemum Vow,' from the Ugetsu Monogatari (1776) by Ueda Akinari." *Durham University Journal* 28 (1967): 108–16.

Blacker, Carmen, and W.E. Skillend. "Muo no rigyo (The Dream Carp)." *Selections from Japanese Literature (12th to 19th Centuries)*. Ed. F.J. Daniels. London: Lund Humphries, 1959, pp. 91–103, 164–71.

Bohackova, Libuse. *Vypraveni za mesice a deste*. Prague: Odeon, 1971.

Chambers, Anthony. "Hankai: A Translation from Harusame monogatari by Ueda Akinari." *MN* 25 (1970): 371–406.

Hamada, Kengi. *Tales of Moonlight and Rain: Japanese Gothic Tales by Uyeda Akinari*. Tokyo: University of Tokyo Press, 1971.

Hani, Kjoko, and Maria Holti. *Eso es hold nesei*. Budapest: Europa, 1964.

Hansey, Alf. "The Blue Hood." *The Young East* 2 (Feb. 1927): 314–19.

Hearn, Lafcadio. "Of a Promise Kept," "The Story of Kōgi the Priest." *A Japanese Miscellany: Strange Stories—Folklore Gleanings—Studies Here & There*. Tokyo: Tuttle, 1967; rpt. 1971, pp. 11–17, 61–71.

Jackman, Barry. *Tales of the Spring Rain*. Tokyo: University of Tokyo Press, 1975.

Sakai, Kazuya. *Cuentos de illuvia y de luna: traduccion del original japones*. Mexico City: Ediciones Era, 1969.

Sasaki Takamasa. *Tales of a Rain'd Moon*. Illustrations by Kaburaki Kiyotaka. Tokyo: Hokuseidō Press, 1980.

Saunders, Dale. "Ugetsu Monogatari, or Tales of Moonlight and Rain." *MN* 21 (1966): 171–202.

Sieffert, Rene. *Contes de pluie et de lune (Ugetsu Monogatari): Traduction et commentaires*. Paris: Gallimard, 1956.

Ueda, Makoto. "A Blue Hood." *San Francisco Review* 1, no. 4 (1960): 42–47.

Whitehouse, Wilfrid, and M.A. Matsumoto. "Ugetsu Monogatari: Tales of a Clouded Moon." *MN* 1 (1938): 242–58, (July 1938) 257–75, 4, (1941): 166–91.

Young, Blake Morgan. " 'Hankai', a Tale from the *Harusame monogatari* by Ueda Akinari (1734–1809)." *HJAS* 32 (1972): 150–207.

Zolbrod, Leon M. "Shiramine (White Peak), from Ugetsu Monogatari (Tales of Moonlight and Rain), by Ueda Akinari (1734–1809)." *Literature East and West* 11 (1967): 402–14.

———. *Ugetsu Monogatari: Tales of Moonlight and Rain*. Vancouver: University of British Columbia Press, 1974.

C. Books and Articles in Japanese

Akiba Naoki. " 'Harusame monogatari' jobun ni tsuite no shōron." *Nihon bungaku ronkyū* 22 (Nov. 1962): 11-16.

Akinari. Ed. Nakamura Yukihiko. *Nihon Koten Kanshō Kōza,* vol. 24. Tokyo: Kadogawa Shoten, 1966.

Akinari. Ed. Nihon Bungaku Kenkyū Shiryō Kankōkai. Tokyo: Yūseidō, 1972.

Akinari, Bakin. Ed. Nakamura Yukihiko and Mizuno Minoru. *Kanshō Nihon Koten Bungaku,* vol. 35. Tokyo: Kadogawa Shoten, 1977.

Asano Akira. "Akinari to Saikaku." *Bungei kenkyū* 33 (Nov. 1959): 10-18.

Asano Sampei. "Akinari den kō." *Bungaku Gogaku* 54 (Dec. 1969): 9-15.

―――. "Akinari den ni okeru ni, san no mondaiten." *KKB* 38 (June 1961): 42-52.

―――. *Akinari zenkashū to sono kenkyū.* Tokyo: Ōfūsha, 1969.

―――. "Harusame monogatari to bukkyō." *JK* 43 (Nov. 1966): 73-82.

―――. "Kakizome kigenkai ni tsuite," *KKB* 35 (Feb. 1958): 41-49.

―――. "Mitsu no fūshiteki sakuhin: 'Kakizome kigenkai.' 'Kuse monogatari,' 'Manihōshū'," *KKK* 23 (June 1958): 42-46.

―――. "Seken tekake katagi wo megutte―Shokoku kaisen dayori, Utamakura someburoshiki ni oyobu." *KKB* 36 (May 1959): 38-48.

―――. "Shodō kikimimi sekenzaru ron." *JK* 15 (Oct. 1959): 46-56.

―――. "Ueda Akinari bannen no no haikai: sono haikai san ni kan wo megutte." *KKB* 40 (July 1963), 36-44.

―――. "Ueda Akinari bannen no haikai: sono haikai san ni kan wo megutte." *KKB* 40 (July 1963), 36-44.

―――. "Ueda Akinari no shussei to kazoku." *JK* 36 (Feb. 1965): 1-10.

―――. "Ugetsu monogatari to Manihōshū." *JK* 22 (July 1961): 1-16.

Asō Isoji. *Edo bungaku to Shina bungaku.* Tokyo: Sanseidō, 1946.

―――. *Kinsei seikatsu to kokubungaku.* Tokyo: Shibundō, 1925.

Bunka ryōran. Ed. Nakamura Yukihiko and Nishiyama Matsunosuke. *Nihon Bungaku no Rekishi,* vol. 8. Tokyo: Kadogawa Shoten, 1967.

Fujii Otoo. "Akinari itsubun." *Kokubungaku kō* 1 (April 1935): 1-6.

―――. *Edo bungaku kenkyū.* Tokyo: Naigai Shuppan Kabushiki Kaisha, 1921.

―――. *Edo bungaku sōsetsu.* Tokyo: Iwanami Shoten, 1931.

Fujii Shiei [Otoo]. "Ueda Akinari no Haichō giron." *KK* 11 (Oct. 1941), 70-79.

Fukunaga Shizuya. "Akinari to Norinaga no ronsō." *JK* 31 (Dec. 1963): 7-19.

Gotō Tanji. "Akinari no kyūsaku to Ugetsu monogatari: Sekenzaru, Tekake katagi no saigen." *Kokubungaku* (Kansai Daigaku Kokubun Gakkai) 9 (Jan. 1953): 25-36.

――――. "Gozasso to Ugetsu monogatari." *Rekishi Nihon* 1 (Dec. 1942): 162-66.

――――. "Ugetsu monogatari shutten wo saguru." *KKK* 265 (June 1958): 52-64.

Hakura Yoshihisa. "Ueda Akinari to Ozawa Roan." *KZ* 55 (June 1954): 126-32.

Hasegawa Tsuyoshi. *Ukiyo-zōshi no kenkyū: Hachimonjiya-bon wo chūshin to suru.* Tokyo: Ōfūsha, 1969.

Ishikawa Jun. "Akinari shiron." *Bungaku* 27 (Aug. 1959), 83-88.

Ishizaki Matazō. *Kinsei Nihon ni okeru Shina zokugo bungaku shi.* Tokyo: Shimizu Kōbundō Shobō, 1967.

Itō Akihiro. "Ueda Akinari no ukiyo-zōshi." *Kinsei shōsetsu: kenkyū to shiryō.* Ed. Keiō Gijuku Daigaku Kokubungaku Kenkyūkai. *Kokubungaku Ronsō*, vol. 6. Tokyo: Shibundō, 1963, pp. 165-85.

Iwahashi Koyata. "Futatabi Ueda Akinari no koto ni tsuite." *KZ* 16 (May 1910): 542-45.

――――. "Haijin Muchō." *KZ* 18 (July 1912): 55-62.

――――. "Reigotsū ron." *Geibun* 14, (Aug. 1923): 47-56.

――――. "Reigotsū yoron." *Geibun* 21 (Feb. 1930); 76-81.

――――. *Ueda Akinari.* Tokyo: Yūseidō, 1975.

――――. "Ueda no hitsuji." *KZ* 33 (June 1927): 29-48.

――――. "Ueda Akinari to Man'yōshū." *Wakatake* 5 (Oct. 1912): 10-14.

――――. "Zuiryūzan ka no Ueda Akinari." *Wakatake* 13 (Mar. 1920): 5-10; (May 1920): 7-13.

Kaguwashi Jinja to Ueda Akinari no shiori. Osaka: Kaguwashi Jinja Keishin Kenkōkai, 1965.

Katsukura Toshikazu. *Ugetsu monogatari kōsō ron.* Tokyo: Kyōiku Shuppan Sentā, 1977.

Kayanuma Noriko. *Akinari bungaku no sekai.* Tokyo: Kasama Senshō, 1979.

――――. "'Harusame monogatari' no kaishaku: iwayuru rekishi monogatari ni tsuite." *NB* 24 (July 1975): 32-45.

――――. "Ueda Akinari no shisō: kokugaku shisō kara mita." *NB* 22 (June 1973): 39-53.

Kitajima Masamoto. *Edo jidai.* Tokyo: Iwanami Shoten, 1958.

Maeno Sadao. "Ueda Akinari no Man'yō gaku." *KBKKK* 4 (June 1959): 62-71.

Maruyama Sueo. "Akinari no haikai to waka." *KKK* 265 (June 1958): 12-19.

――――. "Akinari no Umaki nyūmon no nendai sono ta." *Wagimo* 13 (March 1936): 42-45.

―――. "Roan to Akinari." *KZ* 43 (Oct. 1937): 52–65; (Dec. 1937): 57–73.
―――. "Ueda Akinari to Man'yōshū." *Wagimo* 13 (May 1936): 23–25; (June 1936): 42–47.
Matsuda Osamu. "Sei tōbōsha: Ueda Akinari." *Subaru* 13 (June 1973): 25–37.
Matsuda Osamu, et al, ed. *Ueda Akinari. Zusetsu Nihon no Koten*, vol. 17. Tokyo: Shūeisha, 1981.
Matsuo Yasuaki. *Kinsei no bungaku*. Tokyo: Bunka Shoin, 1965.
Misawa Junjirō. "Akinari den no naka no ayamari hitotsu." *KK* 28 (July 1959): 31–35.
―――. *Shōnen Ueda Akinari den*. Tokyo: Daidōkan Shoten, 1933.
Miyajima Natsuki. "Ueda Akinari." *KKB* 16 (Oct. 1939): 174–95.
―――. "Ueda Akinari ron: sono shisō to seikatsu ni furete." *KKB* 38 (April 1961): 71–81.
―――. "Ueda Akinari shuyō chosaku kaidai." *KBKKK* 4 (June 1959): 40–52.
Miyama Yasushi. "Nubatama no maki ni tsuite." *Kōgakkan Daigaku kiyō* 8 (March 1970): 95–112.
Mori Senzō. "Muchō Okina zakki." *Kamigata* 45 (Sept. 1934): 54–62.
Morita Kirō. *Ueda Akinari*. Tokyo: Kinokuniya Shoten, 1970.
―――. "Ueda Akinari *Kakizome kigenkai*: honkoku to kaidai." *Bungaku kenkyū* 34 (Dec. 1971): 80–90.
―――. *Ueda Akinari no kenkyū*. Tokyo: Kasama Sōsho, 1979.
Moriyama Shigeo. "Akinari kenkyū no gendankai to mondaiten." *KBKKK* 4 (June 1959): 33–39.
―――. "Akinari no ukiyo-zōshi." *KKK* 265 (June 1958): 23–30.
―――. *Chūsei to kinsei no genzō*. Tokyo: Shindokushosha, 1965.
―――. *Hōken shomin bungaku no kenkyū*. Tokyo: San'ichi Shobō, 1960; rpt. 1971.
―――. *Kinsei bungaku no sogen*. Tokyo: Ōfūsha, 1976.
―――. *Ueda Akinari shoki ukiyo-zōshi hyōshaku*. Tokyo: Kokusho Kankō-kai, 1977.
―――. *Ugetsu monogatari, Harusame monogatari: Akinari no bungaku*. Tokyo: Nihon Bungaku Shinsho, 1956.
Muramatsu Sadataka. "Izumi Kyōka to Ueda Akinari." *Gakuen* 246 (Aug. 1960): 2–15.
Murata Noboru. *Kinsei bungei no bukkyōteki kenkyū*. Tokyo: Hyakkaen, 1963.
Nagashima Hiroaki. "Akinari no jitsubo to sono shūhen." *Bungaku* 50 (May 1982): 86–104.
―――. "Akinari shiryō shūi." *Kaishaku* 25 (Nov. 1979): 24–29.
Nakamura Hiroyasu. "Ueda Akinari no shimpi shisō." *Kokubungaku kenkyū* 26 (1962): 96–105.
Nakamura Yukihiko. "Akinari den no mondaiten." *KKK* 265 (June 1958): 7–11.

——. "Akinari ne egakareta hitobito." *KK* 32 (Jan. 1963): 1–11; (June 1963): 50–62.

——. "Akinari no shi Tsuga Teishō," *Rekishi to jimbutsu* 28 (Feb. 1974): 124–35.

——. "Akinari to haikai." *Haiku* 24 (Jan. 1975): 53–59.

——. *Kinsei bungei shichō kō.* Tokyo: Iwanami Shoten, 1975.

——. *Kinsei sakka kenkyū.* Tokyo: San'ichi Shobō, 1961.

——. *Kinsei shōsetsu shi no kenkyū.* Tokyo: Ōfūsha, 1961.

——. "Ueda Akinari den shin shiryō shōkai." *Bungaku* 46 (Oct 1978), 49–64.

——. "Ueda Akinari no monogatari kan." *Kokubungaku* (Kansai Daigaku) 23 (Oct. 1958): 52–60.

——. "Ueda Akinari to sono jidai." *KKK* 41 (July 1976): 6–14.

——. "Ueda Akinari to sono kōyū." *Rekishi to jimbutsu* 27 (Nov. 1973): 152–60.

Nihon bungakū shi. Ed. Hisamatsu Sen'ichi et al. 2nd ed., 6 vols. Tokyo: Shibundō, 1964.

Noda Hisao. "Kai-i shōsetsu no keifu to Akinari." *Kōza Nihon bungaku.* Ed. Zenkoku Daigaku Kokugo Kokubungakkai. 14 vols. (Tokyo: Sanseidō, 1968–71), 8:35–54.

——. *Kinsei bungaku no haikei.* Tokyo: Kōshobō, 1964; rpt. 1971.

——. "Tandai shōshin roku." *KKK* 265 (June 1958): 47–51.

Noma Kōshin. "Iwayuru Genta sōdō wo megutte: Ayatari to Akinari." *Bungaku* 37 (June 1969): 46–55; (July 1969): 39–50.

——. "Kashima insei jidai no Akinari." *Kamigata* 68 (Aug. 1936): 2–10.

Ōba Shunsuke. *Akinari no tenkanshō to dēmon.* Tokyo: Ashi Shobō, 1969.

Ōi Mitsuko. "Ugetsu monogatari 'Aozukin' no bungeisei." *Zeirin* 3 (April 1951): 19–21.

Ōiso Yoshio. "Ueda Akinari wa futari ita." *Kokugo kokubungaku hō* 13 (April 1961): 11–16.

Ōkubo Tadashi. "Akinari to Norinaga: ronsō no kei-i to tairitsu no imi." *KBKKK* 12 (Aug. 1967): 121–26.

Ōwa Yasuhiro. "Shoki yomihon seiritsu no ichimen: Ueda Akinari wo chūsin toshite." *Kinsei shōsetsu: kenkyū to shiryō.* Ed. Keiō Gijuku Daigaku Kokubungaku Kenkyūkai. *Kokubungaku Ronsō,* vol. 6 Tokyo: Shibundō, 1963, pp. 187–205.

——. *Ueda Akinari bungaku no kenkyū.* Tokyo: Kasama Sōsho, 1976.

Rai Momosaburō. "Akinari den kikigaki." *NB* 8 (June 1959): 6–10.

Sakada Motoko. "Ueda Akinari to senchadō." *JK* 31 (Dec. 1963): 62–76.

Sakai Kōichi. "Harusame monogatari." *KKK* 265 (June 1958): 35–42.

——. *Ueda Akinari.* Tokyo: San'ichi Shobō, 1959.

Satō Haruo. *Ueda Akinari.* Tokyo: Tōgensha, 1964.

Shidehara Michitarō. "Kaigai ni shōkai sareta Ueda Akinari." *KBKK* 4 (June 1959): 53–61.

Shigetomo Ki. *Akinari no kenkyū.* Tokyo: Bunri Shoin, 1971.

———. *Kinsei bungaku shi no shomondai.* Tokyo: Meiji Shoin, 1963.

———. *Nihon kinsei bungaku shi.* Tokyo: Iwanami Zensho, 1950; rpt. 1969.

———. "Ueda Akinari no sakkateki shōgai." *KKK* 265 (June 1958): 2–7.

———. *Ugetsu monogatari hyōshaku.* Tokyo: Meiji Shoin, 1957.

Shiina Hiroko. "Ueda Akinari shōron." *Kokubun* (Ochanomizu Joshi Daigaku) 16 (Jan. 1962): 21–34.

Shimizu Masao. "Akinari no haikai." *Bungeikō* 1 (Aug. 1968): 42–50; 2 (Jan 1969): 11–16.

Shindō Tomoyoshi. *Ueda Akinari no Man'yō gaku.* Tokyo: Ōfūsha, 1974.

Suzuki Toshiya. "Kai-i shōsetsuka toshite no Ueda Akinari." *Koten kenkyū* 4 (Oct. 1939): 29–46.

———. *Kindai kokubungaku sobyō.* Tokyo: Meguro Shoten, 1934.

———. *Kinsei Nihon shōsetsu shi: kowaku to gen'yō to no bungei.* Tokyo: Meguro Shoten, 1920.

———. "Shōsetsuka toshite no Akinari." *Kamigata* 45 (Sept. 1934): 17–31.

Takada Mamoru. "Akinari no Bashō kan." *Kinsei bungaku ronsō.* Ed. Waseda Daigaku Haikai Kenkyūkai, pp. 494–508. Tokyo: Ōfūsha, 1970.

———. *Akinari shū. Kanshō Nihon no Koten,* vol. 18. Tokyo: Shōgaku Tosho, 1981.

———. "Akinari wo kenkyū suru hito no tame ni." *KBKKK* 4 (June 1959): 77–80.

———. "Bunka roku nen ni gatsu no Akinari: *Ueda Akinari nempu kōsetsu* yoroku sono ichi. *Koten isan* 18 (May 1968): 38–42.

———. "Kidan sakusha to yumegatari: Akinari, Teishō, Ayatari wo meguttte." *Bungaku* 43 (June 1975): 666–83; (July 1975): 763–74.

———. "Norinaga to Akinari: 'Hi no Kami' ronsō saisetsu nōto." *Bungaku* 36 (August 1968): 21–30.

———. *Ueda Akinari kenkyū josetsu.* Tokyo: Nara Shobō, 1968.

———. *Ueda Akinari nempu kōsetsu.* Tokyo: Meizendō Shoten, 1964.

———. "Ueda Akinari nempu kōsetsu ' hoi." *Kinsei chūki bungaku no shomondai.* Ed. Kinsei Bungaku Shi Kenkyū no Kai, pp. 69–113. Tokyo Meizendō Shoten, 1966, pp. 69–113.

———. "Ueda Akinari no kyōtō." *Dentō to gendai* 3 (July 1972): 40–46.

Takada Mamoru, et al. *Akinari. Shimpojiumu Nihon Bungaku,* vol. 10. Tokyo: Gakuseisha, 1977.

Takeoka Masao. "Fujitani Nariakira to Ueda Akinari to no kankei." *Kokugo* 2 (September 1953): 222–28.

Tanaka Toshikazu. *Ueda Akinari bungei no sekai.* Tokyo: Ōfūsha, 1979.

Teruoka Yasutaka. *Buson: shōgai to geijutsu.* Tokyo: Meiji Shoin, 1954.

————. "Ugetsu monogatari ni tsuite." *Asuka* 8 (April 1943): 3–7.

Tsujimori Shūei. *Ueda Akinari no shōgai.* Tokyo: Yūkōsha, 1942.

Ueda Akinari: kai-i yūkei no bungaku aruiwa monogatari no kyokuhoku. Ed. Kuwahara Shigeo. *Bessatsu Gendai Shi Techō,* vol. 3. Tokyo: Shichōsha, 1972.

Ueda Yone. "Kuse monogatari no fūshi ni tsuite." *JK* 31 (Dec. 1963): 31–43.

Uzuki Hiroshi. "Akinari bungaku no tenkai." *KBKKK* 4 (June 1959): 5–13.

————. "Akinari no bungaku to fūdo: Ugetsu monogatari no fūdosei to hifūdosei." *KBKKK* 8 (Mar. 1963): 71–78.

————. "Shitto to enkon no bungaku." *Asuka* 26, (Apr. 1961): 18–20.

————. *Ugetsu monogatari hyōshaku.* Tokyo: Kadogawa Shoten, 1969.

Washiyama Jushin. *Akinari bungaku no shisō.* Kyoto: Hōzōkan, 1979.

Yamaguchi Takeshi. *Edo bungaku kenkyū.* Tokyo: Tōkyōdō, 1933; rpt. 1942.

————. *Kinsei shōsetsu.* 3 vols. Tokyo: Sōgensha , 1941.

Yamazaki Fumoto. "Tandai shōshin roku ni tsuite." *Koten Kenkyū* 4 (Oct. 1939) 47–63.

D. Books and Articles in Western Languages

Araki, James T. "A Critical Approach to the Ugetsu monogatari." *MN* 22 (1967): 49–64.

Dore, R.P. *Education in Tokugawa Japan.* Berkeley and Los Angeles: University of California Press, 1965.

Hibbett, Howard. *The Floating World in Japanese Fiction.* New York: Oxford University Press, 1959.

Humbertclaude, Pierre. "Essai sur la vie et l'oeuvre de Ueda Akinari, 1734–1809." *MN* 3 (1940): 98–119; 4 (1941): 102–23, 454–64; 5 (1942): 52–85.

Keene, Donald. *World Within Walls: Japanese Literature of the Pre-Modern Era, 1600–1867.* New York: Holt, Rinehart and Winston, 1976.

Lane, Richard. "The Beginnings of the Modern Japanese Novel (*Kanazōshi, 1600–1682*)." *HJAS* 20 (1957): 644–701.

Morris, Ivan, ed. and trans. *The Life of an Amorous Woman and Other Writings by Ihara Saikaku.* Norfolk, Conn.: New Directions, 1963.

Rimer, J. Thomas. *Modern Japanese Fiction and Its Traditions: An Introduction.* Princeton: Princeton University Press, 1978.

Rucinski, Jack. "A Japanese Burlesque: *Nise Monogatari.*" *MN* 30 (1975): 1–18.

Young, Blake Morgan. "A Tale of the Western Hills: Takebe Ayatari's *Nishiyama Monogatari.*" *MN* 37 (1982): 77–121.

Zolbrod, Leon M. "A Comparative Approach to 'Tales of Moonlight and Rain.' " *Humanities Association Bulletin* 21 (Spring 1970): 48–56.

———. *Takizawa Bakin*. New York: Twayne Publishers Inc., 1967.

———. "Yomihon: The Appearance of the Historical Novel in Late Eighteenth Century and Early Nineteenth Century Japan." *JAS* 25 (1966): 485–98.

Index